Atrocities, Diamonds and Diplomacy

Additional Author's Note

On page 52 I refer to Abass Bundu having been 'convicted for selling passports'. This is not accurate. He was charged with this offence but he was subsequently cleared of all charges in 2005.

In the same paragraph I refer to what I was told at the time that Omrie Golley had passed through Conakry 'carrying diamonds'. I wish to clarify that, if true, this was before the passage of the UN resolution banning 'conflict diamonds' and the introduction of the Kimberley Process (see page 184) and therefore was not illegal.

Finally, on page 58 I note that my colleague, Craig Murray, had 'ditched' his wife in Uzbekistan. In fact I now understand that she had left him.

No disrespect is intended to these persons.

Peter Penfold   May 2012

Dedicated to Celia
and to the people of Sierra Leone

Atrocities, Diamonds and Diplomacy

The Inside Story of the Conflict in Sierra Leone

Peter Penfold

Pen & Sword
MILITARY

First published in Great Britain in 2012 by
Pen & Sword Military
an imprint of
Pen & Sword Books Ltd
47 Church Street
Barnsley
South Yorkshire
S70 2AS

Hardback ISBN: 978 1 84884 768 2
Trade Paperback ISBN: 978 1 78159 105 5

Typeset in 11pt Ehrhardt by
Mac Style, Beverley, E. Yorkshire

Printed and bound in the UK by CPI Group (UK) Ltd, Croydon, CR0 4YY

Pen & Sword Books Ltd incorporates the Imprints of Pen & Sword Aviation,
Pen & Sword Family History, Pen & Sword Maritime, Pen & Sword Military,
Pen & Sword Discovery, Wharncliffe Local History, Wharncliffe True Crime,
Wharncliffe Transport, Pen & Sword Select, Pen & Sword Military Classics,
Leo Cooper, The Praetorian Press, Remember When, Seaforth Publishing
and Frontline Publishing.

For a complete list of Pen & Sword titles please contact
PEN & SWORD BOOKS LIMITED
47 Church Street, Barnsley, South Yorkshire, S70 2AS, England
E-mail: enquiries@pen-and-sword.co.uk
Website: www.pen-and-sword.co.uk

Atrocities

'Behaviour or actions that are wicked or ruthless.'

Concise English Dictionary

Diamonds

'Conflict diamonds (sometimes called blood diamonds) are diamonds that originate from areas controlled by forces or factions opposed to legitimate and internationally recognized governments, and are used to fund military action in opposition to those governments, or in contravention of the Security Council.'

United Nations definition

Diplomacy

'The application of intelligence and tact to the conduct of official relations between the governments of independent states.'

Satow's Guide to Diplomatic Practice

'A diplomat is someone who can tell a person to "go to hell" and that person is looking forward to the trip!'

Anon

Contents

Foreword

I have learnt a few things in my forty or so years as an operational soldier. One is that rarely do the experts, the pundits, the bureaucrats and the politicians in Western capitals understand the true nature of a crisis in some far away country as well as the diplomat, soldier and expat who are actually based there. It is only the latter who breathe the same often fearful air as those whose lives are at stake, or meet and thus better understand the leaders, good and bad, competing for power. Soldiers call it 'smelling the cordite,' the necessary precursor to success in battle. If ever this home-spun philosophy held true, as it does, it is in the compelling story of one man's resolute struggle to do the right thing by the benighted, trusting and hugely deserving people of Sierra Leone.

That man is Peter Penfold CMG, a brave and determined British diplomat of the old school. A little headstrong perhaps, but someone who – as we soldiers might say in admiration – one would 'happily go to war with.' His book is a spellbinding account of greed, frustration, intrigue, violence, incompetence and missed opportunity before slowly becoming a story of fresh hope. Peter kindly credits me and some others with helping restore stability in Sierra Leone. We played a role but nothing we did would have been possible without the foundations laid by this remarkable man over three dangerous and difficult years. At the time, to his embarrassment, the people of Sierra Leone almost deified him. To this day he excites there a loyalty, respect and affection that must today be almost unique in its intensity. Yet in the UK he had to retire early and without any of the honours that his forebears would surely have been accorded.

Peter Penfold served as the British High Commissioner in Sierra Leone during a critical period in its turbulent history. He was a key figure in all that went on. Dealing directly with the government and the rebels and witnessing the terrible atrocities heaped upon the Sierra Leone people, as one reads this book his single-minded commitment to this poor West African country becomes increasingly apparent. His actions were in the finest traditions of the British

Diplomatic Service, even if at times his masters in the UK did not fully appreciate what he was doing.

Assisted by a very small team of British soldiers and diplomats, Penfold's attempts after a coup in 1997 to bring an early resolution to the conflict very nearly succeeded. If he had been allowed to do as he had hoped, perhaps much of the next few years' bloodshed would have been avoided. As it was, much to his credit, the successful evacuations and the emergency humanitarian activities in which he played a central role undoubtedly saved many lives. He gave hope to a traumatised population. The Sierra Leone people demonstrated their thanks by making him a paramount chief, the only other non Sierra Leoneans to be given such an honour being The Queen and Prince Philip.

British forces can be rightly proud of what they did to help bring an end to one of Africa's bloodiest conflicts. Operations Palliser and Barrass, with which I was intimately involved, have become benchmarks for successful British military action overseas. But I have always been clear that it was Peter Penfold who set the conditions for our success. His selfless leadership and transparent devotion to the people of Sierra Leone in the three years leading up to our decisive intervention in May 2000 meant we enjoyed the instinctive support of the Sierra Leone Government and the vast majority of the Sierra Leone people. His very personal and informative account of that period reveals some of the intriguing background to our deployment.

The end of the Sierra Leone conflict came after much suffering, at least some of which might have been avoided if different decisions had been taken. Peter Penfold can justifiably be accused of mishandling Whitehall. But as the reader puts down this captivating and most readable of books, few will not be thinking that Whitehall also mishandled this intelligent and experienced diplomat with his huge feel for what was happening on the ground and what perhaps might just work best.

General Sir David Richards
February 2012

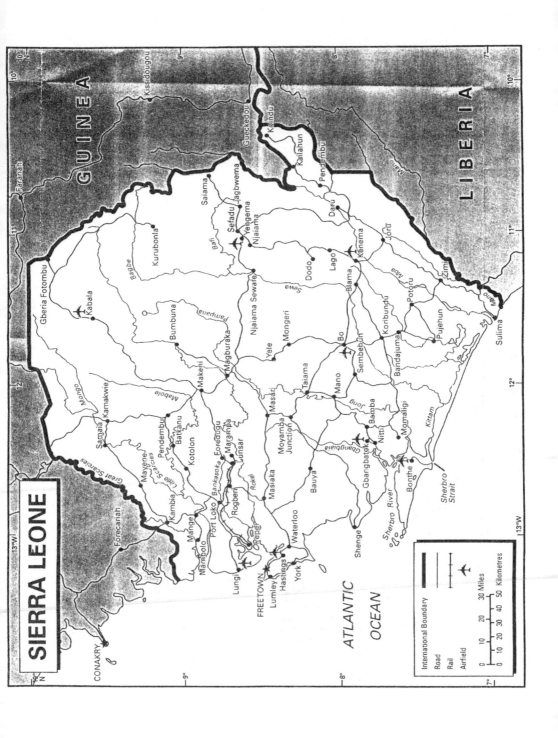

Sierra Leone – A Brief History

With a land mass of 28,000 square miles (roughly the size of Ireland), and a population of around six million, Sierra Leone lies on the West Coast of Africa, between Guinea and Liberia. This beautiful, English-speaking country, rich in agriculture, fishing and minerals (diamonds, gold, bauxite and rutile), derives its name from the Portuguese for 'Lion Mountain Range', given by early Portuguese explorers.

The history of modern Sierra Leone dates from 1787, when British abolitionists of the slave trade purchased from a local chief named Naimbana a strip of land on the peninsula and settled on it 400 freed slaves, calling the settlement Freetown. When Britain outlawed slave trading in 1807 a naval station was established in the natural harbour of Freetown, and slaves freed in naval operations by the ships stationed there were brought back to the settlement, many originally from Jamaica and Nova Scotia. In 1808 Freetown became a British colony and the hinterland a British protectorate from where the colonies of The Gambia and the Gold Coast (now Ghana) were also originally governed.

Sierra Leone peacefully attained independence as a member of the Commonwealth on 27 April 1961, with Her Majesty The Queen as head of state. Sir Milton Margai, of the Sierra Leone People's Party (SLPP), became the country's first prime minister. Disputed elections in 1967 led to two military coups and in 1968, Dr Siaka Stevens, of the All People's Congress (APC), became Prime Minister. Following an abortive coup in 1971, Sierra Leone became a republic, with Dr Stevens as President. Constitutional changes were enacted in 1978, making it a one-party (APC) state. Despite various coup attempts, Dr Stevens remained in power until 1986, when he handed over to his nominated successor, Major General Joseph Momoh. In 1992 Momoh was deposed in a military coup by a group of young army officers led by Captain Valentine Strasser, who formed the National Provisional Ruling Council (NPRC). Shortly before elections to return to a civilian government in 1996, Strasser was removed in a palace coup by his deputy, Julius Maada Bio. The following elections saw the appointment of Ahmad Tejan Kabbah of the SLPP as President, who remained President throughout most of the events of this book. The SLPP was defeated in elections in August 2007 by the APC, and Ernest Koroma became President.

Chronology

1462		Coastline sighted by Portuguese, named Serra Lyoa (Lion Range).
1787		400 freed slaves settle in Freetown.
1807		Britain bans slave trade.
1808		Freetown declared a British Crown Colony.
1896		Britain declares Sierra Leone hinterland a protectorate.
1961	27 April	Sierra Leone attains independence.
1971		President Siaka Stevens declares Sierra Leone a republic.
1991		Revolutionary United Front (RUF) commences hostilities.
1992		President Momoh overthrown in military coup by NPRC.
1995		NPRC signs agreement with Executive Outcomes.
1996	February	NPRC steps down and democratic elections bring in SLPP government under President Ahmad Tejan Kabbah.
	November	Abidjan Peace Accord signed with RUF.
1997	March	Peter Penfold takes up post as British High Commissioner.
	25 May	Armed Forces Revolution Council (AFRC) coup under Johnny Paul Koroma, joined by RUF, Kabbah flees to Conakry.
	May/June	Evacuations of international community.
	August	Ecowas imposes sanctions on Sierra Leone.
	October	United Nations (UN) Security Council Resolution 1132 imposing arms embargo.
		President Kabbah attends Commonwealth Heads of Government Meeting (CHOGM) as guest of Tony Blair. Conakry Peace Plan.
1998	Jan/Feb	Economic Community of West African States, Minority Group (Ecomog) forces push AFRC/RUF out of Freetown.
	March	President Kabbah returns.
		HMS *Cornwall* assists British relief effort.
	May	Sandline/Arms to Africa Scandal – HM Customs investigation.
		After case is dropped, Robin Cook sets up Legg Inquiry.
	June	Penfold made Paramount Chief in Sierra Leone.
	July	Legg report presented to House of Commons.
	Sept/Oct	Treason trials and executions in Freetown.
	November	Foreign Affairs Select Committee inquiry.
	December	Further evacuation from Freetown.

1999	6 January	Rebels re-invade Freetown, committing mass atrocities.
	Jan/Feb	Ecomog, assisted by Civil Defence Force (CDF), regain Freetown and push rebels back.
	June	Human Rights Watch publishes report on atrocities.
	July	Lomé Peace Agreement.
	October	'Vice-President' Foday Sankoh and Johnny Paul Koroma return.
2000	March	Ecomog starts withdrawal as UN begins deployment. General Khobe taken ill, later dies.
	April	Peter Penfold leaves at end of tour.
	May	RUF launch attacks around the country. Fighting around Sankoh's house in Freetown. New British High Commissioner, Alan Jones, arrives. Robin Cook orders evacuation of British community. British troops deployed to assist evacuation – Operation Palliser.
	June	British military training team arrives to train new Sierra Leone army.
	July	UN Security Council Resolution bans sale of 'blood diamonds'.
	August	Soldiers of Royal Irish Regiment taken hostage by 'West Side Boys'.
	September	British forces, led by Special Air Service (SAS), secure release of hostages – Operation Barras.
2001	January	Abuja Ceasefire.
2002	January	Agreement to establish Sierra Leone Special Court.
	February	President Kabbah declares the war is over.
	May	Kabbah and SLPP re-elected.
2003	March	Indictments issued against Sankoh, Koroma, Norman and others by Sierra Leone Special Court (SLSC) for war crimes. June Indictment issued.
	June	Indictment issued against Charles Taylor.
	July	Foday Sankoh dies in detention.
2005		UN Forces withdrawn.
	August	Robin Cook dies whilst hill walking.
2006	February	Testimonies before Special Court on behalf of Sam Norman.
	April	Taylor appears before SLSC in Freetown and later in The Hague.
2007	February	Sam Norman dies in detention following operation.
	August	SLPP led by Berewa defeated in elections by Ernest Koroma and APC.

Author's Note

Autobiography, if there really is such a thing, is like asking a rabbit to tell us what he looks like hopping through the grasses of the field. How would he know? If we want to hear about the field, on the other hand, no one is in a better circumstance to tell us – so long as we keep in mind that we are missing all those things the rabbit was in no position to observe.

Extract from Memoirs of a Geisha, *by Arthur Golden*

This book is an account of my time as the British High Commissioner to Sierra Leone from 1997 to 2000 and the years that followed – very eventful, dramatic and traumatic times for the country and its people, and for me. It is written from a personal standpoint, mainly using notes written soon after my departure from Sierra Leone, though like the rabbit above, it is hardly an autobiography, and certainly not a complete account of *all* that went on in Sierra Leone, nor Britain.

Over a decade on, it relates a seemingly bygone time in British foreign policy when there was more space for diplomacy overseas before the troops were sent in. However, I trust that you will find it interesting and informative. If it leaves you feeling a sense of admiration and commitment for the people of Sierra Leone, or even a little better informed about diplomatic life in far-flung corners of the world, then I will have achieved what I set out to do in writing this book.

I am indebted to my publishers Pen & Sword, particularly Brigadier Henry Wilson and Linne Matthews, for their support, and I acknowledge the help from many friends, but especially my godson, Jack Latham, with the collection of photographs and illustrations. Finally, I am most grateful to General Sir David Richards for writing the foreword to the book.

Peter Penfold
Abingdon, Oxfordshire
July 2011

Prologue

'So you knew that the Sandline contract with President Kabbah included the provision of arms and ammunition?' The question was directed to me from across the narrow table by one of the Customs and Excise investigators. Next to him sat his colleague eyeing me carefully. Next to me sat my solicitor. A tape recorder was on the table between us in the small windowless room. We were in an interview cell in the basement of Her Majesty's Customs and Excise headquarters, close to the Tower of London, and I was being interviewed 'under caution', which meant that anything I said could lead to me being prosecuted for a crime, which in this case carried a maximum penalty of seven years' imprisonment. What on earth was going on?

Just a month previously I had been part of a colourful cavalcade driving through the sunny streets of Freetown, capital of Sierra Leone, lined with thousands of waving and cheering Sierra Leoneans, celebrating the return of their president. The people were demonstrating their joy at the return of their legitimate, democratically elected government, after ten months of misery and hardship. As I passed in the British High Commission Land Rover with the Union Jack flying, they chanted 'Pen-fold, Pen-fold' in recognition of the role that Britain and I had played in securing this success. We made our way through the crowded streets to the National Stadium, filled to capacity with Sierra Leoneans who had been waiting patiently in the hot sun to see their president, Tejan Kabbah, and also General Sani Abacha, the Nigerian leader whose forces had made this day possible.

My return to Freetown, five days previously, had been made possible thanks to the British warship HMS *Cornwall*, whose helicopter had picked me up from Conakry, the capital of neighbouring Guinea, and then sailed me into a devastated and traumatized Freetown. Following my evacuation from Freetown in June 1997, I had spent most of the previous ten months in Conakry, in room 503 of the Hotel Camayenne. It was the hotel in which I had stayed when I had driven along the West African coast in March 1997 to take up my post as British High Commissioner to Sierra Leone. Arriving in Freetown then there was nothing to suggest the dramatic events that were about to unfurl.

Chapter One

Welcome to Freetown – 1997

The sign said 'Welcome to Freetown, Capital of Sierra Leone'. I glanced at the milometer – 1,963km since I had left Dakar. Now, where to go? I wound down the windows of the Land Rover and absorbed the exhilarating sights, sounds and smells of African life. Following what appeared to be the main road into the city, I found myself in the middle of downtown Freetown. The road had petered out and I was surrounded by stalls and market traders selling anything and everything from onions and tomatoes to used clothes and toothbrushes. Everyone was very friendly. I stopped a passing policeman and said, 'I'm the new British High Commissioner but I don't know where I live. Can you help me please?' He looked at me in disbelief and started to walk on but I managed to persuade him that I was serious. He jumped into the Land Rover and directed me out of town and up one of the steep hills that surrounded Freetown. As we drove he told me that he was Sub-Inspector Mambu and that as a member of the police band he had often been to the High Commissioner's residence to play his cornet.

We drove into the residence. The management officer, Dai Harries, was there and a telephone call quickly brought Colin Glass, the Deputy High Commissioner, to the house. They were surprised to see me. Apparently they were not expecting me until that evening. The residence was in a degree of chaos with the painters in and furniture scattered around. But I had arrived. I was excited and ready to start work as the new British High Commissioner to Sierra Leone – the 12th High Commissioner to be appointed by Her Majesty's Government since Sierra Leone's independence in 1961. I sent off a telegram to London the next day, 10 March, which said: 'I crossed the Guinea/Sierra Leone border yesterday morning and reached Freetown having driven 2,000km. I have assumed charge.'

The journey to Sierra Leone had been interesting. I had boarded the MV *Repubblica Di Amalfi*, an Italian container ship, two weeks previously in London's Tilbury Docks, together with my new Land Rover Discovery. The ship had been built to carry both passengers and freight but it turned out that I was the only passenger – clearly freight was more profitable and less hassle than cruise passengers. I was mainly left alone by the all-Italian crew during the day and joined them for dinner at night, when vast quantities of pasta were consumed. Football was the main topic of conversation so fortunately my support for Chelsea allowed me to contribute the odd Italian word like Zola, Di Matteo and Vialli. Thanks to satellite, Italian television was beamed straight to the ship and most evenings were spent watching Italian football. On one evening when we were watching a match between Napoli and Inter Milan the reception was so poor that the officers decided to alter course to get a better picture. For one and a half hours we steamed towards Brazil instead of Senegal!

The Bay of Biscay had been quite rough but as we skirted the Mauritanian coast we entered the calmer waters of the Atlantic. As we crossed the Tropic of Cancer the ship was surrounded by a thick mist. This was the Harmattan, the desert wind that blows across the Sahara picking up sand and depositing it along its trail. We approached Dakar port through the haze, passing Gorée Island on our port side – the infamous island where the slaves were assembled like cattle before being shipped off to the West Indies. Today it is visited by tourists who can inspect the cramped holding cells, where the manacles on the walls cry out of past slaves awaiting their fate on the treacherous journey across the Atlantic to a life of slavery and hardship on the plantations in the Caribbean and the United States. The Dakar pilot came on board and slowly and skilfully manoeuvred the ship through the breakwater and into the port, where I looked down to see Andrew Murro waiting alongside the quay. Andrew was an American friend who had flown across from New York to join me for part of the drive through West Africa.

We spent a day and a half sorting ourselves out, including clearing the Land Rover through Senegalese Customs, and set off. Our first night's destination was Banjul, the capital of The Gambia, the former British colony. We reached Barra, the ferry terminal across from Banjul, in good time and we seemed to be in luck as the ferry had just arrived. However, the ferry terminal gates were closed and we were told that we needed a ferry ticket, which we would have to obtain from an office in a village that we had already passed 2 kilometres back. We went back and bought a ticket for me and the Land Rover. Using a machine that looked like an abacus, the heavily pregnant ferry official explained that she could not issue a ticket for my passenger; this must be obtained at the ferry terminal. Back at the terminal we tried to enter but were told that we had the wrong ticket – my ticket was for a diplomatic vehicle resident in The Gambia; we were just passing through. We drove back to the ticket office. The right ticket issued, we drove back to the ferry terminal and reached the gates, only to see the ferry pulling away. We were told that the next ferry would be another three hours.

This was Andrew's first time in West Africa so I told him about WAWA – 'West Africa Wins Again'. Any time that something does not go as planned you merely shout 'WAWA' and put it down to experience. It was one way to preserve one's sanity in West Africa.

We shouted 'WAWA' many times over the next few days, especially when crossing the borders between The Gambia, Senegal and Guinea, but we finally arrived in Conakry, the capital of Guinea, where Andrew had to fly back to New York. I checked into the Hotel Camayenne and met up with Val Treitlein, the Honorary British Consul. We had closed our embassy in Conakry back in the 1970s and Val kept an eye on British interests. She and her German husband were old African hands and I much enjoyed their company. Val told me that she planned to write a book about life in Conakry that would be entitled *Just One More Signature*. She told of the endless succession of businessmen who came to Guinea to clinch that one big business deal that would make them rich. They arrived smart and eager and checked into the best hotel. After meeting the Guinean officials they would relax around the pool of the hotel just waiting for one more signature to clinch the deal. A few days later they would still be waiting around the pool, a little redder in the face but still confident of getting that signature. A few weeks would go by; they were now very red and somewhat dishevelled in their crumpled tropical suits. By now they had spent so much money on expenses that they dare not return to their head offices without the business deal, which required just one more signature.

I left Val and the Hotel Camayenne for the final leg of my journey to Sierra Leone, not realizing just how much they would become part of my life later that year.

This was not my first time in Sierra Leone. I had previously visited Freetown in the early 1980s when serving as the Sierra Leone desk officer in the West African Department of the Foreign and Commonwealth Office. Even then Freetown was showing signs of wear and tear from the affluent days of immediate post-independence, when Freetown was regarded as the 'Athens of West Africa'.

Sierra Leone's wealth was derived from an abundance of natural and mineral resources – dense mahogany forests, rich coastal fishing waters and fertile soil producing acres of rice and other crops that enabled the population to easily feed itself. The first diamond was discovered in 1930, and the rich alluvial deposits were augmented by deposits of gold, bauxite, iron ore and, especially, rutile. It is from rutile that titanium dioxide is produced, which aids the pigmentation process in paint. Sierra Leone boasted the most profitable rutile mine in the world, which, when it was working, contributed thirty per cent of all government revenue from royalties. However, years of corruption, inefficiency and mismanagement had set the decline of Sierra Leone's once healthy economy.

On independence, in 1961, it was richer than countries like Malaysia and Singapore but by 1977 Sierra Leone found itself ranked as the second poorest country in the world, according to the league table produced by the United Nations Development Programme (UNDP). Gross National Product per capita was less than $200. Seventy-five per cent of the five and a half million population lived in poverty, two thirds in extreme poverty. Life expectancy was forty-two years, infant mortality 162 per 1,000. Sixty per cent of the population had no access to safe and potable water. Illiteracy was eighty per cent. All these figures were far worse than the averages for Africa as a whole.

Within the first month of my arrival I sent, as was customary, a 'first impressions despatch' to Malcolm Rifkind, the Secretary of State at the time. I said that it would take a miracle to get Sierra Leone back on its feet. I took my cue from a sign painted in white on the side of one of the numerous churches driving into Freetown – 'Expect a Miracle'. But I noted that a miracle had already taken place in Sierra Leone – the elections in 1996.

The 1996 Elections

Miracles are ordinary events achieved in the face of extraordinary circumstances. Against all the odds, not least the ongoing rebel war and a further coup just weeks before polling day, democratic elections had taken place in Sierra Leone in February 1996. The determination of the people to hold the elections was truly amazing. After years of corrupt, inefficient and military governments, Sierra Leoneans had decided to embrace democracy. In the face of pressure both from within the country and from the international community, Valentine Strasser's NPRC military government, which had come to power in a military coup in 1991 by removing the government of President Momoh, had agreed to step down and hand over to an elected civilian government. Sierra Leoneans from all walks of life had decided to grab this opportunity to rid themselves once and for all of military governments.

In the forefront of the moves towards democracy were the women of Sierra Leone. As in many other African countries women were not expected, nor encouraged, to get involved in politics, which were traditionally a male preserve. However, a few brave women, including a dynamic civil activist, Mrs Zainab Bangura, had helped organize the various women's groups. Married to a senior politician, she had studied in Britain and then worked in the insurance business in Sierra Leone. But she became increasingly active in civil society and headed an organization called the Campaign for Good Governance. Zainab told me how she would visit the various markets dotted around Freetown and identify the various 'leaders' among the market women. She would then get them together and explain about the constitution and their democratic rights. The women responded enthusiastically. These mostly illiterate and uneducated women quickly grasped the fundamentals of democracy and referred to the constitution as their 'book'. Other civil leaders, trade unionists, students and teachers did likewise, creating a groundswell of grass roots public opinion in favour of democratic elections.

Sierra Leone's widely respected civil servant at the United Nations, Dr James Jonah, was brought back to organize the elections. As an Assistant Secretary-General of the UN, who had been to various trouble spots around the world, he was no stranger to difficult tasks. At one stage he had been considered a candidate to succeed Boutros Boutros-Ghali as Secretary-General, until the Ghanaian Kofi Anan had become the agreed choice. Most of the international community, led by Britain, supported the elections and the British Government put up £3 million to pay for them.

Although Strasser was committed to holding elections, not everyone shared this view, either in the army or outside. A huge conference was held at the Bintumani Conference Centre, built for when Sierra Leone had hosted the Organization of African Unity (OAU) conference in 1980 (and in so doing had crippled the economy), to debate whether the elections should go ahead. All parliamentary parties, civil and professional groups, the army and the police attended. Dr Jonah, recognizing the strength of feeling from the women, skilfully insisted that they should be adequately represented. Another leading female activist, Mrs Shirley Gbujama, was selected to chair the conference. (Both she and Zainab Bangura were later to become foreign ministers.) Despite many attempts to push through resolutions to stop or defer the elections, the majority of the people, led by the women, insisted that they should go ahead.

The RUF sent delegates to the conference. Under the leadership of Foday Sankoh, a former corporal in the army and erstwhile photographer, they had been waging a rebel war in the country since 1991. Sankoh, who had participated in a failed coup attempt against Siaka Stevens in 1971 and had spent most of the 1970s in jail, had previously fought alongside Charles Taylor, the rebel warlord in Liberia. The roots of the RUF were closely linked to Liberia and to Gaddafi in Libya, where both Taylor and Sankoh had received training in insurgency tactics. The RUF claimed that they were fighting for democracy and for the removal of the military government. However, they did not support the call for elections and carried on fighting in the bush. This gave the opponents of the elections the excuse to argue that there should be 'peace before elections'.

Just weeks before elections were due Strasser announced that he intended to stand as 'a civilian candidate'. This prompted his removal in a palace coup by his deputy, Brigadier Julius Maada Bio. Strasser, who sported his Ray-Ban sunglasses on every occasion, had been the world's youngest head of state. He was sent into exile, initially to Guinea and then to the UK, where he was given a scholarship to study law at Warwick University. He ended up living on the dole in North London. Under Bio's leadership, the military government started manoeuvring to cancel the elections. The people, with the women in the lead, marched on the government and demanded that the elections should go ahead in line with their constitutional rights. Carrying copies of the 1991 Sierra Leone Constitution in their hands, the market women told Bio he 'must not touch their book!' Bio backed down and allowed the elections to take place. But on polling day, as thousands lined up to cast their votes, the army turned out in force on the streets and tried to intimidate the people by firing at them. The people bravely stood fast and voted, and then resolutely guarded the ballot boxes to prevent them from disappearing and reappearing stuffed with forged papers, an altogether too common occurrence in African elections. A number of international observers from the UN and the Commonwealth were in Sierra Leone to monitor the elections. Despite some irregularities, they all declared them to be as free and fair as the prevailing circumstances allowed.

Fifteen parties had contested the elections, which, as usual, were dominated by a north/south divide. Prior to the 1991 coup the government had been the northern dominated APC (All People's Congress), the party of the Siaka Stevens and Joseph Momoh, but this time the northern vote was split between the United National People's Party (UNPP), the People's Democratic Party (PDP) and the APC. This allowed the southern based Sierra Leone People's Party (SLPP), the party of the founding father of Sierra Leone's independence, Sir Milton Margai, to win the election with thirty-six per cent of the votes cast.

The slogan for the elections campaign had been 'the future is in your hands' and this had led to the gruesome practice of chopping off people's hands. As elsewhere in Africa, to show that a person had voted and in order to prevent them from voting twice, a mark in indelible ink was put on a finger. If a person was found with such a marking, the RUF rebels hacked off the hand. One such victim was asked how he now felt about voting. Proudly waving his stump, he replied that he had another hand and would use that one the next time to vote. When I heard such stories, it had a profound effect on me. In Britain and in other countries, we took our democracy for granted. How many people in Britain would vote if, in doing so, they risked having their hand chopped off? In Africa great sacrifices were made in the cause of democracy. In South Africa Nelson Mandela endured twenty-seven years in prison for the right to vote; in Sierra Leone people lost their hands.

For the elections the SLPP had chosen as their leader Ahmad Tejan Kabbah. He had been working with the UN in New York for over twenty years after having served as a district officer in the Sierra Leone Public Service. He had little experience of Sierra Leone politics but he was widely regarded as honest, sincere and incorrupt. After years of corruption and inefficiency, he was seen by the people as the one person who could bring Sierra Leone out of the morass into which she had sunk. Kabbah was a Mandingo and a Moslem, born in the north but with tribal roots in the south. Tall and handsome, in his mid sixties, he was a lawyer by training and married to a fellow lawyer, Patricia, a Catholic

Christian. This unusual combination of circumstances made him acceptable to a wide range of the population. He failed to achieve the necessary fifty-one per cent in the first round of voting for the presidency but in the presidential run-off he secured fifty-nine per cent to defeat the veteran politician, John Karefa-Smart, of the UNPP.

President Kabbah set about healing the wounds that had divided the country. He brought into his cabinet some of those who had run against him in the presidential elections, including Thaimu Bangura, the Temne leader of the PDP who had come third in the presidential race. Karefa-Smart chose not to join the coalition but instead formed the official opposition in Parliament.

Kabbah also set about ending the rebel war with the RUF. The latter had come very close to Freetown but in 1995 the NPRC government, unable to secure any help from any Western or African government and faced with imminent attack, had engaged the services of a South African based private security firm, Executive Outcomes (EO). Thanks largely to EO's assistance, the rebels had been repulsed. With less than 200 men, they had retaken the diamond mining area of Kono and by the following year, the RUF had been pushed back against the border with Liberia.

The Abidjan Peace Accord

Peace talks between the Kabbah government and the RUF were started and culminated in the signing of the Abidjan Peace Accord in November 1996. Under the terms of the agreement the members of the RUF would be granted amnesty, they would be demobilized and some of them absorbed into the army. In a confidential annex to the accord a number of the RUF would be given positions in government. One of the conditions upon which the RUF insisted was that the government's contract with Executive Outcomes should be terminated. Despite widespread concerns expressed by many of President Kabbah's advisers, he agreed. The EO staff were withdrawn. Although an offshoot of EO, Lifeguard, continued to provide security for the Sierra Rutile mine and for a diamond mine run by a British firm, Branch Energy.

Prominent among the EO personnel had been a remarkable man, Fred Marafono. A Fijian by birth, Fred was an ex-member of the SAS who had fought with this elite regiment in many parts of the world. After the departure of EO, Fred remained in Sierra Leone and developed a close attachment to the country. His exploits would be colourfully described in the book by Hamish Ross, *From SAS to Blood Diamond Wars*.

A Commission for the Consolidation for Peace (CCP) was set up to implement the terms of the Abidjan Peace Accord, under the chairmanship of the colourful and outspoken Desmond Luke, one of Sierra Leone's leading lawyers and a former foreign minister under Siaka Stevens. A United Nations Trust Fund was established to implement the provisions of the accord, to which the British Government contributed £1.2 million. As the leading bilateral aid donor, the British Government embarked upon a number of aid projects designed to nurture the infant democracy – support for the Parliament, the Public Service, the judicial sector, the press and media and various civil society and human rights groups. It also paid attention to the security sector through projects to support the police and military. A two-man British military training team arrived, headed by a Scots Guard's officer, Major Lincoln Jopp.

I reported to London at the time that I felt for once we were getting things right with our aid programme. For far too long we had seen millions of dollars of aid money in Africa channelled into providing better healthcare, education, transport, communications and so on; but it was all wasted if the problems of insecurity, instability and corruption were not also addressed. The number of schools and hospitals destroyed and people made homeless and hungry as a result of coups and rebellions was endless. This would continue to be the case unless more attention was focussed on security and good government. The previous Tory government under Douglas Hurd and Lynda Chalker's guidance had recognized this and the New Labour government under Tony Blair and Robin Cook was continuing this policy.

In my speech during the presentation of my credentials to President Kabbah at State House I noted that 'one could have stability without development, but one could not have development without stability.' I also noted that I had served in Nigeria in the 1960s during the civil war, in Ethiopia in the 1970s during the revolution, in Uganda in the 1980s during two military coups, so how nice it was at last to serve in 'a peaceful African country'. These remarks were to prove somewhat ironic and prophetic; but for the first few weeks I began to settle into my new home and started to travel around the country.

The British High Commissioner's residence was perched high on one of the hills overlooking Freetown, a couple of miles from the office. It was called 'Runnymede', after the site of the signing of Magna Carta in Britain. A large, modern building, built in the 1960s, it had a grand marble staircase leading down from the entrance hall to the large drawing and dining rooms on the lower floor. Though lacking the character of our previous residence, Government House in the British Virgin Islands in the Caribbean, it was very functional for living and entertaining. The upper floor contained a suite of rooms for our personal use plus a couple of guest bedrooms. The lower floor was encased by large sliding doors, which remained closed most of the time to keep in the air-conditioned cool air, provided by a generator that ran continuously. At times it felt like living in a large fish tank. A large patio surrounded the house leading onto the gardens, which sloped steeply down the hillside.

To help run Runnymede there were Osman, the cook/housekeeper, assisted by Alimamy, John and Fatmata, and Abu, with Toma and Ibrahim, to tend the large garden. They were to become members of our extended African family.

Osman had been working at the residence for four years. A devout Moslem, he came from Lunsar in the north and had previously worked as a pastry chef in one of the Freetown hotels. His cooking was excellent. He could produce a wide range of meals to suit anyone's palate, from Joloff rice and peas – the Sierra Leone national dish – to steak and kidney pudding. But his sense of organization left much to be desired. We would regularly run out of food even when he had been to the market the day before, or he would produce a sumptuous lunch, only to forget that we had guests coming to dinner that evening. If one could deal with the frustrations of Osman, one could deal with anything. But he was friendly and engaging and Celia and I got to love him dearly. We nicknamed him 'Oh dear!' because every time something had been forgotten, he would appear from the kitchen to explain and start by saying 'Oh dear!'

Alimamy's nickname was 'Yes please'. He was very shy and hardly spoke at all, unlike Osman. When questioned about anything, Alimamy had a habit of clutching his testicles for comfort. He had worked out that the best response to any question was 'Yes please'. John and Fatmata were much more on the ball. John was in charge of the drinks. He took his job so conscientiously that he often felt obliged to personally check the drinks before he served them. In quick time he was producing the best gins and tonic in Sierra Leone. Fatmata was the only member of staff to live in. She was very fashion conscious and at weekends on her day off, she would dress up to the nines to go into town to socialize with her friends.

One month after my arrival it was time to hold The Queen's Birthday Party (QBP), at the residence, the highlight of the social year. The Queen's Official Birthday is in June but British Embassies and High Commissions have discretion to vary the date. As it would be held outdoors and as the rainy season would be in full swing in June, it made more sense to hold the QBP in April, the month of Her Majesty's actual birthday. This would prove a good opportunity to meet a large cross section of the Sierra Leone and British community early on in my tour.

Among the guests invited was ex-President Momoh. This caused quite a stir. Momoh had returned to Sierra Leone after his overthrow but was rarely seen out in public. It seemed to me that as an ex-president of a government with whom Britain had maintained relations, it was right that he should be invited. I had another reason for doing so. One of the problems, especially in Africa, is the difference in lifestyle between being a president and an ex-president. As president, you reign supremely in power and luxury, whereas an ex-president, even if he survived not being killed, would often be forced to live in relative poverty with no power and little respect. If ex-presidents were seen to still be worthy of respect, given a pension, invited to official functions, etc, then perhaps more presidents might be prepared to stand down, rather than abuse the democratic system and cling on to power. Ex-President Momoh turned up looking very smart in a natty pinstripe suit. After some hesitation from his fellow guests, he was soon engulfed in animated conversation with many of them. He clearly was thoroughly enjoying himself and said so as he left.

Another important member of my extended African family was my driver, Emmanuel Fillie. His family came from the diamond area of Kono, where they had suffered badly at the hands of the rebels. He was very proud to be the British High Commissioner's driver and was to become one of my closest confidants. Sierra Leone is relatively small, about the size of Ireland, and Emmanuel and I started travelling around the country by road. This was something that my predecessor, Ian McCluney, had not been able to do much because of the insecurity created by the rebel war.

It was in the rural areas that one witnessed the true extent of the poverty of Sierra Leone. Freetown was certainly run down but I had seen similar capitals, and living in Freetown did not leave you feeling that you were in the second poorest country in the world. Outside of Freetown you could begin to see this. But it was not the poverty of malnutrition. Sierra Leone was blessed agriculturally with good soil and ample rainfall and sunshine so no one needed to go hungry. It was the total absence of other amenities – healthcare, sanitation, education, employment, communications, transport, housing – in the rural areas, where there was hardly any sign that a government existed. People just subsisted and survived; their way of life had not changed for centuries.

We visited Bo, the second city of Sierra Leone, in the south, and from there we toured the surrounding districts in the company of a British doctor, Mike Downham. Mike was one of the admirable band of selfless people whom one bumps into in the far-flung corners of Africa who, with meagre resources and basic lifestyle, get on with helping those around them. Originally sent out to study the killer disease of Africa – malaria – he was now running a British aid-funded project setting up rural health clinics. People, who before would have had to walk up to 30 miles to receive medical attention, could now get it on the spot. It was one of the best aid-funded projects I had ever seen.

We visited one of these clinics in the tiny village of Sar, about one and a half hours' drive along rough corrugated tracks north of Bo. I formally opened the clinic and the local headman made a moving speech of appreciation. He invited me to inspect the local school, which apart from the clinic was the only breeze-block building in the village. It comprised two rooms, a tin roof and a mud floor. About fifty children, bright-eyed and smiling, sat cramped on benches in their smart school uniforms. They had no exercise books, pencils or paper. The bare-footed teacher wrote the lesson on the faded blackboard and the children copied it down in chalk on top of their desks. At the end of the day they would have to rub it all out to prepare for the next day's lessons, almost symbolizing that everything they had learned that day counted for nothing. What I found astonishing was that what I read on the blackboard was of a higher standard than one would find in the best-equipped primary schools in Britain.

I had arranged with a printing firm in Freetown to produce some school exercise books with the Sierra Leonean flag and Union Jack and the words 'From the children of Britain to the children of Sierra Leone' on the cover. I presented a box of these together with pencils, rulers and rubbers and a box of chalk. The teacher noted that when he ran out of chalk he would use a dried cassava stick to write on the blackboard. He had not been paid for three months. Even if his salary was available to collect in Bo, there was no public transport, and to go by taxi would cost half a month's salary. There were two dedicated teachers at the school, working a two-shift system. A group of children would come in the morning and another group in the afternoon. Some of the children would have to walk up to three hours a day to get to school from the surrounding villages.

Education was the most sought-after luxury in Africa. Parents and guardians made enormous sacrifices to educate their children. It was the one chance by which they could lift themselves from the subsistence lifestyle in which they were stuck. An educated child represented the opportunity of a job, which would benefit all the family.

From Bo, Emmanuel and I drove to Makeni, one of the major towns in the north, but by a little-used route. The Shell map showed a dirt road but it had all but disappeared in parts, which made the journey very hazardous. Close to Makeni was Magburaka, which was where some of the RUF rebels had started voluntarily coming out of the bush to surrender. They were staying at the Islamic Training College in the town. I wanted to meet them to see what could be done to encourage more to surrender.

The local officials had been alerted that we were coming but we confused them by arriving from 'the wrong direction'. No one had travelled the route we had taken for a considerable time as it had taken us through Foday Sankoh's village and where rebels were still active. Fortunately, I was treated better than poor Bishop Hannington of Uganda. In the 19th century he had arrived in Uganda 'from the wrong direction' and the Kabaka, the superstitious King of Buganda, had him killed for this 'crime'.

A big ceremony had been arranged with all the local dignitaries in attendance – the District Officer, Paramount Chief and local elders. A group of fifty or so RUF rebels were herded into one of the large classrooms. They looked dishevelled, sullen and suspicious. They listened in silence to the endless speeches. One of them was invited to say something. A young boy, no more than sixteen, stood up, quoted disconnected tracts from the *Bible*, and sat down. This was not what I wanted. I had wanted to get a chance to talk to them without all this fanfare. I told them that I would come back the next day but without any ceremonies. As I took my leave, one of the RUF muttered to me: 'If you're coming back tomorrow, bring some Fanta' – soft drinks.

I stayed that night with Bishop George Biguzzi in his modest but comfortable dwelling on the outskirts of Makeni, close to the army barracks. I was immediately impressed by him. This Italian cleric in his late fifties was revered in the north and widely respected throughout the country. During my predecessor's time, the RUF had embarked upon a number of kidnappings and by January 1995, they had been holding seventeen expatriates, including six Britons and seven Catholic nuns, as well as sixty-two Sierra Leoneans. The skilful negotiations for their eventual successful release had been conducted by Bishop Biguzzi and Ian McCluney over the high frequency (HF) radio set at the residence. The Bishop's knowledge of what was going on, especially in the north, was second to none. The Catholic Church had a network of priests, mainly Italian, spread all around the remote corners of the country, and over breakfast the next morning I listened with fascination as the Bishop called up each of them over his radio network to check how things were.

After calling on Paramount Chief Bai Seborah Kasangha II in Makeni the next morning, we drove back to Magburaka. I joined the RUF in one of their dormitories and they continued to view me with their sullen faces. I began to believe that it would take months of 'trauma counselling' before we could ever begin to make an impact on these youths, who had spent the last six years living in the bush committing awful deeds in the name of their supposed revolutionary movement. I reminded them that I had been asked to bring back some Fanta. Emmanuel appeared with a large ice box full of Fantas, Sprites and Cokes and we started handing them out. The change was phenomenal. From a bunch of sullen and morose kids, we suddenly had a group of friendly, animated children. Some of them began to chat confidently with me. One of them told me that after six years in the bush, the bottle of Fanta that he was holding in his hand represented the first thing that someone had actually given to him without him taking or stealing it.

In talking and listening to them, it soon became apparent that they had little knowledge of the Abidjan Peace Accord. The RUF leader, Foday Sankoh, known as 'Pappy', was to them a messianic figure who controlled the organization with a rod of iron. He was supported by a band of ruthless lieutenants, many of whom were Liberians, who went by names such as Mosquito, Superman and Black Jesus. Tight discipline was maintained and the flow of information was closely controlled. For example, the rank and file were forbidden from listening to the radio. Everything that was looted was carefully written down in school exercise books and a portion had to go to Sankoh. The use of drugs was widespread. Children as young as seven or eight were given drugs to complement the daily programme of propaganda and indoctrination. Biblical texts rolled off their lips without any fundamental understanding and with a complete absence of morals and ethics. When the RUF attacked a village, they would burn all the homes and kill or maim the adults – sometimes children were ordered to kill their own parents. In so doing, the RUF became their surrogate family. Those who joined the movement at the age of twelve were by the age of sixteen junior officers with the powers to command adults twice their age. Many of them had no idea how old they were and whether their true parents were alive. Many of the younger ones became 'slaves' to the older commanders. They claimed that there were many who would leave the miserable existence in the bush but that they were afraid to do so; they related tales of arbitrary executions of others who had tried to leave. Hollywood would later capture the essence of this lifestyle in its movie *Blood Diamonds*.

Although the site itself was good, the conditions at the Magburaka camp were poor. There was no bedding, no pots and pans for cooking, no plates and spoons for eating. This annoyed me as our contribution to the UN Trust Fund had been made to supply such materials and I knew that they were sitting in a warehouse in Freetown. I raised this with the UN when I got back to the capital. The UN, together with the Ministry of Reconstruction, Rehabilitation and Resettlement (known as the Triple R Ministry), were responsible for setting up the camps. I was told that Magburaka was not one of the designated sites under the programme. I pointed out that none of the other camps had yet been set up at the designated sites; if the RUF felt more comfortable coming to Magburaka, we should set up a camp there. The way that the first ones who came out of the bush were treated would determine whether others would come. I heard later that another group had voluntarily surrendered near Freetown but had been sent back to the bush, being told that the programme was not yet ready for them!

Meeting the RUF in Magburaka increased my view, widely shared by others, that Foday Sankoh and the RUF commanders were not taking the Abidjan Peace Accord seriously. It later came to light that within hours of signing the accord, Sankoh had sent a message to his commanders in the bush telling them not to take any notice of the document he had signed and that he was merely playing for time to regroup and rearm. Sankoh's attitude towards the peace accord had been encouraged by an international non-governmental organization (NGO), International Alert (IA). A representative of IA had been present during the negotiations in Abidjan, supposedly as an impartial and neutral participant to help the peace process along, but this representative was accused by the UN and others of acting as an advisor to the RUF and of encouraging Sankoh to adopt an entrenched and belligerent attitude.

Other RUF members, like Fayia Musa and the Deen-Jallohs, who had been involved in the Abidjan negotiations and had been appointed by Sankoh as members of the CCP, became disillusioned with Sankoh's attitude. In April they announced that they no longer accepted Sankoh as leader of the RUF. One of the young RUF commanders, Philip Palmer, was appointed acting leader in his place. Through Desmond Luke I met the group, who announced their intention of implementing the Abidjan Accord. I felt a degree of optimism.

In the meantime, Sankoh had flown to Nigeria from Abidjan, where he had been living in comfortable exile, to conclude an arms deal. On arrival at Lagos airport he was arrested by a vigilant Nigerian customs officer for carrying a gun and ammunition. With the agreement of President Kabbah, the Nigerian authorities detained Sankoh, who was ensconced under guard in a luxury villa.

With Sankoh out of the way, Palmer and some of his group went into the bush to meet the notorious RUF commander, Colonel Sam Bockarie, alias 'Mosquito', at the RUF camp near Kailahun on the Liberian border. The group were immediately taken hostage and reportedly tortured. Nothing more was ever heard of them. My optimism began to evaporate.

As well as the set-backs with the RUF, President Kabbah's government was facing increasing problems with the army and the Kamajors. The latter were traditional hunters in the Mende southern area whose role was to defend the villages from intruders, be they animal or human. Much mystique surrounded the Kamajors. Initiated with special rites and armed by magic charms, these fearsome looking warriors were reputedly immune from bullets, as long as they did not go with women or eat bananas. Fred Marafono and Executive Outcomes had organized a training programme for the Kamajors in collaboration with one of the local regent chiefs, Sam Hinga Norman. As a result, the Kamajors had often proved a match for the RUF rebels when the latter had attacked their villages.

Several reports of clashes between the Sierra Leone army and the Kamajors were received. Part of the problem stemmed from the fact that President Kabbah had appointed Sam Norman as the minister responsible for the army. Norman was a suitable choice. As a retired captain in the army, he had received some training in the UK. However, the army claimed that Norman was favouring the Kamajors over the army in terms of the provision of military equipment and food supplies.

Years of military rule under the NPRC government had led to a feather-bedded army. By relative standards to the civilian population, a soldier did very well. The military budget was crippling the economy. Kabbah inherited a situation whereby the military were taking sixty per cent of the entire government revenue. It was customary that the army, as well as being paid wages, received a rice ration. The officers received substantial amounts of rice, which they sold to supplement their wages. They, in effect, became rice traders. The ordinary soldiers did less well but they supplemented their income by using their guns to steal from the civil population. They were soldiers by day and rebels by night and thus became known as 'sobels'.

That there was corruption in the army was indisputable but the extent of the corruption began to be revealed as we attempted to introduce our military training programme. The plan was to train two full battalions, i.e. 1,200 men, in two phases. This was to be done with an American training team who had arrived in the country. The Americans would train the rank and file with basic training, while our two-man team, led by Lincoln Jopp, assisted by Sierra Leone instructors, would train the officers – on a ludicrously meagre budget of £140,000 from the Foreign Office.

Despite the months of preparation, just days before the programme was to commence, the Chief of the Defence Staff (CDS), Brigadier Hassan Conteh, told Lincoln Jopp that he could not provide the necessary 600 men for the training. I went to see Conteh to ask why. He said it was because of the security situation in the country. According to my information the RUF were confined to three small areas in the country and although they were carrying out ambushes on vehicles and the occasional hit-and-runs on villages, they were not posing as significant a threat as they had in the past. I expressed surprise, therefore, that the situation was so bad to tie up an army of 15,000 strong, the number for which the military drew wages and rice rations every month. Leaning back in his swivel chair in his grand office at the Cockerill Defence Headquarters, surrounded by radios and telephones, Conteh admitted that the figure of 15,000 was not accurate, that in terms of fighting troops there were only 6,000 in the Sierra Leone army.

I sought a meeting with Sam Norman and reported on my conversation with his CDS. The Deputy Minister of Defence exploded, saying that he had been trying for months to find out the true number of military forces. He reported to the President and I was asked to attend a meeting at State House, together with Norman, Vice-President Joe Demby, Conteh and the Chief of Army Staff, Colonel Max Kanga. Conteh changed his tune and said it was not a question of numbers but that his men would require new boots and uniforms to take part in the training programme. However, he promised he would find 300 men to start the training.

As a result of the revelations about the army figures, Conteh was told that the rice ration for the army would have to be cut. Rice was the staple food of the people. A Sierra Leonean measured his lifestyle by the price and availability of rice. For the average Sierra Leonean rice was scarce and expensive. Under the corrupt army system, the more senior the officer, the more bags of rice he would receive. A colonel, for example, received thirty-three bags of rice per month, while an ordinary soldier received just one. However, Conteh determined that if there were going to be cuts, it would not be the senior officers who would suffer. He announced that the rice ration for the lower ranks would be reduced. This fuelled much resentment within the army.

These were all worrying signs. The UN Special Envoy, Berhanu Dinka, the US Ambassador, John Hirsch, and I spent a Saturday morning on the veranda of President Kabbah's private home on Juba Hill, impressing upon him the need to address the problems of the army, particularly its antagonism towards Hinga Norman. We passed on rumours that a coup was being planned. The President said that he was aware of the rumours. He would arrange meetings with the army, but there was no urgency.

A week later, on Sunday, 25 May as the dawn broke over Freetown, we awoke to gunshots around the city.

Chapter Two

Coup and Evacuation

T he rainy season in Sierra Leone starts in May and lasts seven months. The hills surrounding Freetown trap the rain clouds, making Freetown the wettest city along the West African coast. However, Sunday, 25 May started with the sun shining – the start of ten very eventful days.

Sunday, 25 May 1997

I usually preferred not to sleep with the air-conditioner going and I awoke around seven o'clock to the distant sound of intermittent gunfire. Still in my dressing gown, I went out to the main gate to check what was going on. The guards at the gate said that they had been hearing the sound of AK47s and mortars firing since about six o'clock. It was not clear exactly from where it was coming.

I went back into the house and telephoned Colin Glass. I spoke to his son, Andrew; his dad was still sleeping. Colin had not heard the shooting over the noise of his air-conditioning. At first he was inclined to think that our local guards were exaggerating and said, 'I bet they've been drinking again on duty.' I rang Hassan Kamara, our local information officer, who lived close to State House, downtown. He reported shooting in his vicinity but did not know what was going on. I then took a call from Zainab Bangura, who had also heard the shooting. She had spoken to the President, who was still in his house at Juba Hill. There were reports that the prison had been broken into and all the prisoners had been released. I rang Colin back and told him to meet me in the office.

I drove down the hill to the office, going past the Wilberforce Barracks, headquarters of the 1st Battalion of the Sierra Leone army. They appeared deserted. A military Land Rover was skewed across the side of the road, abandoned. People were standing around looking apprehensive.

In the office I turned on the local radio and at five minutes to nine, a Corporal Gborie announced that there has been a coup. Barely capable of stringing more than two sentences together, he said that it was purely an internal affair and advised all foreign troops to stay out of it. He ordered all Sierra Leone troops to report to the Cockerill Defence Headquarters. The announcement sparked off another bout of shooting all around the city.

I told Colin to bring all the staff and their families into the office. I telephoned the Resident Clerk in the Foreign Office in London to brief him and followed this up with a reporting telegram. I also spoke to Lincoln Jopp, who was staying at the Cape Sierra Hotel, and to Joe Docherty, the British Council representative, at his home.

The heavy firing continued and we started to receive reports from members of the British and diplomatic communities of wide-scale looting by armed soldiers all around the town. Our friend Corporal Gborie came back on the radio to say that the President had left the country. He appealed to the Nigerians to release Foday Sankoh, to allow him to return and help form the new government. A similar appeal was made to SAJ Musa, a leading member of the former NPRC government, who was currently studying at Warwick University in the UK. All senior army officers were advised to report to State House, which Gborie claimed he and his fellow soldiers now controlled. So I telephoned State House, but there was no reply.

In the first few hours of any coup it was always difficult to find out precisely what was going on, to sort out fact from rumour, but slowly a picture began to emerge of what had happened. A group of seventeen soldiers had broken into an ordinance depot in the early hours and stolen some weapons. They had also got hold of some red T-shirts, which became their unofficial uniform. They attacked the Pademba Road prison in the middle of town and released all the prisoners, including sixty-five fellow soldiers, among whom was a Major Johnny Paul Koroma, a 37-year-old army officer who had previously been convicted on treason charges but whose life had been spared by President Kabbah. From there a group went and shot at the Nigerian soldiers around State House and another group took over the Sierra Leone Broadcasting Service radio station. No officers were involved in the original group. One of the main motives appeared to be to express dissatisfaction with the senior officers over the proposed measures to cut the rice ration. Whether the soldiers thought that the President was actually living in State House was not clear but at the first sign of the shooting, the Nigerian troops guarding President Kabbah at his private home at Juba Hill decided to whisk him away by helicopter.

Many argued subsequently that President Kabbah should have stayed, if not in Freetown, at least in the country. For example, he could have flown to Lungi Airport, under the control of the Nigerian troops, or to Bo or Kenema. But at around 8.00 am, the Nigerians flew him to Conakry, where he took refuge with President Conte. Before being bundled out of his house, Kabbah had made some vain attempts to contact Hassan Conteh, the Chief of the Defence Staff, and Max Kanga, the Chief of the Army Staff, but they had both gone to ground. He tried to record a message to the people, which he could leave with supporters to play over a radio station, assuring them that he was safe and well and that the situation would be brought under control, but he had no batteries for his tape recorder – WAWA.

There was total mayhem. The shooting and looting continued all day, including at the homes of the Standard Chartered Bank manager, the International Monetary Fund (IMF) representative and the High Commission doctor. There were reports that at least two members of the large Lebanese community had been killed and the wife of the Sabena (the then national airline of Belgium) representative had been raped. Many buildings had been set on fire, including the Treasury Building. Several of the soldiers who had been released from the prison were on embezzlement charges. By burning down the Ministry of Finance they had thought that they would be destroying all the evidence against them. This ploy backfired when a few days later, the end of the month came around and there were no records to pay the army. The IMF representative's house was looted several times because the army held the IMF responsible for advising the government to cut the wages bill and rice rations. After the sixth attack the poor chap walked away from his house, leading his traumatized family and clutching only the *Koran* in his hand.

But it was not just the diplomatic corps or the rich expatriates among the Lebanese and Indian business communities who suffered from the looting. As more and more soldiers joined in, they went berserk, looting and terrorising everyone. Even the poorest of the Sierra Leoneans suffered at the hands of the looters. Nobody was spared. By late afternoon a Captain Thomas came on the radio. He declared a dusk to dawn curfew and announced that all land, sea and air borders were closed. He appealed to the international community to show restraint – the designated head of state would brief them in due course. Captain Thomas sounded more authoritative than Corporal Gborie. At least he could read a statement, but the continued shooting did nothing to ease our concerns.

At 9.45 pm, Major Johnny Paul Koroma came on the radio. He introduced himself as the Head of State and Chairman of the Armed Forces Revolutionary Council. The soldiers had used the acronym 'AFRC' out of respect for President Jerry Rawlings, who, after he had come to power in a military coup in Ghana, had established the AFRC government there. Rawlings was the first neighbouring head of state with whom the rebel soldiers tried to make contact. Speaking in a brisk military tone, Koroma outlined the reasons for overthrowing the government and called again for the release of Sankoh, who was designated AFRC Vice-Chairman. He concluded his broadcast with the message, 'The struggle continues. I thank you all.'

In the office we had been busy all day taking calls, receiving visitors and reporting to London. All members of the British community were advised to stay in their homes, keep their heads down and not to venture out. Some of the community did make their way to the office compound and we took them in, but we reluctantly turned away several Sierra Leoneans who also sought sanctuary. I feared that their presence on the compound might endanger the lives of those for whom we were responsible and I did not want to give the soldiers any excuse for breaking into the compound.

As darkness fell we began to settle down for the long night ahead. I had instinctively drawn upon my experiences in dealing with the coups in Uganda in the mid 1980s. We made sure that all our vehicles were out of sight from the road. It was usually the sight of vehicles that first attracted the attention of would-be looters. Our local guards were at the gate but they were not armed and we could not expect them to risk their lives when confronted by armed unruly soldiers – although this was precisely what they bravely did on several occasions.

In Uganda I had learned the importance of getting all the staff and their families under one roof, no matter how uncomfortable it was. Even though most of the staff lived in houses on the compound, I still insisted that everyone moved into the office as we could not be sure that under the cover of darkness looters might not try to climb over the fence and break into the houses. We had young children with us. There were Colin's two children, Andrew and Rachel, and Ann Stephen had her 18-month-old son, Andrew. In all, we numbered around sixteen. Everyone bedded down in various offices. We had one shower in the building, normally used by the drivers and gardeners, and one small kitchen. But on that first night there was little thought of eating, washing or sleeping. We just wanted to survive.

Monday

The night passed quickly. There was some spasmodic shooting but a very heavy rainstorm dampened the enthusiasm of the soldiers for looting. I rang the resident clerk and tuned into the BBC World Service news. The coup in Sierra Leone was the lead item. Journalists telephoned from Britain and elsewhere. In an interview with Radio Scotland I emphasized the role of Colin, the Scottish Deputy High Commissioner, and in the interview with Radio Wales I did likewise with Dai Harries, the Welsh management officer. We truly were a British High Commission!

Internationally, the coup had been widely condemned. African leaders meeting in Harare had called for the immediate restoration of President Kabbah's government and General Sani Abacha, the Nigerian Head of State, had ordered the Nigerian vessel carrying a battalion of Nigerian troops to return to Freetown. There was also talk of Nigerian troops being flown into Lungi Airport.

Lincoln Jopp arrived at around 7.30 am. He had driven up from the Cape Sierra Hotel and was able to give a first-hand account of the scene on the streets. He reported a few people out and about but very few vehicles and no taxis. There were several dead bodies lying around. He had passed only one military road block but had no difficulty getting through in his uniform.

I spoke to the Nigerian High Commissioner, who was also Dean of the Diplomatic Corps, the UN Special Envoy and the US Charge d'Affaires, Ann Wright – John Hirsch, the Ambassador, was out of the country. At my suggestion we agreed to invite the members of the AFRC to a meeting. My residence was agreed by all parties as a neutral venue. Lincoln and I drove up to the residence to await their arrival.

First to arrive were Johnny Paul Koroma and other members of the AFRC, including Gborie and Squadron Leader Victor King. King was the pilot of the one and only helicopter gunship, control of which was vital to the AFRC. Also among them was Captain Albert Johnny Moore, who only a few days previously had been assisting Lincoln with our military training programme. They swept into the driveway in an assortment of vehicles, wearing a motley collection of uniforms and brandishing a wide range of weapons – AK47s, RPGs, machine guns. They were very full of themselves. I greeted them and while we were waiting for the others to arrive, Koroma revealed that he had attended a military training course at Sandhurst, the British military training academy, in 1988/89. I didn't know whether to take this as good news or bad.

The others arrived: Berhanu Dinka, the UN Envoy, Mohammed Abubakar, the Nigerian High Commissioner, Brigadier Ojokojo, the head of the Nigerian forces, along with his number two, Colonel Biu, and Ann Wright, the US Charge. We all moved into the residence dining room and seated ourselves down along the two sides of the long dining table. Koroma sat facing me in the middle with his pistol sticking out from his pocket. Under his army fatigue jacket he wore a T-shirt advertising an American university. His colleagues sat either side and behind him, still carrying their assortment of weapons and ammunition belts, but I had persuaded them to leave their heavier weaponry, the RPGs and machine guns, outside on the pretext that they might scratch the highly polished table.

We invited Koroma to brief us on the current state of security. As if on cue, some shots were fired downtown. He assured us that the situation was coming under control. The dusk to dawn curfew would remain in force; there were still some renegade soldiers carrying out looting in Freetown, acting against the interests of the AFRC, but they were being dealt with. Looted vehicles were being brought to Defence HQ and would be returned to owners. An anti-looting squad had been set up. (Ironically, it used a vehicle looted by the AFRC from the UN. Over the nameplate UNDP had been written in paint, 'Anti-Looting

Squad'.) One of the prime looters was Sergeant Abu Sankoh, who was presently sitting opposite us. His nickname was 'Zagalo', and 'zagaloing' became a euphemism for looting.

We told Koroma that our major concern at that moment was for the safety of our communities. I noted that over fifty British homes had been looted, including, for example, the home of the Barclays Bank manager next door. I invited my colleagues to report on the events of the previous day. They did so in graphic detail, including the deaths of the two Lebanese nationals, the rape of the Sabena wife and the damage to the US Embassy. Ambassador Dinka reported on the vandalism of the UN offices and the looting of the World Food Programme (WFP) stock of grain. In the WFP warehouse there had been enough food to feed all the displaced persons and refugees for six months. Now there was nothing left and it would take three months to resume any feeding programmes. We pointed out that under the Vienna Convention they had an obligation to protect diplomatic and international communities.

Koroma and his colleagues were visibly shaken by these accounts. 'I am ashamed to be a soldier when I hear these things,' said one. Brigadier Ojokojo said he wished to dispel rumours that a Nigerian intervention force was on its way. There was a force coming, he said, but it was merely to assist in the event of an evacuation.

We registered our wish to evacuate some of our communities. Some of Koroma's colleagues expressed concern at the impact both locally and internationally if the international communities were seen to be evacuating as this would be interpreted as a lack of confidence in the AFRC's ability to maintain law and order. They asked for more time to get the situation under control. They hoped to open the airport by the end of the week.

I told Koroma that it was because we did not want to order a total evacuation that it was essential immediately to facilitate the departure of those members of our communities who had particularly suffered as a result of events. I told him that some people, including women and children, had been looted of everything and that I was not prepared to tell such people that they must wait until the end of the week before they could be helped. If the airport was opened immediately, these people could leave under their own steam on scheduled or chartered flights without calling it an evacuation but, I continued, if it was not opened, I would go on the BBC World Service and announce the total evacuation of the British community and, if necessary, call for military assistance to do so.

Koroma had a whispered conversation with Victor King, who was sitting alongside him. King appeared to be the most educated of the bunch sitting opposite us. After this brief discussion, King announced that the airport would be opened the next day. I welcomed the decision and also argued for the International Committee of the Red Cross (ICRC) to be given freedom of access to operate everywhere, as was their right under international law.

After the lengthy discussion of the security situation, we asked Koroma to brief us on the composition of the AFRC and its plans for running the country. He appeared puzzled by the question. He said that the AFRC was not yet fully constituted. He was waiting for the reaction of Foday Sankoh and the RUF. He had received one message from the RUF commander, Colonel Sam Bockarie, congratulating them on the coup. Mohammed Abubakar pointed out that Sankoh was being held in Nigeria at the request of President Kabbah's government. If the new government wanted Sankoh released, the Nigerian government could not react to press broadcasts; they would require an official request. But diplomatically he asked whether it was really in the AFRC's interests to invite Sankoh to join them.

Koroma said he had supported democracy by voting at the last election but there should have been peace before elections; with Foday Sankoh joining them, and by disbanding the Kamajors, there would be peace. Then they could return to the democratic process. But he could give no date at this stage when this would be. They were not like the NPRC; they would not try to cling on to power for ever. (Many people came to regret that they were not, in fact, like the NPRC. At least the NPRC had been disciplined and initially very popular with the Sierra Leone people.)

I found Koroma's remarks incredulous. I told him that democracy was more than just voting in elections. The basis of the democratic process was that governments that lost the support of the people and/or proved to be inefficient or even corrupt should be removed by the ballot box and not by the barrel of a gun. President Kabbah's government had been democratically elected in internationally recognized free and fair elections and welcomed jubilantly by the broad mass of the Sierra Leone population. By perpetrating the coup, he and the AFRC had violated the democratic process, not enhanced it. It was not just to the international community but to their own people they would have to answer. Koroma and his colleagues listened carefully with their heads down. Their cockiness had disappeared. We agreed to all meet again in two days' time.

With the discussion ended, Osman brought in some sandwiches and drinks, which the AFRC members wolfed down enthusiastically. I doubted if they had had much time to sleep or eat during the previous twenty-four hours. On the way out I invited them to sign the visitors' book. Koroma signed with an impressive script. He looked at the photograph alongside the book of Celia and myself on our wedding day at Government House in Tortola and admired my gubernatorial uniform, gold buttons, plumed hat, ceremonial sword, etc. Perhaps he was thinking that this was what the Chairman of the AFRC's uniform should be like?

I took advantage of being back at the residence to pick up a change of clothes and some toiletries. As I drove back to the office I reflected on the naivety of this group of soldiers. Their comments about Foday Sankoh, the disbanding of the Kamajors, their concept of democracy and the absence of any ideas about government all underlined this. They had bitten off more than they could chew. We had to wait and see what the Nigerians would do but we were not out of the woods. Even if law and order was restored, the devastation was such that many essential commodities would be in short supply. I continued to advise the community to keep their heads down and alerted London to the need for a chartered aircraft.

Tuesday

Freetown appeared fairly quiet. The AFRC issued a statement saying that the airport was open and we continued our preparations for evacuation.

I called a meeting of the wardens – selected members of the British community who voluntarily kept an eye on the Brits in their area and acted as points of contact. Only six out of fifteen felt safe enough to come to the office. I briefed them on the latest situation, including my talks with the AFRC and the plans to evacuate dependents and others. Each of the wardens related tales of widespread looting and destruction in their areas. Several of them had been looted themselves. However, they confirmed the good news that as far as we were aware, no member of the British community had been killed or seriously injured.

I also met with the German Charge, Conrad Fischer, and the European Commission delegate, Emilio Perez-Poros. Together we represented the European Union and we had a responsibility for all EU nationals, who, other than the Brits, numbered about 350. The number of British people registered with us was 765, but I was sure that many others would come out of the woodwork as we began to evacuate. Together with some other Commonwealth citizens we were looking at a figure of around 2,000. Only the Lebanese community was bigger, some 5,000, many of whom had taken refuge in the Lebanese Ambassador's small house.

In the office we had settled into some sort of routine. The telephones never stopped ringing and there was a constant stream of visitors at the gates. With Ann Stephen sending and receiving telegrams and her husband Robert helping out in other ways, their son Andrew was left to toddle around the office. There was always someone to keep an eye on him. He was the most unfazed of all of us. He toddled into my office with his football, which I kicked to him using my desk as a goal while I reported to London on events over the telephone. Everyone was busy. Downstairs, Ruth Glass was producing meals from the tiny kitchen, but there was little time to eat them.

The two Nigerian ships carrying Nigerian troops had arrived at Government Wharf, watched anxiously by around 200 armed Sierra Leone soldiers. Demonstrations against the coup had taken place in Bo and Kenema, and there were plans to mount a similar one in Freetown the next day.

Koroma came on the radio in the evening to address the nation. He announced the suspension of the 1991 constitution and the banning of all political parties. Legislation would be by military decree. He said that tribalism had contributed to the problems and then went on to condemn the Kamajors (Mende) but praised the Tamaboras (Temne). He said he supported freedom of expression but announced the closure of all independent radio stations.

Wednesday

The spring bank holiday had come to an end in Britain, so at last we were now in contact with the African Department in the Foreign Office instead of with the hard-working resident clerks. The department had missed all the fun but all they seemed concerned about was what had happened to the Barclays Bank manager. His head office in London had lodged a complaint that we had failed to offer him protection. He had tried to get into my empty residence next door to his home but had been turned away by the guards at the gate. I had left instructions with them that if any British nationals turned up seeking refuge, they should be told to come to the office compound, where we could offer protection. I had explained this to him over the telephone but he remained upset and had gone to another Barclays house in town. This was unfortunate because he was the warden for his area and so other Brits had been unable to get advice from him on what to do.

There were extra troops on the street to stop the demonstration, which had been banned. The local radio also carried a message from Foday Sankoh, in which he told the RUF that they should not go on the offensive but should work with the army, who were no longer their enemies. He ended by saying ominously: 'Let us make revolution. I will join you very soon.'

Colin and Dai were left to pursue the arrangements for the charter flight, which was now expected the following day, as I made my way to the residence for the meeting with the AFRC. Mohammed Abubakar had suggested that we assemble the entire diplomatic corps but I advised against this as I thought that this would intimidate the soldiers and prevent any useful discussions, but we were joined by the Egyptian, Lebanese and Chinese ambassadors. Again, Lincoln Jopp joined us. The AFRC appreciated the presence of another army officer other than a Nigerian. He displayed just the right touch in dealing with them and helped them to relax. Some of the soldiers who had been released from prison even asked Lincoln if he could supply new uniforms for them.

No sooner had we assembled than we heard that Sierra Leone troops had deployed next door in the empty Barclays Bank house. This led to a panic reaction among my diplomatic colleagues. They believed that this was an attempt by the AFRC to kidnap us all. Brigadier Ojokojo radioed his Nigerian troops for assistance and Ann Wright called up her US Marines. While Lincoln went next door to investigate, all the ambassadors jumped into their cars and fled the residence, apart from Berhanu Dinka and myself. Just as Ann Wright was leaving, an advance group of the AFRC, including Victor King, arrived. They were followed through the gates by the US Marines, all tooled up and ready for action. Shortly thereafter, the Nigerian troops arrived. The AFRC delegation radioed Koroma and advised him not to come because they feared he would be kidnapped.

In the driveway of the residence the three sets of forces eyed each other nervously. Tempers were high and the situation was tense. We were close to a fire fight between three groups of nervous soldiers. Lincoln returned to report that the deployment of soldiers next door was because some looters were attempting to steal the Barclays Bank manager's Mercedes. He had sorted it out. The Nigerian troops went off and I asked Ann Wright to make her marines look less threatening. I brought the four AFRC members, plus Ambassador Dinka and Brig Ojokojo, into the residence, sat them down in the living room and offered them drinks of Fanta.

I told the AFRC members that I was aware that a degree of security had returned to Freetown. There was far less shooting and looting and obviously they were trying to get their act together. However, because they were so preoccupied with internal events, were they aware of what the outside world had been saying? Everyone, including the UN and the OAU, had strongly condemned their actions. There had not been one statement of support from any country in the world. Equally, if not more importantly, there was no support from their own people. A demonstration protesting their action had been banned that very morning.

I went on to say that the Chairman's statement had fuelled my concerns. He had said that he supported democracy but had torn up the constitution, banned political parties and now the country was under military rule. He professed support for human rights but, by suspending the constitution, he had taken away all the rights of Sierra Leone citizens. The statement from Foday Sankoh had also worried me. The RUF fighters were now coming to Freetown. These were the very people who only recently had been hacking off people's arms and legs. I feared for my community and the Sierra Leone public. They needed to consider alternatives.

Berhanu Dinka and Ann Wright echoed these views in equally forceful terms. Brigadier Ojokojo put it differently: 'The High Commissioner is a diplomat; he is trained to be patient and understanding. I am a soldier – if someone provokes me, I retaliate as a soldier would.'

King and his three colleagues listened attentively and said they would pass on our views to the Chairman. We agreed to reconvene in two days.

Before leaving the residence, I briefed Brigadier Ojokojo about our plans to evacuate some of our nationals by chartered aircraft. Over the previous couple of days the Nigerians had been quietly reinforcing their numbers. In addition to the two vessels down at Government Wharf, Nigerian military aircraft had been arriving at Lungi. We estimated that they now had around 1,600 troops in key positions, with a further 600 on standby in Monrovia. They were well placed to take over Freetown and force the removal of the AFRC. They would feel that the OAU statement gave them the go-ahead to do so and I was concerned that we should not be attempting an evacuation when hostilities were about to break out. I made the point to Ojokojo that the co-operation Nigeria had demonstrated with the UN, the Americans and ourselves over the past few days augured well for a future improvement in Nigeria's international relations, but this would all be undone if civilian evacuees got caught up in hostilities started by Nigeria. He did not give me a specific guarantee but said enough to reassure me that we should go ahead with the evacuation of women and children.

Back in the office I learned that Colonel Andrew Gale, our defence adviser based in Accra, had hitched a ride on one of the Nigerian C130s and had arrived at Lungi Airport. I much welcomed this extra pair of experienced hands and asked him to remain at Lungi to be our eyes and ears on the ground for the next day's evacuation. Lungi Airport was three and a half hours' drive away by road from Freetown, forty-five minutes by ferry across the bay, or ten minutes by helicopter from the Mammy Yoko Hotel. We did not want to send people across to Lungi and leave them more exposed to danger there, especially if the flight was delayed or, worse still, did not arrive at all. Andrew's presence there would be invaluable, although I did not appreciate at the time just how much so.

While I had been at the residence talking to the AFRC, Colin and the rest of the team had been making the plans for the next day's evacuation. London had chartered a Tristar, with a capacity of 360 seats, which would fly out from Paris via Dakar in Senegal. This was later changed to a jumbo jet. Our biggest problem was how to transport the people from Freetown to Lungi. We were hiring the two Russian helicopters that were based at the Mammy Yoko Hotel but we estimated that with just these two helicopters, it could take up to six hours to move everyone to Lungi. We did not want to start moving people until we were sure that the plane could land but equally, we did not want to risk leaving people too long unprotected at Lungi. We arranged to bring in two more helicopters from Monrovia.

We had to process everybody to make sure that they would have no immigration problems landing in Europe. We were told initially that the flight would return to Paris. Priority would be given to women and children, injured and aged. Priority would also be given to British and European nationals but we also agreed to assist Americans and Commonwealth citizens. Baggage would be restricted to one suitcase, and no pets because of the UK's quarantine laws. Everyone had to sign an undertaking to repay for the flight, or pay on the spot.

Several people had had their passports lost or looted so arrangements had to be made to issue temporary travel documents. All these contingencies had to be covered and the planning went on through the night.

Thursday

Everyone set off early for the Mammy Yoko Hotel, the designated processing point for the evacuation, while I remained in the office to hold the fort with a couple of the local staff. Ruth Glass and her two children and Ann Stephens and her husband and baby would be among those going out on the charter, so we said our hasty farewells.

While I was waiting to hear whether the plane was on its way from Dakar, where it had to refuel, I received a message that Koroma wanted a meeting at midday. The Nigerians told me that he would be requesting political asylum in Nigeria, the US or the UK. I sought instructions from London should he opt for the UK. I was reluctant to advise that we accept him but if it provided a peaceful way out of the mess, then it might be a price worth paying. I was later told that the Nigerians had indicated that they were prepared to accept him, which was a relief for us.

The embassy in Senegal telephoned to say that the charter had left Dakar and was on its way. Andrew Gale reported that all was quiet at the airport. Both Nigerian and Sierra Leone troops were there but they were behaving themselves. I advised Colin over the radio to start ferrying the people across to Lungi. There was the inevitable WAWA. One of the helicopters was taken off for a trip to Conakry and another broke down, but nonetheless, the evacuees started arriving at Lungi. After about four hours of continuous shuttling by helicopter everyone was assembled at the airport and they started boarding the chartered plane under Andrew Gale's supervision.

Suddenly there was a confrontation between the Nigerian and Sierra Leonean troops. What started it was unclear, but guns were cocked and the two sides were squaring off with one another, with our jumbo and evacuees in the middle. Andrew Gale acted quickly and decisively. He was not a tall man, but displaying all the stature and authority of a British colonel, he literally stepped into the breach and calmed the situation down. The women and children continued boarding the aircraft, the doors closed and the plane took off, heading for Gatwick carrying 395 very relieved passengers.

Meanwhile, I was at the residence with the AFRC. Koroma had not come but, in addition to Squadron Leader King and Captain Johnny Moore, he had sent a group of senior Sierra Leone officers – Colonels Sesay, Anderson, Boyah, Williams and Conteh. Also, the veteran politician Karefa-Smart had turned up. Mohammed Abubakar had rung to say he could not attend and Ann Wright and Berhanu Dinka were preparing to evacuate, so that left just Lincoln Jopp and me on our side.

The colonels made a point of explaining that none of them had been involved in the coup. A number of them had, in fact, been arrested and beaten up but they were now trying to bring order to the chaos. They claimed that it was because they had been detained that the looting and devastation had been so widespread. They went over the underlying reasons for the coup and suggested that the events on 25 May had nipped in the bud a far more serious confrontation that was brewing in the country.

I went over the same ground as I had done with the younger soldiers, referring to the breadth and strength of the international condemnation, the obvious absence of local public support, the concern over the increasing presence of the RUF and the limited time left to achieve a peaceful resolution before the Nigerians deployed. I told them that they were deceiving themselves if they believed that bringing law and order to Freetown and making overtures about respect for democracy would be enough to win over the support of the international community and the public. I used an aphorism I had heard Karefa–Smart make at a public speech, that when one stumbled and fell, one did not look at where one landed but back to where one stumbled. In their case it had been the overthrow by military force of a democratically elected civilian government where they had stumbled; unless this was put right, it was a waste of time trying other measures. I pointed out that the President had the means to address all their grievances, e.g. status of the army, conditions of service, a more representative government, within the old constitution. They did not need this violent change. If they stepped down peacefully, it could be argued that the coup had helped focus on what were the key issues that needed to be addressed.

The colonels nodded in agreement. At one stage I thought they were going to announce that they would take over from the AFRC as a transition until President Kabbah came back, but the moment did not materialize. We agreed to meet the next day.

Thanks to Colin, Dai, Andrew and others, the evacuation had gone well. It had been an operation with immense logistical problems set against a tense, dangerous, fast-moving situation. Everyone who had turned up wanting to leave got on the plane. No one had been turned away. The passengers had been patient and good-humoured throughout. To my surprise, Dai produced a wad of US dollars. Apparently, a good number of the evacuees had preferred to pay for their passage in cash, rather than sign the undertakings to repay. This was to prove fortuitous.

The Americans were planning to evacuate all their nationals the next day by an American warship, the USS *Kearsarge*, a helicopter carrier that had on board 356 marines. They publicized their intentions, which led to the AFRC announcing that all land, sea and air borders were closed. Our jumbo had been the last plane to leave, along with a Lebanese flight taking the Lebanese women and children to Beirut. This further closure of the borders was something I had wanted to avoid, as it meant that any further evacuations would be set against an even more hostile environment. I had hoped to string the AFRC along until we had got everyone out that we needed to. The announcement by the Americans would lead to an increasing number of people wanting to leave.

Koroma came on the radio. Quoting from Shakespeare and the *Bible*, he announced that peace had been achieved thanks to the AFRC, and he declared three days of prayers and fasting. Did he not realize that we had been fasting and praying for peace since Sunday's coup?

Friday

The night had passed very quietly, almost eerily so. After constant shooting every night, it was more difficult to sleep through the deafening silence as you asked yourself why they were saving their ammunition. The situation remained tense. It was still not clear what the Nigerians would do. Increasing numbers of the RUF were now in Freetown and they were making up for having missed the initial looting spree by the soldiers, but in their own gruesome fashion. Outside one supermarket, which they had ransacked, they had left a familiar calling card – a dead body with its arms and legs hacked off and a dismembered penis stuck in the mouth. The RUF were now calling the shots with the AFRC. The bunch of colonels I had met the previous day were now being detained by the RUF at Defence Headquarters. The soldiers had let the RUF genie out of the bottle and now they could not get it back in. After consulting Desmond Luke, who knew the mindset of the RUF as well as anyone, I cancelled the meeting with the AFRC that day. Desmond had felt that the possibility of hostage-taking was real.

I proposed to London that we should advise all members of the British community who had no good reason to stay to leave, taking advantage of the USS *Kearsarge*. I also proposed we reduce our own staff to the bare minimum to enable us to function – Colin, Dai, Andrew, Lincoln and me. I invited Emilio Perez-Poros, the European Commission (EC) delegate, to join us on the compound. The EC had a helicopter permanently standing-by in Monrovia. This could prove useful if we needed to move quickly. Similar offers were made to Ann Wright and Conrad Fischer, but they had both received instructions from their capitals to close down their missions completely and leave.

The whirr of the *Kearsarge* helicopters could be heard throughout the morning as they lifted people from the Mammy Yoko to the ship. One person they had airlifted was Sam Hinga Norman, who had been hiding on top of the lift shaft of the Mammy Yoko Hotel. He was the only one of Kabbah's ministers who had tried to resist the AFRC when they had taken over. The AFRC and RUF had been looking for him everywhere to kill him. The *Kearsarge* completed its day's evacuation but, as expected, more people had emerged wanting to leave. They were advised to make their way to the Mammy Yoko or Cape Sierra hotels on the other side of the Aberdeen Bridge, which were being guarded by a detachment of Nigerian soldiers behind a defensive line. The Americans said that they would bring the *Kearsarge* back the next day to help lift the remaining expatriates, including more Americans. They were liaising with Roger Crooks, the American manager of the Mammy Yoko, and as the US Embassy was now closed, we offered to assist.

Saturday

Andrew and Lincoln were out and about assessing the situation and contacting any members of the British community they could find to advise them to leave, and Colin and Dai were dealing with the endless stream of enquiries. Stretched so thin and being so busy, I had some concern for our own safety as it was not impossible that a group of RUF could have broken into the compound and overrun us in the office before we knew what was going on. I asked Emilio Perez–Poros to position himself in the office at the end of the building overlooking the main gate in order to keep an eye out. In my office at the other end of the building, I suddenly heard a commotion outside. I went running down the corridor, shouting to Emilio, 'What's going on?' There was a crowd of around fifty AFRC supporters at the front gate shouting and jumping up and down. Fortunately, they moved on without attempting to break in as Emilio came running out of the bathroom, still zipping up his pants. Having sat patiently for hours watching the gate, a call of nature meant that he had missed the one moment of excitement.

The USS *Kearsarge* sent a message saying she would not be able to come in until the next day but we learned from the Honorary French Consul that there was a French naval ship nearby. I telephoned the French Ambassador in Conakry, who had only recently presented his credentials to President Kabbah in Freetown, and asked if there was any chance of bringing his ship in to lift off the French nationals and any others. He contacted the Quai d'Orsay in Paris and clearance was given for the ship, a corvette called the *Jean Moulin*, to come and help. She would take a couple of hours to reach Freetown so Colin, Dai, Emilio and the French Consul went off to round up any Europeans and get them to the Aqua Club, where we had agreed to bring in the French ship. I got in touch with Defence Headquarters for agreement for the *Jean Moulin* to enter Sierra Leone waters to lift off distressed European nationals.

The *Jean Moulin* arrived and at the Aqua Club a rubber zodiac dinghy carrying a couple of French *matelots* and a French officer, all looking very smart in their dark blue shorts and long white socks, came up onto the beach. The officer carried a laptop computer linked to the ship. In just a couple of hours, 261 persons were processed and boarded, including 157 British nationals, plus the French, other Europeans, a few Americans and the Papal Nuncio. The *Jean Moulin* sailed serenely off to Conakry. It was a very slick operation.

The *Jean Moulin* was followed out of the bay by a small fishing boat stacked to the gunnels with mainly Indian nationals. The hard-working and influential Indian Honorary Consul, Ken Azad, had previously organized an air charter for the wives and children of the Indian community at the same time that our charter had left Lungi. They were flown to Abidjan. But now many of the remaining Indian business community wanted to leave. They had been having a very difficult time at the hands of the RUF. The rusting fishing smack tried desperately to keep up with the sleek French corvette, but less than a mile out to sea it was shipping water and started sinking. It turned around and barely made it back to Freetown.

Sunday

It was just a week since we had awoken to the sound of gunfire around Freetown. From early morning the *Kearsarge* helicopters started ferrying a further batch of evacuees to the ship. She left around midday, followed by another boat that had been chartered by the Lebanese to take around 600 of their nationals to Conakry.

Desmond Luke telephoned to try to arrange 'one final meeting' between the AFRC and the international community. I pointed out that apart from the Nigerian High Commissioner and myself, there was no one left to represent the international community. We fixed a meeting at the residence for the afternoon and as Lincoln and I drove up to the residence, many Sierra Leoneans lined the street. They had been monitoring the comings and goings to the residence all week and one could see the look of hope and expectation in their faces that a solution would emerge from these talks and that they could go back to living their normal lives. We shared their hope, if not their expectation.

Desmond Luke and Mohammed Abubakar, plus the latter's deputy, Joe Keshi, arrived at the residence. For the previous twenty-four hours they had been trying to hammer out an agreement on paper with the AFRC, which in essence allowed for the dissolution of the AFRC, the reinstatement of President Kabbah, an amnesty for the coupists and the implementation of the Abidjan Peace Accord. They hoped to get a response from the AFRC at the meeting.

Eventually, Colonels Anderson, Conteh and Boya arrived, together with Karefa-Smart, who this time did not sit alongside the AFRC delegation, but down at the end of the long, highly polished, dining table. Karefa-Smart had attracted a great deal of criticism from the public for having 'sided' with the AFRC and he started the meeting by explaining that he was not there as a member of the AFRC delegation, but as a 'facilitator'.

It emerged that the colonels had not even discussed the draft agreement with the other AFRC members and the RUF. Instead, Anderson attacked Mohammed Abubakar about the increasing numbers of Nigerian troops that had arrived. I suggested that the way to stop the troops arriving would be to reach an agreement along the lines negotiated. Abubakar, Luke and I urged them to do so. I noted that we had been meeting all week and that this was the 'final' meeting I was prepared to convene. I said that after I left the residence, I would go to my office, switch on the radio, and hope to hear an announcement from the Chairman accepting the points of the agreement. Anderson looked at me across the table and, fingering the gun he had strapped across his breast, he said a little menacingly: 'Then perhaps, High Commissioner, we should not let you leave.' There was a chilled silence in the room. I broke it by laughing and saying I had to go back to the office because my staff were waiting lunch for me!

After the colonels had departed, Abubakar told me that the decision to deploy had already been made by Abacha. It was now down to the Nigerian military commander to decide when, not if. Only an announcement from Koroma that evening could stop the operation the next day.

Back in the office, after we had eaten an excellent Sunday roast lunch prepared by Osman – the first proper meal we had eaten all week – Joe Keshi came round. He had been negotiating some further points with the soldiers. The agreement now covered twenty-one points, including the provision of money, homes and cars for those leading members of the AFRC who would be flown to Nigeria. It seemed that these were as important points of detail as to what would happen to the country. Mercedes Benz was the car of choice.

Lincoln drove back down to the Cape Sierra Hotel and Joe and I, together with Colin, Dai and Andrew, sat round the radio hoping to hear an announcement. At 9.00 pm Colonel Anderson telephoned to say that they had reached agreement among themselves but they could not find the Chairman to make the broadcast. He asked whether another member of the AFRC could do it but we advised that only the Chairman's voice would carry the necessary authority, otherwise it would not be believed.

The radio carried on playing music until around midnight, and then the radio station closed down without any announcement from the Chairman. It later emerged that the RUF had detained Koroma to prevent him from making any broadcast. Our opportunity to nip the troubles in the bud before they got worse had been lost. We tried to snatch some sleep before impending events.

Monday

Morning broke to the sound of heavy shelling. Andrew and Dai went outside and from a vantage point on the compound they could see down on the town and beyond to the Aberdeen Bridge and the Mammy Yoko Hotel. Using his army binoculars, Andrew reported that the two Nigerian vessels anchored off in the bay were firing shell bursts in the air. They did not appear to be landing anywhere and seemed to be just warning shots. The BBC reported that Nigerian ships were bombarding Freetown – a slight exaggeration.

Lincoln, who had made his way to the Mammy Yoko, reported by radio that under the cover of a group of Sierra Leone peace protesters, the AFRC and RUF had mounted four positions with mortars and launched an attack on the Mammy Yoko Hotel. The sixty or so Nigerian troops at the hotel, under the command of Colonel Biu, had returned fire and were holding their ground. As we monitored the situation from our compound the shelling and firing intensified and I was now in constant contact over the telephone with Roger Crooks, the American manager of the hotel, and his British assistant, Steve Lawson. They reported that there were around 800 very frightened civilians crammed into the basement.

I contacted the USS *Kearsarge*, out of sight over the horizon, and briefed the ship on the situation. I was asked whether there were American nationals at the hotel. I replied that that was almost certainly the case but now was not the time to be checking passports – everyone at the hotel needed help.

By now Lincoln was up on the roof with a British expatriate, Will Scully. Will was a former member of the SAS who had been brought out to assist with the security of one of the gold mines up-country. In effect, the two of them took over the defence of the hotel: Lincoln spotted the AFRC/RUF positions and Will took them out. At one stage a Land Rover approached the hotel full of wild RUF carrying RPGs and machine guns. With precision accuracy, Will fired his RPG and scored a direct hit. Colonel Biu, who had been watching the poor performance of his own men, and enthused with Will's success, told his men, 'That's what I want.' Will replied calmly, 'That's what I do.' Will was later to record these dramatic events in his book *Once A Pilgrim*.

We lost radio contact with Lincoln and Steve Lawson reported the grim news over the telephone that Lincoln had been injured. He had received the back blast from an RPG fired carelessly by one of the Nigerian soldiers and then had sustained shrapnel wounds to his head and back. This was extremely worrying news.

As the AFRC and RUF continued to shell the hotel, there was now very little fire being returned as the Nigerians had run out of ammunition. From on top of the hill we could see that the hotel had now caught fire. The situation was getting out of control.

I telephoned Defence Headquarters. I spoke to a major and told him that his forces should stop firing at the hotel, where there were 800 civilians trapped in the basement. The Major claimed that his forces were not firing at the hotel. I told him that I was in touch with those in the hotel and indeed that I could see what was going on from my compound. I warned him that they had ten minutes to stop the firing. If not, I would get in touch with the American warship and tell them that innocent civilians, including Americans and British, were under attack and advise that they should deploy their marines against the AFRC and RUF forces. The Major said he would get back to me and ten minutes later, he did so to say that he had instructed his forces to stop firing. He assured me that it was safe for the civilians to leave the hotel.

The firing had indeed stopped and although the smoke continued to rise from the hotel, there was an uneasy quiet. But could we rely upon the word of the Major in Defence Headquarters that his instruction had been passed to all those mounting attacks around the hotel, especially the RUF, who had not demonstrated much capacity to take orders from anyone? Andrew volunteered to drive down to the area and speak to those on the ground. Securing the biggest Union Jack we could find to his Land Rover, Andrew set off, with instructions to maintain a running commentary over the radio on what was happening. He reached the Lumley Beach Road but then we lost contact. It was not until much later that we discovered what had happened to him.

In the meantime I had spoken to the *Kearsarge* and asked whether they could send in their marines to get the people out of the hotel now that the firing had stopped. They were concerned that by deploying, they could start the firing again and further endanger the lives of the civilians. They advised that the people should leave the hotel and walk along the beach. If they came under fire, this would give the excuse for the marines to go in and rescue them. If they did not come under attack, they would evacuate them, although as it was now getting dark this would not happen until the following morning. This all sounded very risky to me – as Will Scully said later in his book, a little like tying a goat to a stake in order to encourage the lion to come along and eat it.

I spoke to Colonel Anderson at Defence Headquarters. He again assured me it was safe for the civilians to come out of the hotel but as neither he nor we had heard from Andrew Gale, I suggested that the ICRC should be used to escort the people from the building.

I managed to talk to Lincoln over the telephone in the hotel. At least he was alive. I briefed him and Will Scully on my conversations with the *Kearsarge* and Defence Headquarters. Will reported that the ICRC representative had appeared at the hotel and was proposing to escort all the civilians out of the hotel under the Red Cross flag and across the Aberdeen Bridge. Will asked me what they should do.

They were in a real dilemma. It was obviously not safe to stay in the hotel. Even if they brought the fires under control, the situation in the basement was untenable. They had no food or water and the hot humid atmosphere was unbearable. If they walked out with the ICRC across the Aberdeen Bridge, they would have to pass through the RUF, and heaven knows what they would try to do. If they walked along the beach, they would be totally in the open. To wait there all night until the evacuation in the morning made no sense. They would be totally exposed, stuck right in the middle of the line of fire between the *Kearsarge* and Defence Headquarters. I told Will that as the man on the ground, he was best placed to make the decision. I sensed that he was frustrated with my answer. I felt for him but took some comfort that there was a man with his experience among all those civilians.

Graham McKinley contacted us from the Cape Sierra Hotel. Graham was a former defence adviser, Andrew Gale's predecessor, who had retired from the UK forces and was now a resident businessman in Freetown. All week he had been helping us with the evacuations and had been monitoring events at the Mammy Yoko Hotel nearby. He advised that in his view it would be safe for the civilians to come out of the back of the Mammy Yoko and make their way to the Cape Sierra. I passed on this advice to Will Scully and Roger Crooks. The choice was put to the traumatized civilians in the basement. About half of them, mainly Sierra Leoneans, left with the ICRC representative, and walked across the Aberdeen Bridge, the rest, mainly expatriates, slipped through the back of the hotel and made their way to the Cape Sierra Hotel to await evacuation by the *Kearsarge* the next day.

All this time we had been wondering what had happened to Andrew. As darkness fell, he finally arrived back at the office and recounted his experiences. He had visited the AFRC/RUF positions that had been shelling the Mammy Yoko. He had told them about the ceasefire that had been agreed by Defence Headquarters. They had agreed that he could go into the hotel to bring out Colonel Bio to work out the terms of the ceasefire, together with some wounded Nigerian soldiers. They had driven in Andrew's Land Rover under cover of the Union Jack and a white flag to Defence Headquarters. As soon as they had arrived, a group of RUF lined them up against a wall and were going to shoot all of them on the spot. Andrew protested that they had come voluntarily under a flag of truce. After much arguing, the RUF backed down and allowed Andrew to remove the injured Nigerian soldiers to the military hospital.

After all the drama of the day's events there was not much time to rest. We now had to prepare for the next day's evacuation of those rescued from the Mammy Yoko and any others. A telegram arrived from London saying that we were to close down the mission and join the evacuation. This came as a shock. We were not prepared to leave ourselves. We had too much to do dealing with the others, and in my view it would have been better for us to withdraw in some order. It was not a simple thing to close down a diplomatic mission. It was not just a question of walking out through the front door and turning off the lights. We had to destroy all our classified files, blank passports and communications equipment as well as make arrangements for all our local staff. Obviously we needed to get Lincoln out but the rest of us were OK. I called the others together. None of them wanted to leave. Once the next day's evacuation was out of the way, we could better organize ourselves. We could then call up the EC helicopter in Monrovia, close the mission and leave in good order. I reported this to London, but they insisted that we leave on the *Kearsarge*. We worked through the night burning and shredding. There was no time to pack our personal effects or secure our homes, or get any sleep.

Tuesday

The night had passed quietly after all the noise of the previous day. I checked with the *Kearsarge* and sent a final telegram to London, signing off from Freetown.

I called together those members of the local staff who had been with us at the office, including the guards, and explained that we had been told to leave on the American ship that morning. I trusted that it would only be a few days before we were back. I wished them all well and looked to them to guard our property while we were away, but on no account should they risk their lives unnecessarily – their lives were more important than our buildings. I handed over the keys to Solomon Lebby, the assistant management officer, and we drove off.

We drove down Spur Road and then past the golf course along the Lumley Beach Road. The sight we saw was like a John Wayne movie. Scores of heavily armed American Marines were everywhere. We came to a well constructed road block where a very young US Marine stopped us and asked for our identification. I told him that we were the staff of the British High Commission, plus the European Commission Ambassador. He radioed the information ahead and we were waved through. There were a couple of US armoured personnel carriers on the beach and machine guns mounted alongside the road, which had been floated in under cover of darkness from the USS *Kearsarge*, which remained out of sight over the horizon. All the guns were pointed towards Cockerill, the Defence Headquarters.

We learned later that the Americans had been especially concerned with any attempts by the AFRC to deploy the helicopter gunship, which was parked at Cockerill. They had instructions to destroy it if there was any attempt to make it airborne. In one tense moment a Sierra Leone soldier had been observed walking towards the helicopter. The US Marines monitored the scene carefully. Unaware that there were a dozen guns pointing at him, the Sierra Leone soldier continued to approach the helicopter but then for some unapparent reason, he turned around and walked back to the building. The moment had passed. If the Americans had opened fire, I had no doubt that the AFRC/RUF resistance would have crumbled totally.

On the beach across from what remained of the Chez Nous restaurant, large helicopters were taking off and landing. Hundreds of civilians were walking along the Lumley Beach Road from the direction of the Cape Sierra Hotel. Outside the restaurant they formed orderly queues as if in Disneyworld and were processed into lines of ten, sitting down on the ground under the watchful eyes of the marines. At a given signal each group was directed towards the helicopters, which, in a swirl of dust and sand, whisked the people off out to sea and onto the *Kearsarge*. It was a most impressive operation. In the space of about four hours, 1,260 people were lifted off Lumley Beach – reportedly the fastest evacuation of civilians in history.

Over the previous week a total of over 4,000 expatriates had been evacuated by sea and air, including nearly 1,000 British passport holders.

Within minutes we were being led by a US Marine onto a helicopter. As soon as we were on board, it took off. I peered through the window at the swirling sand as the beach disappeared below us. Farewell Freetown.

Chapter Three

Living in Conakry

From the USS *Kearsarge*, I had been flown to Conakry, where Val Treitlein and a team from the British Embassy in Dakar were valiantly dealing with the hundreds of evacuees from Freetown. Soon after settling into room 503 of the Hotel Camayenne, I received a call from the Foreign Office in London. The Secretary of State wanted to have a word with me. Though I had never met him, I recognized the voice of Robin Cook on the other end. 'Peter, I want you to know how grateful and proud we are of you. Well done!' I reminded him that it had been a team effort and thanked him for calling personally. I was touched that the Secretary of State had taken the time to call. He later issued a statement paying tribute to me and the staff 'who have done a magnificent job in very dangerous and very difficult circumstances, both in trying to achieve a negotiated resolution to the crisis in Sierra Leone and also in handling the evacuation of so many foreign nationals. We are very, very proud of the work that has been done. I pay tribute to Peter Penfold and all those who worked with him.'

This was to be followed later by a letter from No. 10 Downing Street signed by the Prime Minister, Tony Blair:

> I should like to add my personal thanks and best wishes to you, Colin Glass and Dai Harries for your exceptional work helping to evacuate British nationals from Sierra Leone in what were obviously appallingly confused and dangerous circumstances. I know that you also did your best to bring the various factions together and to avoid bloodshed. Your efforts do great credit to the Diplomatic Service.

Many other plaudits were received thanking us for the assistance rendered, both from foreign governments and individuals, including Sierra Leoneans living in Britain such as Ibrahim Suma and Momodou Sillah, the Sierra Leonean Labour Councillor in Hackney, who were both to remain staunch supporters throughout my time in Sierra Leone. There were a few complaints that we did not do enough. One of these was in a letter to Robin Cook from Rupert Bowen, the country manager of Branch Energy. He had been out of Freetown at the time of the coup and when he and his wife appeared at the gates of the High Commission the next day, he complained that he had been kept waiting fifteen minutes and was not offered a cup of tea. His wife was evacuated on our chartered plane and Bowen left later on the *Kearsarge*. The letter did not endear me to Bowen.

The spin doctors in the Foreign Office had been anxious to capitalize on events. They arranged an interview with the *Daily Mirror*, which produced a two–page centre spread under the headline 'Hero of Hell City – True Brit of envoy as 800 rescued'. London was delighted with the result. They said that it was the first time that they had had such a positive article about the Foreign Office in one of the tabloids.

I had gone to see President Kabbah on arrival in Conakry. President Conte had accommodated him in a villa on a compound not far from the Camayenne and across from the Sierra Leone Embassy. The villa was one of several set in large grounds dotted with palm trees, with camels wandering around and all behind a 10 foot high perimeter wall. It was where former Sierra Leone Presidents Momoh and Strasser also had taken refuge when they had been forced to flee. The Guinean soldiers at the entrance to the compound had looked at me quizzically sat in the back of the dilapidated taxi that I had hired as I explained in my poor French that I was the British Ambassador from Sierra Leone. They were not altogether convinced but they let me in.

The President looked drawn and tired. I briefed him on the discussions we had held in the residence with the AFRC and told him that I was surprised that he had taken so long to issue any statement to his people. They needed to hear from him. He mentioned the problems he had had with batteries for his tape recorder before he had left Freetown. After our meeting he issued a statement saying that his government accepted all the points we had negotiated in the residence with the AFRC and that he was prepared to adhere to them if the junta stood down and allowed the restoration of the legitimate government. The statement fell on deaf ears.

It was felt that it would only be a matter of weeks before we could reopen the mission in Freetown and so it was decided by Tony Lloyd, the minister responsible for Africa, and Richard Dales, the Director for Africa in the Foreign Office, that I should remain in Conakry and set up an office there to stay alongside President Kabbah and his ministers as a clear demonstration that the British Government continued to recognize his government as the legitimate government of Sierra Leone. It would also enable us to maintain contact and provide support for our locally engaged staff (over seventy strong) and safeguard the substantial British Government estate there worth millions of pounds. In the meantime the British aid programme was suspended and would resume 'once, but not until, President Kabbah is restored.'

My bedroom (room 503) at the Hotel Camayenne became the office of the British High Commission to Sierra Leone, in exile. Running a diplomatic mission from a hotel room was not easy. The wad of US dollars that Dai had produced following the evacuation proved useful in setting up the office until we had established a bank account in Conakry, which required endless signatures.

Val Treitlein operated her honorary consul's office out of her home and was busy dealing with the flow of evacuees as well as the normal day to day Guinean business. We did receive some assistance from the resident German Embassy in the spirit of European Union co-operation but generally we relied upon the hotel telephone and fax facilities for communication. The age of internet communication and sophisticated mobile phones had not yet arrived. A satellite phone received from the Foreign Office never worked. Classified communication was especially difficult. The Foreign Office sent out a classified fax machine but then insisted that we keep it locked away in a security cupboard that accompanied the machine, but the cupboard was too big to fit into the hotel room and therefore both cupboard and machine had to be sent back. We stood for hours alongside the hotel's fax machine to avoid prying eyes seeing our messages going back and forth.

For a while both Colin and Dai were stationed with me, which allowed us short breaks back home from time to time, but then Dai was posted to Mozambique. The High Commission's locally engaged accountant, Brima Samura, had fled Freetown and turned up in Conakry. He was able to help us with our accounts – no easy task given that we were operating in four different currencies: pounds sterling, US dollars, Sierra Leone leones and Guinea francs. The only other 'member of staff' was Alphonse, the Guinean driver of our dilapidated taxi, who benefitted greatly from the generous weekly allowance we were paying him. Regrettably, he chose not to use this influx of funds to improve his taxi with modifications like air-conditioning or unbroken windows, let alone new tyres or brake pads.

Most days I would telephone Solomon Lebby, our assistant management officer, back in Freetown, who was performing miracles keeping the staff in good heart and our properties untouched. A young, handsome Sierra Leonean, with a penchant for colourful ties and braces, he had been working at the High Commission for around twelve years. His efforts during these difficult times would later be recognized by the award of the MBE by The Queen.

Every day, Solomon went to the office and the residence to check on the staff and that everything was OK. Johnny Paul Koroma had moved into a house right next to the office compound. We were not sure whether it was because he felt safer that Ecomog were unlikely to shell a building alongside the British High Commission or just that the soldiers guarding Koroma liked to enjoy the light from our compound's generators when the rest of Freetown was in darkness. We would find all kinds of ingenious methods of sending in the salaries for all the staff each month and Solomon would distribute them. Our staff were therefore among the very few in Freetown to receive regular salaries and the High Commission compound and residence remained among the very few properties not to be looted by the soldiers.

Initially, Conakry was full of those who had fled Freetown but as the weeks turned into months, the numbers of international personnel dwindled. Most of the international agencies and NGOs returned to Europe and North America.

However difficult life for us was in Conakry, it was far worse for the thousands of Sierra Leoneans who had fled there. For years Sierra Leoneans had looked down their noses at Guineans. De Gaulle had taken his spite out on the Guinean President, Sékou Touré, for not going along with French plans for 'controlled decolonization' by pulling the French out of Guinea lock, stock and barrel – the story went that even the telephone and electricity wires were removed. Guinea was left in a desperate state. By contrast, Sierra Leone was then a rich and developed country and Guineans came to Sierra Leone to shop and seek employment. Now the situation had been reversed and although Guinea was not rich, it enjoyed a degree of stability and development far beyond Sierra Leone's. The Guineans did not welcome the influx of Sierra Leoneans, a position that was exacerbated by the language difference.

The United Nations Commision for Human Rights (UNHCR) had established a refugee camp in Guinea at Fourecariah near the Sierra Leone border, but many Sierra Leoneans preferred to stay in Conakry. Many of them were from the professional classes, and life in a refugee camp held little attraction. However, in Conakry most of them had no homes, no jobs and no income. Some of them managed to find menial employment and others rented shacks on the outskirts of the city. A major problem was the education of their children. They could not put them into Guinean schools so they set up their own, informally. Several of the students who had fled became impromptu teachers.

A constant stream of Sierra Leoneans appeared at the Hotel Camayenne seeking help. I did what I could. I would invite many of them to have a meal with me in the restaurant, knowing that for some, this would be the only meal they had had for days. They came from all walks of life – government ministers, teachers, students, businessmen, market women – the effect of the evacuation had been to bring everyone down to a common level.

Zainab Bangura had had to flee Freetown with her husband and teenage son and she continued organizing the civil society groups in Conakry. Her energy and commitment was amazing. She got together the various women's groups, trade unionists, teachers and students. She was constantly in touch with those back in Freetown, reporting on events, issuing statements, organizing meetings. I started attending some of these meetings, talking to them about democracy, urging them not to lose hope. Some of the younger Sierra Leoneans formed a new organization – the Movement for the Restoration of Democracy (MRD). Others would be constantly going in and out of the country, at great risk to themselves, to promote the resistance to the junta. These times were very inspirational. Many felt that we were not just fighting for the cause of democracy in Sierra Leone, but for the cause of democracy in Africa as a whole. In line with the statement issued by Kofi Anan, the UN Secretary-General, we were sending a message that military coups were no longer acceptable in Africa. The Overseas Development Organization (ODA) (predecessor of the Department for International Development, DFID) made some funds available to support such activities. ODA officials visited regularly from London. They were very committed and it was a pleasure working with them.

For those left in Sierra Leone, life was even more miserable. Out of a population of over a million in Freetown, less than a third remained. People had either fled the country or moved back to their villages in the rural areas. To reach the Guinea border one had to run a gauntlet of over twenty road blocks manned by the soldiers and RUF, each demanding a payment to pass. Only those who had nowhere to go remained in Freetown. Less than ten per cent of shops and businesses were open, the banks remained closed. Despite continuing threats from the AFRC, very few people went to work, either to maintain their boycott of the regime or because there was no work to go to. As a result of the widespread looting and destruction, many offices were bare, devoid of even desks and chairs, let alone computers. It was a joke that many of the RUF had complained that many of the 'televisions' they had looted did not pick up the Sierra Leone television service. With the banks closed, money was in short supply. Anyone receiving any income found him/herself maintaining dozens of 'relatives'.

The looting continued, often accompanied by rapings and maimings. By 7.00 pm everyone returned to their homes and locked and bolted their doors and windows. Some of the Lebanese and Indian businessmen who had remained would even weld up their stores every night.

The junta's control of the rest of the country was even less tenuous. The main towns of Bo, Kenema and Makeni, where there were army bases, remained nominally under the control of the regime, but with even less appearance of government activity. Outside of Freetown the strongest presence of the AFRC and RUF was in Kono District, centre of the diamond mining industry, where the local populace was forced to mine for diamonds. The AFRC's writ did not extend to the south of the country. There the Kamajors kept control in support of the Kabbah government.

Koroma continued to issue statements trying to give the impression of a government in control. Endless people were appointed to official positions, often without being consulted in advance. An announcement would be carried over the radio that so-and-so was now an AFRC minister and that he should report to his new ministry. For the individual involved this was often the signal for him/her to flee the country.

The RUF in Freetown

From time to time a few international journalists managed to visit Freetown to report on the situation, which was easier said than done because of the absence of scheduled flights, and limited accommodation. Only one hotel was functioning in Freetown, the Cape Sierra.

Michael Ashworth of the *Independent* visited and spent seven days waiting for an interview with Koroma. He was finally allowed to see one of the RUF leaders, Eldred Collins. Sitting in an office in State House wearing a cowboy hat and dark sunglasses and with a bandoleer of linked ammunition slung across his T-shirt on which was written 'Save the planet', Collins claimed to Ashworth that everything was normal and peaceful. Ashworth asked him why then were the banks closed? Collins said that they were not. Ashworth, who had spent the previous week trying to change some money, pointed out that they were. Fingering the gun by his side on the desk, Collins looked him in the eye and said, 'I am telling you, the banks are open.' In relating the story to me back in Conakry, Ashworth, who had served in the army himself and was familiar with hot spots around the world, said he was convinced that if he had argued further with Collins, the latter would have shot him on the spot. Ashworth filed several reports on the chaos and disorder in Freetown. While he was waiting at State House he witnessed a battered Mercedes full of soldiers with RPGs and AK47s sticking out of the windows come screeching around a corner. It narrowly missed a group of men and ploughed into a concrete pillar. The driver jumped out and kicked the car and the passengers jumped out and kicked the driver.

Most of the RUF were constantly high on drugs. The use of drugs was a common feature of the RUF both in the bush and now in Freetown. Children as young as ten years old were weaned on a local drug known as 'brown brown', a powder, brown in colour, which was heated and inhaled, like cocaine. Marijuana, and another plant known as 'kumbajarra', traditionally used for keeping snakes away from homes, was grown widely. The two were mixed together with gunpowder and injected straight into the brain. It was quite common to see RUF kids walking around in a daze with a plaster on their forehead.

Soon after I had arrived in Conakry I had sent a report to Ann Grant in the Foreign Office headed 'Why We Should Not Deal With The RUF'. In it I noted how the RUF were now controlling Koroma and the AFRC. I detailed the terrible atrocities committed by the RUF. Although some outsiders had attempted to paint them as a well-meaning liberation movement, I described them as 'a bunch of brutal thugs, surrounded by a mass of confused, simple people, led by a power crazed, untrustworthy zealot'. The idea that we should try to negotiate any deal with such people that would leave them in a position of power and influence, I found unacceptable. Even taking into account their lack of basic education and understanding, how could one envisage such people as ministers or senior officials in any government? For some time there had been an acceptable face of the RUF in the lead-up to the Abidjan Peace Accord, people like the Deen-Jallohs, Fayia Musa, Dr Barre and Philip Palmer; but events had shown that such people did not wield any real power and influence within the RUF. Where were they now that the RUF was in power? Probably tortured and killed by the very people they were purporting to represent. I concluded that we should not apply pressure on President Kabbah to do a deal with the RUF. It was not in our interests; it was not in Africa's interests; it was not in Sierra Leone's interests; and, as they had demonstrated most courageously, it was not what the Sierra Leoneans wanted.

The RUF fighting had been described as a 'civil war' but I felt that this misrepresented the true situation. A civil war suggested two opposing sides, both with a clear political agenda, both attempting to win the hearts and minds of the people, with a clear dividing line, on either side of which the people supported the occupying forces. This was not the case in Sierra Leone. The RUF were out for power for power's sake, merely to satisfy their greed. They 'controlled' only those areas where their forces were present, and even in these areas, they were generally unpopular. I was not alone with these views. Dr Joe Opala, an American anthropologist and historian, who had lived in Sierra Leone for twenty years and was about the most knowledgeable expatriate expert on the country, was to write:

> We must recognize that Sierra Leone did not suffer a civil war, but an episode of civil chaos. Once this is recognized, we should also recognize that negotiations with Sankoh are not the most important part of restoring order. Sankoh is a symptom of civil chaos, not its cause.

His words were to prove most prophetic, though regrettably they failed to influence the US Government's thinking at the time of the Lomé negotiations.

I received a polite reply to my report from Ann Grant, saying in effect that in order to achieve peace, one often had to sit down with unsavoury characters.

Civil Resistance to the Junta

This might have been the considered view in London but it was clearly not what the Sierra Leone people felt. In Freetown and elsewhere in the country most of the people continued to ignore the AFRC junta. Inevitably there were a few Lebanese businessmen who remained to do their deals with the junta but they were in the minority as most of their colleagues had fled the country. One who remained but refused to have anything to do with the junta was Alhaji Hussein Jawad. Born in Sierra Leone of Lebanese parents, this remarkable man continued to build his Family Kingdom hotel complex close to the Mammy Yoko Hotel even though it seemed unlikely at the time that people from outside would ever enjoy the facility. His determination gave hope to the Sierra Leone people that at least there was one businessman who had faith that things would improve at some time in the future. He was to become a close friend.

Perhaps the most remarkable show of solidarity against the junta was taken by the students. Notwithstanding the importance attached to gaining an education, they passed a resolution refusing to return to classes until the AFRC had stood down. As a result all the schools and colleges remained closed. In August they attempted to mount a demonstration on the streets of Freetown against the junta. It was ruthlessly put down by the soldiers. Several students were murdered and others were imprisoned. It became an offence against the junta to be a student. One student recounted how his cousin was ordered by the RUF to hack off his hand. When he put forward his left hand, the RUF rebel immediately insisted that he put his out his right hand 'because he was a student' and should not be allowed to write again.

With the imposition of sanctions, food and fuel stocks became scarce. At one stage the junta managed to get a tanker through the Ecomog cordon, so that after weeks of no fuel for electricity or for vehicles, it was suddenly in supply. One would have imagined that the poor people of Freetown would have welcomed this respite from the tough life they were living, but in fact the opposite was true. On the day that the tanker reached Freetown my telephone in the hotel in Conakry never stopped ringing from people in Freetown saying, 'I thought the international community was supposed to be operating an embargo. How did you let that tanker get through?' Residents of Freetown would ring their relatives in Conakry telling them not to send in any food supplies to them. Although they were hungry, they knew that any food sent in would be stolen by the soldiers and rebels, and thus prolong their stay in power.

ODA's decision to suspend our aid programme, which I supported, was criticized by some British NGOs. The latter claimed that we were using humanitarian aid as a political tool, which would lead to innocent civilians dying. The matter was raised in the House of Commons. Guided by the views of the many Sierra Leoneans in the country with whom I was in touch, I had no doubt that our policy was right. In the rural areas outside the junta's control the people were able to grow sufficient food for their needs. In Freetown and the other major towns, the junta requisitioned any food brought in. This whole debate was to become the focus of an Open University course on development.

This civil resistance was to last nine months. It was a remarkable demonstration of determination and sacrifice.

The international pressure on the AFRC to stand down continued. The OAU had been the first to condemn the coup. They had been meeting in Harare at the time of the coup, and the OAU statement calling for the immediate restoration of the democratic government was issued by President Mugabe in his capacity as Chairman of the OAU. It was followed by similar statements from around the world. The UN Secretary-General Kofi Anan had issued a particularly strongly worded statement:

Last week, military elements in Sierra Leone toppled a democratically elected government. Africa can no longer tolerate, and accept as *faits accomplis*, coups against elected governments, and the illegal seizure of power by military cliques, who sometimes act for sectional interests, sometimes simply for their own. Armies exist to protect national sovereignty, not to train their guns on their own people. Some may argue that military regimes bring stability and predictability, that they are helpful to economic development. That is a delusion. Look at the example of South America, where the militaries are back in their garrisons, democracy thrives, and economies soar. Accordingly, let us dedicate ourselves to a new doctrine for African politics: where democracy has been usurped, let us do whatever is in our power to restore it to its rightful owners, the people. Verbal condemnation, though necessary, is not sufficient. We must also ostracize and isolate putchists. Neighbouring states, regional groupings, and the international community all must play their part.

The OAU had designated the sub-regional grouping Ecowas (Economic Community of West African States) to pursue the return of the legitimate government in Sierra Leone. Following an Ecowas foreign ministers' meeting in Conakry on 26 and 27 June, a communiqué was issued calling for a combination of three measures, namely dialogue, sanctions and the use of force, in order to achieve the reinstatement of the legitimate government. A subcommittee of foreign ministers from Nigeria, Ghana, Guinea and the Ivory Coast was established to ensure implementation within a time frame of two weeks. The Nigerian force still in Sierra Leone, joined by elements of the Guinean army, was identified as part of the regional Ecomog force that had been deployed in Liberia for some time to help bring order there. The time frame of two weeks proved far too optimistic. The Liberian Foreign Minister was added to the subcommittee, to be known as the C5, following the 'democratic' elections that brought Charles Taylor to power. Several meetings were held as the tortuous attempts to find a peaceful solution continued culminating at the end of the year with the Conakry Peace Plan.

It was, of course, not surprising that Nigeria was playing this leading role. Nigeria, by far, dominated the affairs of West Africa. In size and population it was ten times bigger than the rest of West Africa combined. However, her influence presented problems for us and other Western countries at the time. Nigeria was being ostracized by the international community because of the dictatorial military regime headed by Sani Abacha, which showed little respect for human rights and few moves towards a democratic system. Though we maintained diplomatic relations, sanctions against Nigeria were in place and her membership of the Commonwealth had been suspended. It was therefore ironic that she should be playing the leading role in securing the return of democracy in Sierra Leone. On my and others' advice, British ministers decided to 'ring-fence' the activities of Nigeria with regard to Sierra Leone; although we welcomed what she was doing there as a force for good, we noted that this would not stop us criticizing her for what was going on in her own country.

While Nigeria was in the forefront of the regional efforts, Britain led the international efforts to secure the restoration of the Kabbah government. We arranged for Shirley Gbujama, Kabbah's Foreign Minister, to attend a conference at Wilton Park on 'Stability in Africa' and followed this by organizing and funding a conference in London in November entitled 'Restoring Sierra Leone to Democracy', to which over 200 people were invited to listen to speeches by President Kabbah and Tony Lloyd. The most moving presentation was delivered by Zainab Bangura. While she was speaking, stills were flashed up on a screen behind her of some of the atrocities committed by the RUF and AFRC. Some people in the audience wept at the sight of decapitated bodies lying in pools of mud and blood.

From the London conference, Kabbah was flown in a specially chartered flight, together with his delegation comprising Thaimu Bangura, Shirley Gbujama, James Jonah, Momodou Koroma, Cyril Foray, the Sierra Leone High Commissioner, and myself, to Edinburgh to attend the Commonwealth heads of government meeting as the special guest of Tony Blair. Nearly forty heads of state attended the meeting, including Nelson Mandela, who grabbed the headlines by promoting the cause of the relatives of the Lockerbie bombing. Kabbah had several bilateral meetings, including with Tony Lloyd, whom he asked whether the British Government would be prepared to supply arms and ammunition to help achieve the restoration of his government. He was turned down.

In their communiqué issued at the end of the conference, all the Commonwealth heads of government condemned the coup in Sierra Leone and called for the immediate reinstatement of President Kabbah, whom they welcomed to the meeting. The CHOGM communiqué also welcomed the UN resolution imposing petroleum, weapons and travel restrictions on the junta in Sierra Leone. The UK delegation in New York had been actively involved in drafting this resolution, Number 1132, which was passed on 8 October. Sitting in Conakry at the time, I was aware of the UN resolution but did not receive a copy from the Foreign Office, nor, more importantly, a copy of the later UK Order in Council putting the UN resolution into effect in Britain. At the time that did not seem important.

With all their efforts to promote the restoration of the Kabbah government, the officials in the Foreign Office in London became increasingly frustrated at the seeming lack of energy shown by President Kabbah himself to get back to Sierra Leone. Kabbah acquired a nickname in Conakry among his fellow Sierra Leoneans of 'Pretty Soon', as whenever he was asked when they would get back to Sierra Leone he would reply 'pretty soon'. The British Government had said that it wanted 'an African solution to an African problem', but it was not prepared for it to be determined by an African timeframe.

London asked me to urge Kabbah to be more proactive. A stream of directives were issued from London telling Kabbah to do this or do that. For a government that was seemingly embarrassed about its colonial past, the instructions I received from the Foreign Office on what to say to President Kabbah were more forthright than when I had been serving as a governor of one of our colonial dependencies.

Though I shared London's frustration, to be fair to Kabbah, he was limited in what he could do. He had no source of funding. Apart from a few energetic ministers like Momodou Koroma and Shirley Gbujama, and others like James Jonah and Zainab Bangura, he had few reliable people to whom he could turn. There was still an element of mistrust between Kabbah and Sam Hinga Norman. When I had first arrived in Conakry, I had discovered that they were not even talking to one another. Kabbah referred to Norman as a 'loose cannon'. I advised that the best way to deal with a loose cannon was to tie it down and ensure that it was firing in the right direction! I urged both Kabbah and Norman to bury their differences and work together for the good of the country. Sam Norman later told me that this was the best advice I had ever given him.

In terms of a fighting force under Kabbah's direct command, other than a few loyal army and Special Security Division (SSD) with Ecomog at Lungi Airport, he only had the Kamajors, who had ensured that the south of the country remained loyal to the Kabbah government. They had now been joined by other similar tribal groups from around the country, the Kapras, the Gbethis, the Donsos and the Tamaboras, to form the Civil Defence Force (CDF). Norman was given the challenging task of co-ordinating the activities of the CDF from within the country but under the control of a committee headed by the Vice President, Joe Demby, stationed at Lungi with Ecomog and answerable directly to the President.

Norman initially based himself in Monrovia, from where he would cross over the border into Sierra Leone, until Charles Taylor came to power. Taylor's support for Sankoh and the RUF meant that Norman's life was at risk in Monrovia and he moved permanently into Sierra Leone, where he was helped by the Fijian ex-SAS soldier Fred Marafono with the training and operations of the CDF. A training camp was set up, Base Zero, in the Bonthe area. Vital to its operation was 'Bokkie'. Bokkie was the nickname for an Mi-17 helicopter that originally had belonged to Executive Outcomes. When EO pulled out, the helicopter was taken over by another private security firm, Sandline, of which much more later. Bokkie provided a vital airbridge between the Ecomog base in Monrovia and the Ecomog forces at Lungi, and also for the CDF at Base Zero. It was flown by an outstanding ex-EO South African pilot, Johann Joubert, or Juba. The exploits of Bokkie being flown by Juba with Fred wielding his GPMG (General Purpose Machine Gun) from the open door became legendary. They were expertly told in Hamish Ross's book, *From SAS to Blood Diamonds War*.

Norman claimed to Ecomog that the CDF could muster up to 37,000 fighters from the various chiefdoms in support of the Ecomog operation. The CDF undoubtedly fought bravely for Kabbah's restoration, but they continuously lacked logistical support and equipment. Militarily Kabbah was essentially dependent upon the Nigerians and the Guineans and he did not want to do anything to displease them. He rarely left the confines of his villa in Conakry; not to the refugee camp at Fourecariah, not even to his embassy directly opposite the villa complex where hundreds of his fellow countrymen were gathered. Mostly the trips he made were outside Guinea, to Nigeria to see Abacha.

Thanks largely to the British Government's efforts, not one country in the world, not even Libya or Cuba, for example, recognized the illegal AFRC junta – a significant diplomatic achievement. However, to ensure that support for the Kabbah government did not waiver among the international community, it was important to promote an image of a semi-functioning government ready to return and pick up the reins of governing the country. The ODA arranged a workshop in the UK whose task was to prepare a 'ninety-day action plan' covering the priorities of the first three months of President Kabbah's government after restoration. Thirty Sierra Leoneans were flown back to the UK from Conakry and joined by others, including leading British businessmen such as Clive Dawson, who was working hard behind the scenes to support the restoration. The plan was presented at the London conference 'Restoring Sierra Leone to Democracy'.

In Conakry, a Sierra Leone government office was set up using ODA funds. We rented a run-down building, which had been an Indian restaurant on one of the main thoroughfares, and stuck up a sign saying 'Government of Sierra Leone'. A very tight rein was kept on the UK funds made available for the purpose. I told President Kabbah that it was not our intention to subsidize the cost of all his ministers, several of whom, in my opinion, had proved themselves useless. Programmes were run from the Conakry Government Office to promote the cause for the restoration of democracy in Sierra Leone, including monitoring the UN sanctions imposed upon the junta.

The basis on which we felt confident to promote the return of the Kabbah government was not only the legitimacy of the democratic election but the will and determination shown by the Sierra Leone people that this was what they wanted. It was important, therefore, to support them in their struggle and encourage them not to lose hope in the face of the sacrifices they were making, especially inside the country. But how to get this message across? The AFRC had banned the independent newspapers and radio stations. Radio was by far the most influential sector of the media. With such a high illiteracy rate and a television service reaching just the couple of hundred sets in Freetown, it was through the radio that people were kept informed. The BBC World Service, especially its two African programmes, *Network Africa* and *Focus on Africa*, was required listening for all Sierra Leoneans. The situation in Sierra Leone dominated the African news and often the programmes carried heartfelt messages from Sierra Leoneans requesting help to rid them of the oppressive junta in Freetown.

Following a discussion with Mukesh Kapila in the ODA, we decided to fund a clandestine pro-democracy radio station. One of Sierra Leone's leading academics and a former newspaper editor, Dr Julius Spencer, was brought back from the United States to set it up. Radio 98.1 Democracy was an instant success. Operating initially out of a tent at Lungi Airport behind the Ecomog lines, the radio broadcast to the people of Freetown sixteen hours a day. It reported on the international support for President Kabbah's government and the calls for the AFRC to stand down. Thanks to an effective network of informers in Freetown, mainly students, the station was able to report in detail on the activities of the AFRC and RUF, highlighting their crimes and misdeeds.

Radio 98.1 really got up the noses of Koroma and his cohorts. No sooner had they held a meeting among themselves, than details of what had been discussed was being broadcast to the people. The junta was continually trying to discover from where the radio station was broadcasting. They warned people not to listen to it. One 80-year-old woman was killed for just doing so. Along with the BBC's *Focus on Africa*, Radio 98.1 became the main source of information to the Sierra Leone people about what was going on in their country and outside. It was a source of much strength and encouragement to the residents of Freetown, who went to bed with their radios underneath their pillows to dampen the reception, listening to Spencer and his colleagues.

We deliberately did not publicize our support for Radio 98.1 for fear of reprisals being taken against our staff and properties but from time to time I would give a live interview by telephone from my hotel room in Conakry in which I encouraged the people to keep faith with democracy and not to lose hope. Because of these interviews and my other activities, I became one of the 'enemies of the AFRC revolution'. When John Flynn, a retired member of the Diplomatic Service, was made the Secretary of State's Special Representative to Sierra Leone, the AFRC misinterpreted his appointment as my successor. One of the few pro-AFRC newspapers allowed to operate, *We Yone*, produced an editorial headed 'Good Riddance to Penfold'.

Conakry Peace Plan

Towards the end of 1997 spirits were raised with the signing of the Conakry Peace Plan, which had been pushed through by Tom Ikimi, the enigmatic Foreign Minister of Nigeria. The plan called for an immediate ceasefire and the disarmament of all combatants leading to the restoration of President Kabbah under a power-sharing arrangement by 22 April 1998. There were many problems with the plan. Firstly there was the question of whether the AFRC could be trusted to honour their side of the agreement. People had not forgotten earlier in the year when a previous AFRC delegation, when meeting the C5 ministers in Abidjan, had agreed for the AFRC to step down. Before the ink was dry on the document, Koroma had announced from Freetown that he intended to remain in power until the year 2001. Secondly, there was the danger that the AFRC would interpret the agreement as giving them *de facto* recognition as the Government of Sierra Leone, something that we had been studiously avoiding; and thirdly, would the people of Sierra Leone accept such a power-sharing agreement after holding out so resolutely against the AFRC and RUF?

President Kabbah's government had not been involved in the Conakry meeting, although Solomon Berewa, his Attorney-General, had sat in as an 'observer'. A copy of the Plan had been faxed through to Kabbah while he was in London. James Jonah, among others, voiced concerns about it, but Kabbah, under strong pressure from the Nigerians, said he was prepared to go along with it. The international community supported the Plan. Tony Lloyd saw the shortcomings but, in the absence of anything else, felt that the Plan represented the best chance of a peaceful solution. The AFRC demanded an immediate lifting of the UN sanctions. But this was refused.

In early December we learned that the AFRC was still bringing in weapons. They had rehabilitated the old airstrip at Magburaka and a consignment of arms and ammunition originating in Ukraine had been flown in from Burkino Faso. Steve Bio, the brother of the former head of state, had made the arrangements. It appeared that the AFRC had little intention of standing down. This view was further reflected in copies of letters that President Kabbah acquired, which revealed that dissident elements in the UK, such as Abass Bundu, a former foreign minister convicted for selling passports, and Omrie Golley, a discredited Sierra Leone lawyer, were advising Koroma to play for time. They argued that the longer the AFRC stayed in power, the more likely the solidarity displayed by Ecowas and the international community would begin to fragment. There was the added bonus that the longer the AFRC stayed in power, the more they could exploit the diamonds and make themselves and their supporters rich. On at least one occasion, Golley passed through Conakry carrying diamonds for the AFRC junta.

The year 1997 had not been easy for me and Celia. Although I had managed to get back to the UK on several occasions, we had been unable to spend much time together. Originally she had been expected to join me in Freetown on completion of her studies at Oxford, where she was studying theology and philosophy. The coup and evacuation had totally disrupted these plans. While I was stuck in Conakry, she continued her studies, but the separation was having an effect. London agreed that I could have a complete break from Sierra Leone affairs for six weeks over Christmas and New Year. It was not an ideal time to be going away. With the junta reneging on its commitments under the Conakry Peace Plan, the situation in Sierra Leone was becoming tense. I argued with London that in my absence there should be cover in Conakry over the holiday period. Colin Glass was not due to come out until early January and with his family commitments I did not want to disrupt his Christmas/New Year plans, so Dai Harries was asked to interrupt his Portuguese language training prior to his posting to Maputo to provide cover. The arrangements were put in train.

Chapter Four

Contacts with Sandline

Before leaving Conakry on 19 December I called on President Kabbah at his villa to wish him a merry Christmas and to check whether he had any messages to take back to London. As usual we met alone in the large living room on the ground floor of the villa. He sat sprawled out on the luxurious leather settee and I sank into one of the large armchairs. Although our meetings were always very relaxed, we still maintained the diplomatic courtesies of addressing each other, 'Your Excellency'.

During the meeting he showed me in confidence a faxed copy of a draft contract that he had recently received. I read it quickly. The contract was between a Canadian mining company called Blackstone and the Government of Sierra Leone. In return for mining concessions from the government, Blackstone would make available to a company called Sandline up to US $10 million for the purchase of equipment and the provision of personnel and training to support President Kabbah's restoration. I did not recall that the draft contract made any specific mention of arms, but given the amount of money involved I assumed that arms would be included as part of the package. I had not heard of Blackstone but the company Sandline and its boss, Tim Spicer, had been brought to my attention only recently in watching CNN reports on the television in my hotel room about its activities in Papua New Guinea.

There was much confusion about the linkage between Branch Energy, Executive Outcomes, Lifeguard and Sandline, partly of their own deliberate making in order to blur the various connections. The Foreign Office had arranged for me to call on Branch Energy as part of my pre-posting briefing. The British company had mining concessions to mine kimberlite in Kono District. After his evacuation from Freetown, Branch Energy's representative, Rupert Bowen, had reappeared in Conakry towards the end of the year. Given the letter he had sent to Robin Cook, I did not go out of my way to meet him, but from time to time he turned up at the bar of the Hotel Camayenne. When President Kabbah terminated the contract with the South African based firm,

Executive Outcomes, as part of the Abidjan Peace Accord, an affiliated company, Lifeguard, remained in Sierra Leone to provide security at the Branch Energy mine and also at the Sierra Rutile mine, owned by a multi-national conglomerate including Hanson Trust. Spicer always maintained that his Bahamian registered company, Sandline, had no connection with Branch Energy or Executive Outcomes, but it may be more than coincidental that Sandline's London offices were at the same address as Branch Energy and that some of EO's personnel were also used by Sandline.

President Kabbah asked me whether the British Government was likely to provide a similar package of assistance. I told him that the British Government was firmly committed to the restoration of his government, but we preferred to see this achieved by peaceful means through the implementation of the Conakry Peace Plan. I saw no likelihood that we would provide arms and ammunition. I was confident of this view not just because of the conversation that he had had with Tony Lloyd in Edinburgh, but I had previously attended an inter-ministry meeting in London and had raised the question of us supplying boots and uniforms for the 1,000 or so soldiers and policemen loyal to Kabbah who were with the Ecomog forces at Lungi. The reaction at the meeting, even for this type of equipment, had not been positive.

Kabbah sought my advice on the contract. I made it clear that the decision was for him to make. He referred to the positive help given by EO in the past and noted that at his last meeting with Abacha in Abuja the latter had encouraged him to seek help 'from wherever' for his loyal forces to strengthen Ecomog. Although he did not wish to mortgage the future of his country by signing deals like this, he noted that when he did return he would need to get a grip on the diamond mining industry. This had traditionally fallen into the hands of unscrupulous individuals and corrupt ministers and officials with the result that the country's diamond wealth had never benefited the economy. He would probably go ahead and sign the contract. As neither he nor I considered that the UN sanctions applied to his government, no mention was made of them. Kabbah said that he would ask Spicer to get in touch with me when I was in the UK.

I flew back to London on the overnight flight and on the following day I went up to the Foreign Office from my home. Celia came with me to pick up her passport and to do some Christmas shopping. Spicer had telephoned and we arranged to meet for lunch after my meeting in the Foreign Office.

As always when I returned to London I went into what was known as the 'third room' of the African Department, where the head of section, Tim Andrews, and the desk officer, Lynda St Cooke, worked. They were the main officers with whom I maintained contact on virtually a day to day basis. I introduced Celia and she collected her passport, which was being processed for a visa. I handed in my 'Annual Review', one of the key documents of any post overseas. It was, as its name suggested, a review of all the events of the past year, and was done in the form of a despatch to the Secretary of State. As I was going to be away for the whole month of January, I was keen to get it into the system. Amongst other things it reflected my thoughts on where we stood with the Conakry Peace Plan and my view that only a credible threat of force would persuade the junta to honour its obligations under the Plan.

I reported on my meeting with Kabbah and mentioned that I would be seeing Spicer. It was made clear to me that Spicer had been in touch with the department, though it was not to be until much later that I learned of the extent of these contacts. He had frequently telephoned the department, especially John Everard, the deputy head of the department, about events in Sierra Leone, and only earlier that month representatives of Branch Energy/Executive Outcomes had had a meeting in the office. Later, in the Legg Inquiry, both Tim and Lynda were to have only a hazy recollection of our meeting – indeed, they said that they were not sure whether it took place at all.

My main purpose in seeing Spicer, as indeed the department's, was to gather information on the security situation in Sierra Leone. In Conakry I was pretty well informed about what was going on given our range of contacts. The main gap in my knowledge was trying to find out what the Nigerians were up to. The strain in our relations with Nigeria, and in particular the embargo we had imposed on contacts with the Nigerian military, meant that it was difficult to find out what Ecomog was doing. Through the operation of its helicopter Sandline had personnel working alongside Ecomog at Lungi and this was a valuable source of information that was available to Spicer.

I met up with Spicer in a restaurant on the Old Brompton Road. Tony Buckingham, the boss of Branch Energy, was with him. Reference was made to the draft contract but they seemed mainly interested in my views of President Kabbah – whether he was honest, whether he could bring stability back to Sierra Leone. The lunch lasted less than an hour as I was anxious to meet up with Celia. Spicer promised to keep me informed on developments.

Celia and I spent an enjoyable Christmas at the Compleat Angler on the Thames at Marlow and whilst there Spicer telephoned to confirm that Kabbah had signed the contract. On our return to Abingdon we prepared to fly off to Canada to spend New Year with Celia's sisters in Toronto. As I was going to have a complete break from Sierra Leone affairs for the whole month of January, I needed to ensure that any information I had was with the department. I wrote a letter to Ann Grant, the head of the African Department. In addition to Spicer's information, I had spoken to Dai Harries in Conakry and also to the staff in Freetown so I was able to report to Ann that Christmas had passed off quietly in Sierra Leone.

In the letter I noted, 'I have been in touch with Tim Spicer over the holidays. Kabbah has signed the deal with Blackstone for EO/Sandline to provide $10 million of equipment and training for the civil defence militia. This will begin to flow in January.' I also reported to Ann the conversation that I had had with Richard Dales, the Director for Africa, just before Christmas, in which I had expressed some reservations about the decision to appoint John Flynn as the Secretary of State's special representative. I knew that Ann had been closely involved in the decision and I wanted to ensure that she knew my views. I also mentioned the awards about to be announced in the New Year Honours. On my recommendation the other four members of the team had all received awards – Colin, an MBE, Dai, an OBE, Andrew, The Queen's Gallantry Medal, and Lincoln, the Military Cross. I had spoken to some of them over Christmas and they were embarrassed that I had received nothing.

I kept a copy of the hand-written letter, which I posted in the little post box around the corner from my house before going off to Heathrow to catch the flight to Toronto. It surprised me subsequently to learn that this letter, dated 30 December, had gone missing. What was especially curious was that when I returned from holiday attempts were made to explain to me why the department had not put me up for an award in the New Year Honours. Why should they do so if no one had seen my letter?

After New Year while I was still in Toronto, Lynda St Cooke telephoned to ask me to break my leave and attend some meetings with John Flynn in New York. I met up with John at the offices of the UK mission to the UN. He had flown in from Caracas, where he had previously served as Ambassador. He had been appointed the Secretary of State's special representative mainly on the strength of his experience in Angola, where, as Ambassador, he had played an important role in trying to resolve the conflict in that poor country. John had also served elsewhere in Africa, but he had no West African experience. The UK mission had arranged various meetings for us, including with the Swedish Ambassador as Chairman of the UN Sanctions Committee, and the US delegation to the UN. Sir John Weston, our Ambassador, also kindly arranged a lunch in his small but fashionable New York apartment, to which, among others, he invited James Jonah.

Whilst in New York I was able to spend an enjoyable evening with Andrew Murro reminiscing on our trip along the West African coast and then on 27 January, Celia and I flew back to London.

While I had been away Spicer had gone into the Foreign Office for a meeting with Craig Murray, John Everard's successor, and Tim Andrews. In the subsequent inquiries it proved impossible to reconcile the two versions of what had been discussed at this meeting. In essence Murray claimed that Spicer had not revealed that arms were included in the Sandline contract with Kabbah and that they had made it clear to Spicer that the provision of arms would constitute a breach of the arms sanctions. On the other hand Spicer claimed, equally adamantly, that he had made it clear that arms were involved but that at no time did the officials point out that this would be in breach of sanctions. In the inquiry set up to investigate the Sandline affair Sir Thomas Legg referred to the 'diametric' conflict of evidence about the 19 January meeting. In the findings of his report he noted:

> There is a conflict of evidence about what happened at that meeting which cannot now be fully resolved. Our conclusion is that Mr Murray and Mr Andrews probably left the meeting unaware that Sandline was supplying arms to President Kabbah. We have found no reason why they should have chosen to give Sandline encouragement or approval. We do not find that they did so. We also conclude that Mr Spicer could have left the meeting unaware that supplying arms to President Kabbah would be a breach of the arms embargo. Thus he may have assumed that he had been given tacit approval.

At Spicer's request we had arranged to meet again after my return to the UK. On 28 January I went to the offices in the King's Road, the same as those for Branch Energy, where we discussed the general security situation in Sierra Leone to help bring me up to date. Spicer gave me a copy of a strategy paper that he had prepared on the assistance that Sandline were offering the Kabbah government, which became known as the 'project python' paper. Again, as with Kabbah, as it was widely accepted that the sanctions were directed against the illegal junta, I had no reason to believe that Sandline was breaching the UN sanctions order and therefore made no mention of them. I went into the African Department the next day and I handed over the 'project python' document to Tim Andrews. Tim subsequently told the Legg Inquiry that he did not understand it and sent it to the Ministry of Defence for an explanation.

John Everard had now left the department and I met his successor for the first time, Craig Murray. Murray would later come to prominence as the Ambassador to Uzbekistan, from where he ditched his wife and took up with a local lap dancer. Upon his early retirement from the Diplomatic Service, he ran as an independent candidate in the 2005 elections in Britain in the Blackburn constituency against Robin Cook, but for now he was trying to impress his Foreign Secretary.

Murray had only been in the department for a couple of weeks when we met. Apart from a brief tour a few years back in Nigeria he had no African experience, but he was already formulating his ideas on what to do about Sierra Leone. It seemed to me that he was considering ditching President Kabbah and going for some power-sharing arrangement with the AFRC and the RUF. This worried me. There was nothing wrong in looking at alternative policies, but acknowledging that President Kabbah's government was the legitimate government was fundamental to the policy that we had been pursuing for the previous eight months. Not only was Craig Murray unaware of the sacrifices the

Sierra Leone people had made to bring in their democratic government but also, if we shifted our position, it would encourage the weaker African governments to switch allegiances. The new and courageous policy adopted by the OAU of saying that once and for all military coups were no longer acceptable in Africa would be totally undermined. I went home that evening deeply disturbed and I prepared a paper entitled 'Sierra Leone – The Way Forward', which, while looking at ways of getting the Conakry Peace Plan back on track, re-emphasized the position of not abandoning President Kabbah's government.

I went back into the office the next day and handed in a copy of my paper. Ann Grant asked to see me, and together with Craig Murray, we had a meeting in her room. Ann was particularly concerned to be briefed on my meeting with President Kabbah before Christmas. I went over this in detail, and also outlined to her my two meetings with Spicer, noting that I had handed over the 'project python' paper to Tim Andrews the previous day. Ann's concern was not regarding my contacts with Spicer *per se*, but whether my meeting with Kabbah and my subsequent meetings with Spicer could be interpreted as signifying that I supported the use of force. I made a distinction between the threat to use force to ensure compliance with the peace agreements and the actual use of force. She asked me to draft a note setting out my discussions with President Kabbah and Spicer so that she could assess the position.

Over the weekend I prepared a memo to Ann Grant as requested. In the memo I referred to Sandline's 'purchase of arms and equipment and the provision of training'. I also referred to my earlier letter of 30 December. On the Monday I made a special trip into the office to hand in the memo. As it was graded confidential I could not post it from Abingdon. In the words of the subsequent Legg Inquiry, this memo became 'a crucial document in our investigations', but to all intents and purposes nobody took any notice of my memo. Ann Grant went off on a trip and did not read it until after her return a week later. Murray claimed he did not see it until the end of the month. Andrews saw it but claimed that he had spent most of the time trying to find my letter of 30 December.

Although Murray had claimed that he not seen my memo, he had read my paper on 'The Way Forward' and John Flynn's report from the discussions in New York. Murray submitted a memo to Richard Dales saying that in his view there was a dichotomy in our policy thinking on Sierra Leone. He claimed that I had advised President Kabbah to go for the military option and he criticized Flynn for advocating military assistance to the Nigerians. He recommended an early termination of my posting. In his reply Richard Dales told Murray that there was no dichotomy in our thinking. Her Majasty's Government's policy was that the Conakry Peace Plan should be implemented by Ecomog, under the cover of a UN Security Council resolution, monitored and assisted by UN advisers/observers and 'using limited necessary force or the threat of force to ensure compliance by the junta.' In other words, Richard Dales was confirming the policy that I had been advising in my Annual Review. Murray later told the Legg Commission that he was upset by Richard Dales' response and that this was one of the reasons why he chose not to let me know that I was under investigation.

Murray also advised Dales that in his most optimistic estimate the High Commission in Freetown would not reopen for at least another six months. On this he was also wrong. I was to be back in Freetown to reopen the High Commission within a month.

Chapter Five

President Kabbah Restored – 1998

B y the time I arrived back in Conakry on 10 February, the Ecomog forces had already started to retake Freetown. For the previous eight months their forces had sat patiently at Lungi and at Kosso camp on the outskirts of Freetown, but they were frustrated. Every now and again the AFRC and RUF forces had launched raids on the Ecomog positions trying to provoke them into action in the misguided belief that any Ecomog retaliation would be condemned by the international community and thereby force Ecomog's withdrawal from Sierra Leone. Each attack was repulsed successfully, often inflicting heavy casualties on the drug-induced junta forces. In one foolish attack reputedly 300 RUF youths were slaughtered. But Ecomog also suffered casualties. At the beginning of February an Ecomog vehicle was blown up by a landmine planted by the junta and a number of Nigerian soldiers were killed.

The new Ecomog commander, Colonel Maxwell Khobe, and his men were becoming increasingly frustrated at having to sit there and take these provocations. Abacha, sitting in Abuja, was also no doubt increasingly concerned at the losses his forces were suffering. No publicity was given back in Nigeria for these deaths but he could not keep having Nigerian soldiers being flown back to Nigeria in body bags without it being noticed and leading to a groundswell of resentment among the Nigerian public. The cost of the Ecomog operation in Sierra Leone was enormous; some experts put it at over $3 million per week. As time went on Abacha needed increasingly to have something to show for this drain on the Nigerian coffers. There was no sign that the junta was serious about standing down. Abacha decided to go for the military option. Whether he told President Kabbah in advance became a matter of debate but, given that Nigeria was calling all the shots, it mattered little. Sierra Leone was now a pawn in Nigerian politics.

Ecomog Retakes Freetown
By 8 February the fighting was in earnest. Khobe led his forces into the city. Right from the start it was obvious that Ecomog planned to retake Freetown.

Abacha was astute enough to realize that for Nigeria to win the glory and the recognition of the international community, restoring Kabbah was not enough. It would have to be achieved with the minimum loss of life and destruction of property.

Julius Spencer accompanied Khobe and his forces into Freetown and continued broadcasting live reports on Radio 98.1. As they came along the Kissy Road, 98.1 announced where the Ecomog forces were and advised the civilian population to stay off the streets and remain in their homes. In this way Ecomog knew that anyone they saw on the streets were junta supporters. After the radio had announced that an area was cleared the people came out and cheered the Ecomog forces, offering them food and water. In this way civilian casualties were kept to a minimum. It was a most effective use of radio broadcasting in warfare and a further feather in our caps that the radio had been financed by the British Government, so that indirectly we again contributed to saving lives.

In Khobe, Nigeria had selected a remarkable military commander. He led his men from the front, advancing into Freetown just carrying his swagger stick. His men believed that he was invincible and when he ordered his force to divide into two, all of them wanted to stay with him. At one point the group of soldiers he was with were pinned down by a 12-year-old RUF fighter who was sniping at them from a building. Khobe's men wanted to blast the building with RPG rounds, but Khobe ordered them to keep firing warning shots until the youth ran out of ammunition. They then captured the youth and moved on. Coming under a further attack Khobe was wounded, suffering shrapnel wounds to his leg, but he refused to withdraw and continued to lead his men. A legend was made.

By 12 February Freetown was secured. The junta forces had either surrendered or fled. Khobe had deliberately left a backdoor open to enable the junta forces to escape around the peninsular and out through Tombu. The city had been taken with remarkably few casualties, either military of civilian.

Back in Conakry we followed the events closely by telephone and radio reports and when word came through that Ecomog forces were around the Cotton Tree and had taken State House, there was jubilation. By contrast London appeared to be preoccupied as to whether the Ecomog deployment was legal or not. They wanted to condemn the Ecomog action because there had been no UN resolution allowing it. These thoughts were far removed from the feelings of the people in Freetown and Conakry. I went and saw President Kabbah and asked him when he would be returning. He said, 'Pretty soon!'

The Royal Navy Sails In

The decision was taken in London to pre-position HMS *Monmouth* off the coast so that she would be available to help me get back and be on-hand to offer assistance to President Kabbah's government. Major Peter Hicks was flown out to be my military liaison officer, or MILO, as the Ministry of Defence referred to him. At the same time the ODA sent out a consultant, David Hill, to help co-ordinate emergency and humanitarian assistance. Colin was already with me so from a solitary existence for so long, I suddenly had all these staff, and a British warship to boot.

We sought diplomatic clearance from the Guinean government for HMS *Monmouth* to come into the port at Conakry and I went down to see the captain. We were keen to get *Monmouth* into Freetown and I sought diplomatic clearance from President Kabbah. I assumed that this would be a formality. However, he said that he would need to speak to the Nigerians. I was somewhat concerned. Although President Kabbah was dependent upon Ecomog and the Nigerians for the security situation in the country, we were anxious that his government re-assume the running of the country as soon as possible and be seen to be doing so. We had not supported the restoration of his government all this time to see Sierra Leone become a feudal state of Nigeria. Kabbah was flying off to see Abacha in Abuja and said that he would discuss the *Monmouth* visit with him. I pointed out that we could not keep a Royal Navy vessel hanging around indefinitely and suggested that once he had spoken to Abacha he should pass the clearance for *Monmouth* to go into Freetown to our High Commission in Abuja.

The Nigerians, or more particularly, Ikimi, their Foreign Minister, were not keen to see a British ship in Freetown. He had made a big thing of the fact that it was African, i.e. Nigerian, troops that had restored the democratic government to Sierra Leone while the rest of the world stood idly by. He did not want to share the glory with Britain or anyone else. Ikimi was a very difficult character. Undoubtedly he was able but he appeared to have a chip on his shoulder with the UK. He even refused sometimes to take telephone calls from Graham Burton, our High Commissioner in Abuja. Ikimi had the ear of Abacha and he persuaded the latter that a British ship in Freetown would steal some of the glory and be used to spy on the Nigerians. Kabbah was in a difficult position. He did not want to annoy us but equally he was not prepared to go against the Nigerians. He tried to wriggle out of it by suggesting that we should ask the Nigerians for permission for *Monmouth* to go in. We said that we were not prepared to do any such thing. His government was in charge and therefore responsible for issuing diplomatic clearances for visiting ships. However, HMS *Monmouth* was already coming to an end of her six-month deployment so it was decided that she should head back to the UK. She was to be replaced by HMS *Cornwall*, which, as it turned out, proved to be fortuitous.

Before HMS *Monmouth* left some of her crew were able to witness a remarkable demonstration in Conakry. Enthused with the news of the success of Ecomog in Freetown the Sierra Leone civil society groups in Conakry decided to mount a victory rally. Again Zainab Bangura was in the forefront of arranging this event. She and other civil leaders organized a march through the streets of Conakry, culminating at the football stadium, which they hired. Hundreds of Sierra Leoneans took part, bringing traffic to a standstill as the bemused Guineans looked on. Francis Okelo and I were invited to address the crowd on behalf of the international community. I took the captain of Monmouth and some of his officers along. As I stood up to speak the crowd started chanting, 'Pen-fold, Pen-fold, Pen-fold'. I was embarrassed. Fighting to have myself heard over the drone of a portable generator set up to work the microphone system, I said, 'Today is a happy day for Sierra Leone, for Ecowas, for the international community, and for all democracy-loving people throughout the world.' And indeed it was.

Back in Sierra Leone, although the Ecomog forces had taken Freetown, they now had to reclaim other parts of the country. CDF forces had retaken the diamond mining town of Tongo at the time of the fighting in Freetown but the next major town to be secured was Bo.

Throughout the previous nine months, Mike Downham, our British doctor, had remained in Bo. From time to time we had been able to get messages to and from him while we were in Conakry. He had faced many difficulties but resolutely stayed to help the people of Bo. However, when the fighting to take the town by Ecomog and the Kamajors started he was finally forced to flee. His offices were ransacked and his vehicles stolen by the fleeing junta forces. Mike set off on foot, together with a bunch of about thirty displaced children, to find safety in the bush. They walked for about 30 miles. Mike telephoned me at the hotel in Conakry on his satellite phone from the bush to report on these events. As usual he played down the danger and the efforts he had made to keep all these people alive. Being stuck in the bush he could not keep his satellite phone on all the time because the batteries would run down so we arranged a daily contact. For five days he would ring me at the prearranged time. It was always a relief to hear from him, and I was able to telephone his aged mother in the UK and let her know that her son was OK. After Bo had been secured, Mike led his charges back on foot again.

London was now seriously considering my return and the reopening of the mission. They insisted as a precondition of my return that I should be accompanied by a close protection team (CPT). These are members of the Royal Military Police (RMP), teams of which are positioned in various embassies or high commissions in so-called hot spots around the world. I was quite familiar with the RMPs. Throughout my time in Uganda we had had teams there and indeed on more than one occasion they were called upon to demonstrate their skills. One particular incident, which took place in my house in Kampala, was later written up in a book called *The Bullet Catchers*. A three-man team flew out to Conakry to swell our numbers, and Mal Scott, the team leader, flew in with Colin and David Hill into Freetown while the rest of us waited in Conakry.

Colin rarely showed emotion at the best of times, a dour Scot in the traditional sense, but even he could not fail to be caught up in the jubilation displayed by the staff at the High Commission on his return.

In the meantime HMS *Cornwall* had arrived to replace *Monmouth*. She was a much bigger ship with a larger crew. She was commanded by Captain Anthony Dymock. I immediately took to this very experienced naval officer.

President Kabbah was now back from Abuja and I again sought his clearance for *Cornwall* to go into Freetown, this time with me on board. I pointed out that the *Cornwall* would be used to spearhead our emergency assistance. Again he was hesitant. This was becoming very serious. I realized that if ministers felt that Kabbah had refused twice to allow us to send in a British ship to provide emergency and humanitarian assistance, this would significantly affect our future policy towards Sierra Leone. They really would believe that President Kabbah was a stooge of the Nigerians and Sierra Leone could kiss goodbye to any further UK assistance. This would also affect international assistance and I encouraged Ambassador Okelo to join me in making representations to the President. London was rattled by the attitude of President Kabbah and recommended *Cornwall's* withdrawal. She pulled out of Conakry port, but within hours of the ship preparing to sail away I obtained the President's agreement for the *Cornwall* to go into Freetown.

Return to Freetown
The ship's helicopter was sent to pick us up from Conakry Airport. I checked out of the Hotel Camayenne and settled the bills. The occupancy of room 503 finally came to an end after 276 nights. Together with Peter Hicks, the two RMPs, an engineer from Accra and two press officers flown out by the Ministry of Defence in London, I drove with Alphonse for the last time to the airport, the others following in the Camayenne's minibus. I had also arranged for us to take back to Freetown Shirley Gbujama, the Sierra Leone Foreign Minister, and Emilio Perez–Poros, the EC representative, who had flown back to Conakry just after Christmas. We all flew off from Conakry and landed on the deck of the *Cornwall* while she was still a couple of hours' sailing from Freetown. It occurred to me that yet again I would be arriving in Freetown without ever having seen Lungi International Airport.

It was a dry but overcast day as HMS *Cornwall* slowly approached Freetown. Using Anthony Dymock's binoculars I scanned the city looking for evidence of the terror and destruction that the city had gone through during the previous nine months. It was difficult to spot any new destruction; the city looked as run down as it had always been. What was noticeable was the absence of people and vehicles. We seemed to be coming into an abandoned city. Nonetheless, there was an air of excitement as Shirley and I picked out familiar landmarks such as Fourah Bay College and St George's cathedral spire.

As the ship slowly came alongside the Kissy Docks we spotted on the quayside some familiar faces – Colin, Solomon, Emmanuel, plus Momodou Koroma, Julius Spencer and Val Collier. They were part of the advance task force to re-establish the Government of Sierra Leone. Momodou and Julius had come in with the Ecomog forces while Val, head of the Public Service, had remained in Freetown throughout. We disembarked and set foot on Sierra Leone soil again. I hugged Solomon and Emmanuel and said to Momodou, 'There you are; I told you one day we would be back!'

As we drove away from the port and through the city to the residence, the streets were eerily quiet. There was no traffic. We saw probably no more than half a dozen vehicles. Perhaps more surprisingly, though there were people around and even a few traders were manning their street-side stalls, we saw no soldiers or policemen. The people we saw had a weary, haggard look. We drove up the hill to the residence. John, Fatmata, IB and the guards were all there to welcome me back. Osman and Alimamy came rushing out from the kitchen. There were tearful embraces.

I went to check on our pet parrots, two African greys called Lori and Lorito. All this time they had remained on our upstairs balcony, no doubt wondering what the hell was going on. Their well-being had been a constant source of concern for Celia and from time to time I had managed to smuggle parrot food into them. Lorito immediately showed how pleased he was to see me after all this time by giving me a nasty peck on the finger.

Thanks to the staff the residence was in remarkably good shape. It was almost as if I had just been away for a weekend. The only serious damage we had suffered was a broken window downstairs from a shrapnel blast, which had splintered dramatically but still stayed in place. It remained a permanent reminder of these dramatic days throughout my tour, often photographed by visitors to the residence.

The next few days were extremely hectic. HMS *Cornwall's* crew set about distributing food and medicines and making emergency repairs to the electricity and water supplies. David Hill co-ordinated the work of those NGOs that were around. The Crown Agents flew in a plane full of office equipment, desks, chairs, photocopiers and generators to help the government start to function again. Every morning we would all meet in my office and plan the day's activities. My residence became a meeting place for all and sundry. At any time, day or night, people would stop by for a chat and a meal. There was little food around but thanks to the *Cornwall* we could usually rustle up some sausages and beans – a veritable feast, especially for the Sierra Leoneans who had stayed throughout.

The *Cornwall's* helicopter proved invaluable for getting around the country. It was constantly flying into Bo, Kenema or Makeni, taking food and medicines. Other than Ecomog we were the only ones able to visit these places. Anthony

Dymock and I and the close protection team flew to Makeni. The town had only just been secured by Ecomog a couple of days previously. The helicopter landed in a swirl of dust on the football ground. There were a few people standing around and they eyed us nervously. I jumped out and walked straight up to them saying, 'It's the British High Commissioner and the British ship HMS *Cornwall* come to see how you are.' A number of them recognized me from previous visits.

They gathered round enthusiastically. 'Who do you want to see?' they asked.

I've come to see my good friends Paramount Chief Bai Sebora Kasangha and Bishop Biguzzi.'

'We'll take you; come this way.'

As we made our way through the streets of Makeni, the numbers swelled behind us kicking up a dust storm. Some ran on ahead and one could hear the buzz, 'It's the British High Commissioner, it's the British High Commissioner.' As the people appeared from their damaged houses, they waved and cheered. By now we had a crowd of several hundred strong accompanying us. We walked for about a mile and turned into the Pastoral Centre. This was where Bishop Biguzzi had taken refuge with nearly three dozen nuns, priests and other expatriates. From time to time we had exchanged messages with couriers while I was in Conakry and on one occasion he had come out for a break, only to bravely go back into Sierra Leone to look after his diocese. My pulse was racing in eager anticipation of seeing him again.

A long driveway led to the building that housed a school and hospital. I recognized the familiar face of the Bishop in his white robes. He started walking towards me. As we approached one another the crowd drew back and formed a circle. We came together and embraced. It was a scene right out of Stanley and Livingstone. We sat under a tree in the grounds and were shortly joined by Paramount Chief Kasanga. We also greeted each other warmly. These two remarkable men had kept the town together. They were the only symbols of order in the midst of utter chaos and devastation.

We had with us the ship's chaplain, Garth Petzer. A South African by birth, he was co-ordinating all of the *Cornwall's* relief activities. Another remarkable man, he combined the efficiency of a naval officer with the caring of a priest and the commitment of an African. We were so lucky to have him with the *Cornwall* as not many Royal Navy ships carry a chaplain on board. Garth went off to the hospital with the Australian lady doctor based in Makeni.

An Ecomog officer arrived to announce that the entire top brass of Ecomog had just arrived, including General Shelpidi, the Ecomog Force Commander who was based in Monrovia. He wanted to address the people of Makeni. Paramount Chief Kasanga was asked to organize it. We went off to a junction on the outskirts of the town where an assortment of looted goods had been assembled. The crowds gathered and eventually a convoy of vehicles arrived bearing Shelpidi and other Ecomog officers including Colonel Khobe. The crowd started chanting 'Khobe, Khobe'. He was undoubtedly the hero of the hour. Shelpidi and Khobe addressed the crowd and I was asked to say a few words.

The Ecomog party went off and we took a tour of the town, including what was left of the district administration offices and the police headquarters. They were totally gutted. They had been looted and set on fire by the junta's forces. There were still unexploded shells around the police station. We said our farewells and flew back to Freetown.

A couple of days later we made a similar trip to Bo. By now Francis Okelo and James Jonah had arrived from Conakry, so they came with us. The helicopter flew fast and low, barely skimming the tree tops and following the river beds over the unfamiliar terrain. The pilot, looking dashing with a red bandana tied around his neck, told me that it was safer to fly this way because by the time any rebels saw us we would be already long gone.

We arrived in Bo to an enthusiastic welcome. There were signs of fighting and devastation everywhere. We unloaded the food and medicines that we had brought with us. While we were doing this, James Jonah had stood unobtrusively to one side. At first people did not realize that he was with us, but as it gradually dawned on them they gathered around him eagerly, all wanting to shake his hand. Even in this Mende heartland, Jonah, a Krio, was a real hero to them. This was the man who had ensured that their democratic elections had taken place and who had continued to speak out forcibly against the junta.

We met up with Mike Downham. He was looking terrible. As well as suffering sore feet from his trek into the bush he had come down with a bad bout of malaria. We insisted that he came back with us and spend a couple of days recuperating on board the *Cornwall*.

Photographs were taken at the CDF headquarters with a bunch of Kamajors bedecked in their unusual and distinctive garb, including necklaces and mirrors to make them 'bullet-proof' and then we toured Bo to witness the scale of the looting and destruction that had taken place. As in other towns and villages, anything that was not bolted down was looted by the soldiers and the RUF. Most of the looted goods would find their way across the borders to Guinea and Liberia.

President Kabbah Returns

Freetown was now preparing for President Kabbah's return on 10 March. He was to be accompanied by General Abacha and the Presidents of Guinea and Niger. Momodou Koroma and his team were responsible for the programme. A visit by three heads of state is demanding at the best of times but set against the backcloth of a devastated city recovering from ten months of junta misrule, the organization would be mind-boggling. We offered to help. We provided some of our vehicles as there were no government vehicles around. All of them had been looted. An official luncheon would be held at the Cape Sierra Hotel and the

Cornwall's catering crew helped in the kitchen and provided some plates, knives and forks and other equipment.

We drove out to Hastings airfield on the outskirts of Freetown on the appointed day. It was hot and sunny. The plan was that President Kabbah would fly into Lungi Airport from Conakry at 9.00 am, where Vice President Dr Demby would formally welcome him back. Kabbah would then greet his overseas guests and they would all fly across to Hastings, where other dignitaries and the diplomatic corps would be assembled. We would then all drive in a cavalcade into Freetown to the national stadium for the welcome home rally.

We all waited at Hastings – Francis Okelo, Emilio, John Hirsch, who had flown back specially the day before, Anthony Dymock, looking resplendent in his white naval uniform, Colin and myself. There was an air of excitement and good humour. This really was a special day. Such an event had never happened before in Africa since the time Emperor Haile Selassie had returned to Ethiopia after the Second World War – the return of a head of state who had been forcibly and illegally removed. From time to time aircraft would arrive bringing in some of the President's ministers and others who had been with him in Conakry. James Jonah and Desmond Luke arrived. I saw my Nigerian colleague Mohammed Abubakar disembark from one of the aircraft. I had not seen him since the day of the evacuation and went up and greeted him warmly. What a way to come back – with his head of state.

The Vice President arrived. A small, unassuming man, Joe Demby had remained at Lungi under difficult conditions throughout the junta's occupation of Freetown as an important symbol that the Kabbah government retained a presence in the country. I had not seen him since our meeting in his office when we discovered that the army was cheating on its pay and rice rations. If only that had been handled differently.

Finally, after a couple of hours we heard the drone of the President's aircraft. A buzz went around the large crowd that had assembled. It landed and taxied round to where we were all standing in the hot sun. It was immediately surrounded by Ecomog soldiers. Shelpidi and Khobe were there. The door of the plane opened and President Kabbah appeared in his flowing African robes. He was followed by General Abacha, dressed likewise. A cheer went up from the crowd assembled at the airport straining to see the President and his entourage who were immediately engulfed by all the Nigerian officers and soldiers. It was perhaps symbolic that Kabbah should be greeted on his return to Sierra Leone by Nigerians; after all, it was thanks to them that he had been able to return to his country.

Everyone climbed into the vehicles. Ikimi, the Nigerian Foreign Minister, was stranded without a car. I had already offered to give a ride to James Jonah, and Colin was taking the Liberian representative, but I was asked whether we could also give Ikimi a lift. It would have been lovely to see Ikimi riding in a

British High Commission vehicle. I am sure that Graham Burton in Abuja would have been amused by it, but I felt that Ikimi would not have seen the humour of the situation and I did not want to ruin Mohammed Abubakar's day, so I arranged for one of the UN vehicles to take the distinguished Foreign Minister from Nigeria.

The long convoy of some two dozen assorted cars and trucks started the drive into Freetown with Presidents Kabbah and Abacha sitting together in the front. The streets were lined with people, young and old, cheering and waving. As our car went past with the Union Jack fluttering in the breeze, cries of 'Jonah' or 'Penfold' went up. We waved back to the happy people. By the time we had reached the stadium we were already five hours behind schedule. The stadium was packed with Sierra Leoneans who had been waiting in the hot sun since early morning. We took our seats in, thankfully, the shaded part of the stadium. I sat below President Conte, alongside his ADC, who was wearing a brilliant red tunic. His first task was to pass up the ashtray he always carried for his president. Conte was an ardent smoker and never went anywhere without his cigarettes and ashtray. I imagined smoke-filled discussions with him if I had been accredited to Guinea.

The crowd cheered as President Kabbah made his way up to the top of the VIP section of the stadium following behind Abacha. The various speeches started – the Vice President, the UN Assistant Secretary General, the head of the Anglican Church, Bishop Julius Lynch, and other civil society leaders. They all said much the same thing – this was the day they had all been waiting for; democracy had been restored. There were loud cheers every time someone mentioned Ecomog, Nigeria or Abacha. Even references to Britain and the United Nations were received enthusiastically by the large crowd. But the loudest cheers were reserved for Khobe and for Radio 98.1. Finally the time came for the speech by the person all the crowd had been waiting for – General Sani Abacha. The crowd went wild. The trade union leader had already declared in his speech that Kissy Street was to be renamed Sani Abacha Street. This was the person for whom they had waited in the hot sun to hear. They knew only too well that this was the person whose commitment had made this day possible, whatever the rest of the world thought of him.

Abacha delivered a statesmanlike speech, noting the significance of the occasion, and then grabbing him by the hand, Abacha 'introduced' President Kabbah. The cheering started all over again as Kabbah announced, 'I'm back.'

By the time Kabbah had started his speech it was five o'clock in the afternoon. The people had been waiting since 7.00 am. They had had enough. They had heard Abacha. They had seen their president. They started to drift away even while Kabbah was still speaking so that by the time his speech came to an end the stadium was half full. The Mayor of Freetown, Mrs Florence Dillsworth, wrapped up proceedings, and we all left. Abacha headed straight for the airport together with the Guinean and Nigerien Presidents. His task was completed and the squalor of Freetown held no attraction compared to the luxury of Abuja. The formal lunch became an informal supper for anyone who wanted it. By now I was feeling pretty tired so after spending a little time with those assembled I made my way home. This historic day came to an end. The democratic government had been restored, and Britain could take pride in the role she had played in achieving this.

Over the next couple of weeks we continued to focus all our energies on emergency and relief assistance. The crew of HMS *Cornwall* set about their tasks with zeal and determination. For many of these young lads it was their first time out of Britain; only a couple of weeks previously they had been in Portsmouth setting off on their first voyage. They were deeply moved by what they saw and were rightly proud of what they were doing. One particularly harrowing experience for a group of young sailors who went on one of the trips to Bo was to help exhume a mass grave of victims of the junta. Over fifty bodies had been dumped in a pit in the hospital grounds, creating a serious health hazard. The crew of Cornwall, under the supervision of Garth Petzer, exhumed the bodies, carried out an ecumenical funeral service and cremated them – a very gruesome task. Now that the government was back the people were very keen to see the schools reopened and the education of their children resumed. But many of the schools had been damaged. Teams from the ship went around and, together with the local communities, carried out repairs. After a school had been repaired UNICEF provided supplies of school materials such as text books and pencils so that the schools could be reopened.

As the time approached for *Cornwall* to leave, Anthony Dymock hosted a lunch on board for President Kabbah and some of his ministers. The President was effusive in his thanks to the ship and to Britain. Britain had stood by her old friend Sierra Leone in her hour of greatest need and was continuing to do so.

In addition to *Cornwall's* activities David Hill was out and about co-ordinating the ODA's effort with the NGOs. ODA, under the new Labour government, had been renamed the Department for International Development, so we all had to learn a new acronym DFID. David had previously worked for a British NGO in Somalia. This lanky, bearded Brit, walking around in his sandals, became very popular with the Sierra Leoneans. He worked tirelessly in helping the distraught Sierra Leoneans. His affable, uncomplaining manner made him a joy to work with.

But while we in Sierra Leone were busy with all these humane activities, the department in London was beginning to get caught up in the 'Sandline affair'. Lord Avebury had written to the office accusing Sandline of having broken the UN arms embargo. A debate in the House of Commons, instead of drawing praise for Britain's role in restoring democracy to Sierra Leone, focussed on illegal arms sales. The British press had hardly covered President

Kabbah's return; instead they were preoccupied with my meetings with 'mercenaries'.

This was all very puzzling to us in Freetown. As far as we were concerned, the UN sanctions were directed against the junta. In any event, the arms that Sandline had supplied had arrived at the end of February, too late to be used by Ecomog and Kabbah's forces. Indeed, President Kabbah was threatening to go back on his agreement with Blackstone because the arms and ammunition had arrived too late. When 30 tons of equipment did arrive towards the end of February Ecomog had merely locked it away in a warehouse at Lungi.

By mid April, HMS *Cornwall* had left and we had completed the most immediate relief and humanitarian assistance. Ann Grant sent me a fax suggesting that I return to the UK for a brief visit to assess the UK's next priorities and objectives. I had already issued invitations for 27 April for our reception to celebrate The Queen's Birthday, so it was agreed that I would fly back immediately afterwards. We celebrated Her Majesty's Birthday in traditional style with a large reception at the residence, to which practically everybody came, including the entire diplomatic corps, which at the time, I noted, could have fitted into a taxi. A moving speech was delivered by the new Foreign Minister, Dr Sama Banya, on behalf of the President, and we toasted the continued health and happiness of Her Majesty and President Kabbah. The next day I caught a flight to Conakry, and from there flew back to London.

Chapter Six

Arms to Africa Scandal

The day before I left Freetown I received a fax from Tim Andrews giving details of the meetings planned for me in the Foreign Office but also asking ominously that I should bring any Sandline papers back with me. Waiting for me at home on my return on the Saturday was a message asking me to contact immediately the head of the personnel department. He told me that I was not to go into the Foreign Office, nor was I to have any contact with anyone in the department. I was required to give an interview to HM Customs and Excise about Sandline and he pointed out that the interview would be given 'under caution'. I was not clear exactly what this meant, but it seemed to me that I needed legal advice. I was not permitted to consult the Foreign Office legal advisers but advised to use the firm of Kingsley Napley, who had been used by the office for the Scott Inquiry. I went to their offices in London and met with Stephen Pollard, who had recently defended Nick Leeson in the Barings Bank affair, and his assistant, Sophie Purkis.

The accusations against me were detailed in a letter from Spicer's and Sandline's lawyers, SJ Berwin, to Robin Cook, which referred to the military assistance given by Sandline to President Kabbah's government, and claimed, 'At the suggestion of your High Commissioner in Freetown, Mr Peter Penfold, President Kabbah asked our clients to provide such assistance.' The letter further claimed that 'Mr Penfold himself called at our clients' office premises on 28 January 1998, just three weeks before the equipment now in issue was delivered, and was given full details of the arrangements including the number of personnel involved and the nature of the military equipment that was to be provided. He was also given a copy of Sandline International's strategic and tactical plan, its Concept of Operations, for its involvement in the Sierra Leone arena.'

The letter identified meetings with others in the Foreign Office – John Everard, Craig Murray, Linda St Cook and Tim Andrews, and with Colonel Hicks and Colonel Gale. As a result of all these meetings, the letter concluded,

'Our clients were assured throughout that the operation had the full support of Her Majesty's Government.'

Reading through the Berwin letter in Stephen Pollard's office I told him that although some of the allegations made were patently untrue, I could not deny the fact that I had met Spicer and that details of Sandline's proposed assistance had been discussed; but what was all the fuss about? The UN sanctions were directed against the junta and therefore where was the illegality? I had brought with me the text of the UN sanctions resolution and some of the other accompanying documentation, but we did not have a copy of the UK Order in Council, under the terms of which Sandline was being prosecuted. Stephen Pollard immediately arranged to have a copy faxed to his office.

When I read the UK Order I noticed at once something strange about it. Whereas the UN sanctions resolution had merely referred to 'Sierra Leone', the UK Order had attempted to define what it meant by 'person connected with Sierra Leone'. This included 'the Government of Sierra Leone'. As the main plank of our policy had been to continue to regard President Kabbah's government as the Government of Sierra Leone and not to give any recognition to the AFRC junta, there could be no doubt that under the terms of the UK legislation, it was illegal to sell arms to President Kabbah's government. Interestingly, the UK Order made no specific mention of the AFRC junta, although it was caught up in a catch-all phrase of 'any other person in, or resident in, Sierra Leone'. I could now see why HM Customs and Excise had decided to act against Sandline, but how did this confusion arise? Surely those in the office would have pointed out to HM Customs that the aim of the sanctions was against the junta, and not against President Kabbah's government?

Stephen Pollard, Sophie Purkis and I went along to the headquarters of HM Customs and Excise at Lower Thames Street, close to the Tower of London. We were led downstairs to the basement of the building. I was warned of my rights, signed various bits of paper and then taken along to one of the interrogation cells. Two Customs and Excise officials sat across a narrow wooden table, while alongside me sat Stephen. A double cassette player was on the table and I was advised that the proceedings were being videoed.

I was again warned that I was being interviewed under caution. My attention was drawn to the Sierra Leone (United Nations Sanctions) Order 1997, in particular section 3, which stated that 'Except under the authority of a licence granted by the Secretary of State, no person shall do any act calculated to promote the supply or delivery of any goods specified under the Order.' I was warned that the penalty for doing so was seven years' imprisonment. Customs had already visited the Foreign Office and taken away various files. Stephen had had access to these papers and some of them had been very revealing. They had shown the amount of contact that had been going on between Spicer and the department, of which I was unaware. Reference was made to some of these documents, including my memo of 2 February detailing my contacts with Sandline. I went over the two meetings that I had had with Spicer. The Customs officers seemed surprised to learn that I had not had any meetings with Spicer in Conakry or Freetown. I explained to them my understanding of the UN sanctions resolution and how every document that I had received in Conakry and Freetown indicated that the sanctions were directed against the junta. I produced these documents, some of which had not been made available to them from the Foreign Office files. These included the Foreign Office's press briefing note on the UN sanctions, the CHOGM communiqué and a letter from Ann Grant to the Sierra Leone Foreign Minister. All of them clearly referred to 'sanctions against the junta'.

The interview went on for over two hours. The Customs officials were very professional and not unfriendly but, as I later told the Legg Inquiry and the Foreign Affairs Committee, I found the whole affair very distasteful. Here I was, a member of the Diplomatic Service, being interrogated by another branch of the same government, which I had served faithfully and professionally for thirty-five years, with the threat of seven years' imprisonment hanging over my head.

A couple of weeks later I was asked to attend another interview with Customs after they had interviewed others in the Foreign Office. I had no idea what my colleagues had said, but I was not pleased to learn subsequently that none of them had been questioned 'under caution'. The same two Customs officers were there but this time they were joined by a Customs legal Adviser. I went over in more detail the differences that I perceived between the UN sanctions resolution and the UK Order in Council. Since my previous interview I had received a telephone call from a close friend in the Service who was now serving overseas. He had previously been a legal adviser in the Foreign Office and we had gone around the Caribbean together as a team trying to persuade Caribbean governments to enact tougher anti-drugs legislation based on the UK model. The UK newspapers had taken some time reaching him and he was ringing to give me moral support. When I mentioned the inconsistencies between the UN sanctions and the UK Order, he pointed out that under the terms of the United Nations Act of 1946, the UK Act from which the powers are conferred on Parliament for implementing UN sanctions orders, it was not allowed for the UK legislation to either add or subtract from the original UN sanctions. In his view there was a possibility that the UK Order was *ultra vires*. I made these points to the Customs legal adviser, who listened attentively without commenting.

As well as copying their letter all around the ministries in Whitehall, SJ Berwin had released it to the press. The 'Arms to Africa' scandal dominated the front pages and editorials as more and more information came to light. It was revealed, for example, that HMS *Cornwall* had helped repair Sandline's helicopter while the ship was in Freetown. I became subject to intense press interest. My picture appeared under headlines such as 'Foreign Office accused of aiding mercenaries' while I was accused of colluding with 'dogs of war'. For a time the media were camped outside our home in Abingdon and we would have to sneak through the garage at the back just to get some shopping.

Robin Cook's 'ethical foreign policy' was questioned, and he became subject to intense scrutiny, especially by the tabloids, who called for his resignation. The *Daily Mirror* carried a full page photograph of him walking head down along Whitehall under the heading 'Sierra Alone'.

The opposition's knives were out in Parliament, where emergency questions were being tabled. Shadow foreign affairs spokesman Michael Howard attacked the government over 'this murky business'. Responding, Robin Cook said that he had not been informed about the matter. Whilst stoutly defending his fellow ministers, Tony Lloyd and Baroness Symons, he distanced himself from his officials. I found it baffling that at no time was I asked to go into the office and explain to Robin Cook what had happened. He and his ministers and senior officials were having to spend increasing amounts of their time answering the various accusations being bandied around, but without the benefit of being briefed by those officials most in the know of what had gone on, i.e. the members of the African Department and myself. Not surprisingly they kept shooting themselves in the foot.

Sir John Kerr, the relatively new Permanent Under-Secretary at the Foreign Office, was summoned before the House of Commons Foreign Affairs Committee to answer questions. He was given a hard time. Again hampered by inadequate briefing, he, 'having refreshed his memory', retracted some of the statements he had made earlier to the Committee, which appeared to contradict what Robin Cook had told the Committee.

The Foreign Office spin doctors kept making boobs. They leaked to the press that while I was stuck in Conakry I had been unable to send any reports to the Foreign Office from May 1997 until April 1998. But they had to immediately retract the story in the face of the evidence of my almost daily reports (faxed from the Hotel Camayenne), copies of which were now with Customs and Excise. Other attempts to tarnish my reputation were made. The press were fed a story that I had been withdrawn from the British Virgin Islands ahead of time and in disgrace. When it was pointed out that I had completed my full tour and had been awarded the CMG for my services in Tortola the story was dropped.

However, the more that I was attacked, the more people came forward to defend me. One most unexpected show of support came from, of all people, the Prime Minister. Whilst speaking to reporters Tony Blair went out of his way to praise me, saying that I had done 'a superb job'. He referred to the media coverage as 'a lot of hoo-ha' and pointed out that 'the good guys had won.'

President Kabbah sent a four-page letter to Tony Blair attacking my critics and supporting me. He wrote, 'Peter Penfold was a source of moral strength not only to me personally, but to all patriotic Sierra Leoneans – widely perceived by many as not only a hero, but a victim of the very forces that conspired but failed to destroy our country.'

I was touched by his support, not least because the President had taken the time to write it just when he had received the tragic news that his wife, Patricia, had died of cancer in a London hospital. I felt very sorry for him. Within a matter of weeks, he had lost his two closest supporters. General Abacha had recently died unexpectedly, and now his wife. I immediately sent him a fax from home offering my sincere condolences. I hoped that my government was not so preoccupied with the 'arms to Sierra Leone scandal' not to send an official condolence message.

On 16 May a rally was held in my support in Freetown. Twenty thousand people took to the streets in what one person described as the biggest demonstration ever to have taken place in recent times – schoolchildren, teachers, trade unionists, market women, church leaders. They chanted endlessly, 'Peter Penfold – Bring Him Back' and carried placards saying, 'We support Peter Penfold', 'Don't funny Peter Penfold', 'Penfold – Father of Democracy' and 'God bless Penfold Tenfold'. There were also placards supporting Tony Blair and the British Labour government, and some attacking Lord Avebury, who was seen as the arch villain. Although the government had given permission for it to take place, it was the ordinary (extraordinary) people who had arranged it, led by Zainab Bangura. The Minister of Education had specifically said that if children took part they should not do so in their school uniforms, but the kids ignored this instruction and turned out in their colourful uniforms waving the British and Sierra Leone flags. Similar, though smaller, demonstrations also took place in other towns in Sierra Leone.

A couple of days later HM Customs and Excise dropped its investigation. In a statement issued to the press it said, 'Even though offences may have been committed, the circumstances leading up to the supply affect the fairness to the extent that any prosecution could well fail and would certainly not be in the public interest.' In some respects I, and I suspect Tim Spicer, were disappointed that we had not gone to court in order to fully clear our names, but at least I hoped that it was now all behind us. Not so.

Legg Inquiry

In response, Robin Cook was quick to announce the setting up of a public inquiry. Sir Thomas Legg QC, aged sixty-two and former Permanent Secretary at the Lord Chancellor's Department, was appointed to head it, to be assisted by Sir Robin Ibbs, a former chairman of Lloyds TSB bank. They were asked to find out what government officials and ministers knew about breaches of the arms embargo and whether they gave such breaches any encouragement or approval. There were immediate accusations by Diane Abbott MP, among others, that Government was seeking to fix the outcome of the inquiry. In a speech during yet another Commons debate on Sierra Leone, she said, 'I know that one way to fix an inquiry is through the terms of reference. How strange that after all the debates on UN sanctions ... this well trumpeted inquiry should be set up with nothing in the terms of reference about whether UN sanctions had been breached.' I felt that she had a point.

As part of my preparation for appearing before the Legg Inquiry, Stephen obtained permission to view the documents that had been made available to Sir Thomas Legg. This led to Stephen, Sophie and me going into the Foreign Office one afternoon to look at the papers. It was a very strange experience to go into a building that for so many years had been my place of work accompanied by a couple of lawyers. We were escorted to a room close to the African Department and left with a pile of documents. Again I was fascinated to see papers on Sierra Leone that I had never seen before. As many of the papers were classified we could not take copies away, but it was useful to read them nonetheless.

With Stephen's and Sophie's help I finalized my written statement to the Legg Inquiry, which ran to sixteen pages and included twenty annexes. Although not strictly within their terms of reference, I went over in detail the history and developments of the sanctions orders starting from the Ecowas sanctions in June of 1997 leading to the UN sanctions resolution of 8 October. I listed the endless documents I had seen that referred to sanctions against only the junta, and I included a letter issued by the Assistant Secretary General for Legal Affairs of the United Nations that had concluded that the supply of arms to Ecomog was not in breach of the UN sanctions.

On 8 June I went off for my appearance before the Legg Inquiry. They had been provided with comfortable offices in Queen Anne's Gate overlooking St James' Park. Stephen and Sophie came with me. Sir Thomas Legg was welcoming and friendly. Sir Robin Ibbs was more taciturn but I suspected that he had a sharper mind. They explained that they were not out to get anybody, they just wanted to establish the facts. They thanked me for my statement, which, they said, had helped put things into perspective. Both Sir Thomas and Sir Robin appeared to have some difficulties understanding the workings of the Foreign Office and its posts overseas. I went over in detail my meetings with President Kabbah and Tim Spicer. I explained that I had not encouraged either of them in their dealings; nor had I discouraged them, and therefore, by not positively discouraging them, I accepted that both of them could have felt that their contract had a measure of support. But all of us were firmly of the view that the supply of arms would not be in breach of the UN sanctions. When Sir Thomas asked me who else in the Foreign Office was of a similar mind, he seemed surprised to hear me say that as far as I was concerned, they all were. I cited various documentary evidence to support this. Three days previously the UN Security Council had passed a further resolution making it absolutely clear that the arms embargo did not apply to the Kabbah government or Ecomog. I was unaware of this at the time of my interview, and the Legg Inquiry didn't mention it in any of its findings.

My session with the inquiry lasted about three hours. They could not say for certain whether I would be required to appear again, but they had no objection to me returning to Sierra Leone to resume my duties as High Commissioner. I made a booking on the Sabena flight to Conakry for the coming Saturday, 13 June.

Paramount Chief

Conakry Airport was as chaotic as ever with the Guinean health official demanding to see everyone's certificates against smallpox, yellow fever, cholera – as if Guinea was the healthiest country in the world! To reach the exit you had to run the gauntlet of dozens of customs officials, each one wanting to inspect every piece of baggage. WAWA. Alphonse was on hand to meet me and we drove the familiar route through the bustling streets of Conakry in the half-light of early evening to the Hotel Camayenne. Room 503 was not available, but I was given room 403, the room immediately below it, so everything seemed identical. I took a shower, phoned Celia and then watched the movie on the French channel before going to sleep.

Alphonse came back to pick me up the next morning. He asked to borrow some money – another piece of his taxi had fallen off. We drove out to the airport where I was joined by Desmond Luke, who was now the Chief Justice, and Charles Margai, the Minister of Internal Affairs. They said that they had been delegated to accompany me back to Freetown. Instead of flying as normal to the international airport at Lungi, our charter plane flew directly to Hastings. As it landed and taxied round in front of the wooden huts that represented the terminal, I looked out through the window and could see a crowd gathered. I stepped off the plane and was immediately surrounded by cheering Sierra Leoneans. The drums were playing and there was lively singing from a group of women in their white and green dresses. I was escorted to the terminal building. A number of familiar faces were around – Colin, Solomon, Emmanuel and Zainab. I was introduced to King Naimbana II, the Temne tribal chief for the Western Area. He sat me in a chair and announced to everyone that I was to be made a paramount chief. He produced a traditional costume made out of bark cloth and proceeded to put it over my head. He placed a hat made of the same material on my head. A pair of trousers were also produced but we agreed that it would not be dignified for me to drop my pants in front of the assembled crowd so I handed them to Mal, head of the close protection team. The television cameras were on hand. The King made a little speech and handed me my staff of office – a wooden stave with a brass knob. I was now Pa Komrabai Penfold of the Western Area. I was led back outside and the singing and dancing went wild. I went up to the drummers and the singing women and started to dance with them. This brought more loud cheers. I was then led to my Land Rover and climbed inside.

A line of cars both preceded and followed us into Freetown. Apparently the ceremonies were still not over. With horns blaring and people shouting and waving we entered the city limits. Bunches of schoolchildren lined the route and waved as we went past. As we came up to the PZ roundabout the crowds got thicker. The vehicles stopped and I got out of the car. I was led over to a hammock made of rope with a wooden awning perched over the top of it, painted in red, white and blue on the outside, and blue, white and green, the colours of the Sierra Leone national flag, on the inside. On the front of the awning was painted in bold white lettering, 'Sierra Leone welcomes back HE Peter Penfold.' The whole structure, which must have been considerably heavy, was supported on the heads of four strong Sierra Leoneans.

I was lifted bodily into the hammock and we started to process along the street surrounded by hundreds of smiling and cheering Sierra Leoneans. Most of them were waving home-made Union Jacks and Sierra Leone flags. Being carried in a hammock is the traditional mode of travel for a paramount chief, but it was not easy. I had never been briefed on how one travels by hammock. Did I stretch my legs out or let them hang either side? I tried to sit up as we proceeded uphill so that I could look at what was going on. One woman followed alongside me, fanning me with something that looked like a large table mat made out of straw. Every now and then her hand slipped and I would receive a nasty whack on the back of my neck. Immediately behind came Paul, one of the close protection team. Quite what he would be able to do to protect me in such a crowd, I had no idea, nor, did I guess, did he. The route was lined with Sierra Leoneans of all ages cheering and waving. I waved back. We went along Siaka Stevens Street. What the late President, who had declared Sierra Leone a republic in 1971, would have made of all this, I did not know. Here was I, a white man, a representative of the former colonial power, being carried in a hammock through the streets of the capital of this African country nearly forty years after independence.

The procession continued until we reached the Cotton Tree, the centre of Freetown, where in the olden days the freed slaves would gather. I was lifted out of the hammock and carried to the steps of the Law Courts building. The crowd was now a couple of thousand strong. Before mounting the steps I went back to the hammock to shake the hands of the four porters who were sweating profusely. I then went up the steps of the building and was seated in front of the cheering crowd. Behind me sat a number of VIPs on white plastic chairs.

King Naimbana came to the microphone and announced that I had been made a paramount chief and that henceforth I was to be known as Chief Komrabai Penfold. Zainab Bangura made a rousing speech thanking Britain for coming to Sierra Leone's help in its hour of need. 'We thought that Britain had turned its back on us, but this battered nation found a friend in Komrabai Penfold, for which we will be ever grateful.' Moslem and Christian prayers were said and then another of the women's representatives led the crowd in singing a hymn of praise.

I was invited to speak. I started by saying, '*Am gladdie tbe bak een me oon hoos*,' the Krio for 'I'm pleased to be back home.' The crowd went wild. I said I was honoured to become a paramount chief, which I accepted on behalf of Her Majesty The Queen, the British Government and the British people. I noted the commitment of the Sierra Leone people to democracy and the sacrifices they had made to keep it. I promised them the continued support of the British Government and people. There were more loud cheers and singing. After another speech from the trade union congress leader, it was time to get back into the vehicles. Again I was surrounded by seething masses all wanting to shake my hand. We made it to the Land Rover and Emmanuel slowly drove away past the American Embassy and the Nigerian High Commission. We turned up the hill towards Runnymede. A number of those who had been involved in the earlier proceedings had come to the residence. We sat and drank and talked. It was good to be back among so many friends.

The next day in the office I had to send a telegram reporting on my return. There were already too many people back in the UK who believed that I had gone native, so I tried to keep the report light-hearted. I sought instructions on what was the official mileage rate for travel by hammock and asked how many porters I was entitled to, pointing out that when Colin had to deputize for me, with his bulk he would require an additional allowance of porters. I also suggested that close protection teams would require training drills before they came out on how to escort a hammock-travelling High Commissioner.

Although I had played down my appointment as a paramount chief to London, in Sierra Leone it was taken very seriously. The system of paramount chiefs went back several centuries. By the fifteenth century Sierra Leone was divided into numerous small kingdoms that were governed by extraordinary warriors, hunters or traders. Titled 'owners of the land', they exercised complete authority within their domains. In 1896 the British declared the interior of Sierra Leone a protectorate, while Freetown and the peninsular were declared a colony. They designated the rulers in the protectorate 'paramount chiefs' and presented each with an official symbol of office – a cane staff topped with a brass knob bearing the British coat of arms. Although the paramount chief was still the highest ranking personage of his domain, he had to share the powers of leadership with a British district commissioner who oversaw several chiefdoms. A paramount chief primarily kept law and order and collected taxes. He also recruited labour for projects such as building roads. The district commissioner retained responsibility for settling land disputes and judging criminal cases. This was the system of 'indirect rule' by which Britain exercised her colonial authority in Sierra Leone and in many other parts of the Empire.

In 1898 the colonial administration imposed a new tax, the 'hut tax'. In many ways it was a forerunner of the poll tax in Britain in the 1980s, and as in Britain, the people revolted. A Temne warrior chief, Bai Bureh, led the revolt. The British authorities eventually regained control and to break the power of the chiefs, they divided the kingdoms into smaller units. These were still called chiefdoms and were still headed by paramount chiefs. Some of the newly appointed rulers were paramount chiefs who had not taken part in the revolt. As long as the new paramount chiefs did not oppose the district commissioners, they governed for life. From the 1930s, with the introduction of local government administrations, the chief's powers were shared with government officials and a group of councillors chosen by the elders, but they continued to exercise much control and influence.

There were 149 paramount chiefs spread throughout Sierra Leone. Many of them could trace their lineage back to the original chiefs and rulers. Twelve chiefs, one from each national district, sat in the Parliament, like a mini House of Lords within the House of Commons. The chiefs were the real power and influence in the country. They were the persons to whom the people turned for any advice or guidance. They ruled their people but they were also answerable to them. If the people were not satisfied with the performance of their chief, he, or she (there were some lady paramount chiefs, but only in the south), would be removed. So although they represented an ancient traditional system of authority, they were also part of a modern democratic system of government. Because of the chiefs' immense influence the rebels had killed several of them or had driven them from their homes. For example, in Kailahun District alone, eight out of the fourteen chiefs had been murdered by the RUF. Several chiefs were now living temporarily in Freetown or the other major towns.

Since independence The Queen and Prince Philip had been the only non-Sierra Leoneans to be appointed paramount chiefs. As a paramount chief I was entitled to direct access to the President at all times. President Kabbah took to calling me 'Chief' instead of 'Your Excellency'. The accepted form of greeting from one paramount chief to another was 'My Good Friend'. (A few years later when Tony Blair was made a paramount chief of a small village in the north, I congratulated him in a letter addressed to 'My Good Friend'.)

Being made a paramount chief increased my stature in the country but also added to my workload. The number of people wanting to see me trebled and I received half a dozen letters a day seeking favours and requests such as for a job, or money, food or clothing, or asking me to intercede in a dispute. I was asked to become 'Grand Chief Patron' of all types of organizations or 'Special Chief Guest' at the opening of ceremonies or church services. As I did not have a designated chiefdom it was felt that all and sundry could approach me. Also, because I had been given the title 'Komrabai', which meant 'elder of the chiefs', many of the chiefs themselves would approach me for assistance.

One aspect of the appointment sounded interesting. I was told that a paramount chief was entitled to ten wives. I passed this information on to Celia. As my number one wife it was her duty to help select the other nine for me. I'm still waiting!

Colin went off on leave to be with Ruth and the children for the summer holidays, which left me alone in the office. It was like being in Conakry again. I had to open up the office, supervise the cleaners, then go off to see the President, come back and type up and send off my own telegrams – so much for being a paramount chief!

A message came through that the Legg Inquiry wanted to see me again. I pointed out that if I returned we would have to close down the mission because there were no other UK based officers left to assume charge. This did not appear to worry the department. Sandline and Legg had priority over all other matters. I spoke to Richard Dales and he undertook to find someone to come out and cover so that at least the mission could stay open. One of the young second secretaries in the High Commission in Accra was bundled on a plane and sent down to Freetown to look after the shop. I flew back to London.

Allowing for the cost of bringing an officer up from Accra to keep the mission in Freetown open, as well as the costs for my travel, my further two-hour interview with the Legg Inquiry must have cost the British tax payer in the region of £5,000. Sir Thomas was under intense pressure from Robin Cook to complete the inquiry in time for the minister to present its findings to the House before the summer recess. I had been the first to appear before the inquiry and now they needed to check some things with me in the light of the evidence presented by others. I had not seen what the other interviewees had said. Because of the injunction imposed by the office that I should not visit the Foreign Office, nor discuss the Sandline affair with anyone, it was not until the Legg Report was finally published that I was to discover fully what had been going on and what had been said by others. The same injunction about not discussing the Sandline affair applied equally to my colleagues in the Foreign Office, although, as they continued working alongside one another in the office, it was difficult to imagine that they managed to adhere to this restriction.

Altogether, the Legg Inquiry interviewed seven ministers and forty-nine officials. It also received evidence from certain witnesses outside the public service, including Tim Spicer, Rupert Bowen and Lord Avebury. Several of those interviewed, including the two ministers in the Ministry of Defence, George Robertson and John Reid, Clare Short, the DFID minister, and Captain

Dymock, admitted that they were unaware that the arms embargo applied to the Kabbah government. I had given the inquiry a copy of the letter issued by the Assistant Secretary General for Legal Affairs in the UN saying that the supply of military equipment to the Kabbah government was not in breach of the UN sanctions but it chose not to mention this in its report.

The report ran to 167 pages. Its main findings were:

No minister gave encouragement or approval to Sandline's plan to send a shipment of arms into Sierra Leone, and none had effective knowledge of it. Some officials became aware, or had notice, of the plan. The High Commissioner gave it a degree of approval, which he had no authority to do, but he did not know that such a shipment would be illegal. No other official gave any encouragement or approval. All concerned were working to fulfil Government policy, and there was no attempt to hide information from ministers. However, officials in London should have acted sooner and more decisively than they did on the mounting evidence of an impending breach of the arms embargo, and they should have told ministers earlier and more effectively. As a result, ministers were given no, or only inadequate, notice of the matter until the Berwin letter arrived. The failures at official level were caused mainly by management and cultural factors, but partly by human error, largely due to overload.

The Legg Inquiry was very thorough in what it did. Its shortcomings were related more to the questions that it failed to address, such as whether UN sanctions had been breached or the UK Order in Council was legal, but Sir Thomas had done the job he was expected to do – he had absolved ministers of any responsibility. All the blame was laid at the hands of officials, me in particular. It noted:

The High Commissioner, Mr Penfold, was told of Sandline's plans, in mid-December 1997 by President Kabbah, and later that month by Mr Spicer, and gave them a degree of approval. However, the full effect of the arms embargo had not been properly explained, and Mr Penfold and others were not aware that the unlicensed supply of arms to the elected government of Sierra Leone was illegal. Mr Penfold should have done more to inform himself about the arms embargo, and should have reported his contacts with President Kabbah and Mr Spicer back to the Foreign and Commonwealth Office more promptly and effectively.

The shortcomings of my colleagues in the office were highlighted, but were criticized less harshly:

At the beginning of February 1998, the head and several officials in the Africa command received definite written notice from Mr Penfold that Sandline's plans included the supply of arms. They did not immediately appreciate the full significance of the information, and they did not act upon it. As a result, when they subsequently referred the matter to Customs, they did so only on the basis of newspaper allegations drawn to their attention by Lord Avebury. They did not give Customs the more definite evidence by then available to them from Mr Penfold. Because FCO officials at working and middle-management levels did not appreciate the importance and sensitivity of the matter, they did not bring it promptly or prominently to the attention of ministers. And when top management received some, though inadequate, notice in early April, they sought more information before warning ministers.

At the end of its findings the Legg Report made the following observation:

> We wish to put our criticisms of officials into context. There were individual failures and misjudgements. But most of the trouble originated from systematic and cultural factors. We consider that the officials involved are loyal and conscientious. They were very busy during the period we have investigated and they worked to good effect in other respects. They have already endured an anxious period of criticism and uncertainty. We hope that this report will help the FCO to close the chapter as far as they are concerned. If any disciplinary proceedings are judged necessary, we hope they will take place soon.

Robin Cook tabled the report in the House of Commons on 27 July. In his address to the House he praised my 'great courage and commitment' during the coup, which 'has won high standing for Britain in the country where he represents us,' but he went on to criticize me for not 'having taken steps to inform himself more fully about the scope of the arms embargo' and for showing 'a lack of caution in his dealings with Colonel Spicer and to this extent gave Sandline a degree of approval for which he had no authority.'

He accepted all the findings of the Legg Report and said that 'there will be no scapegoats, and this should be the end of the matter as far as individual officials are concerned.' He went on to outline a number of measures to be introduced into the workings of the Foreign Office to tighten up the implementation and monitoring of sanctions, and he confirmed that guidelines would be issued regarding official contacts with private military firms. A circular was issued later to all members of the Service at the end of July saying that any contacts with private security firms should be cleared in advance; hitherto there had been no such restrictions or guidelines – a clear case of shutting the stable door after the horse had bolted.

On Robin Cook's instructions Sir John Kerr sent me a letter drawing attention to the criticisms of me in the Legg Report. I was formally reprimanded for my dealings with Sandline and giving a degree of approval to the Sandline contract, for failing to inform myself about the scope of the arms embargo, and for failing to report effectively on my meeting with President Kabbah on 19 December. I was reminded that for the duration of my tour in Freetown I was expected to have only an 'official' relationship with President Kabbah. Sir John concluded his warning letter that 'none of those involved in this will have a block on their careers as a result. The Personnel Command will ensure that the relevant Selection Board bears this in mind.'

Whether the Selection Board did bear this in mind is highly questionable. I was to apply for sixteen posts after my tour in Sierra Leone was completed and was turned down for all of them. Instead I was 'encouraged' to take early retirement.

Although I was far from happy with the result of the Legg Inquiry, I really did hope that it was all now behind us. The events surrounding Sandline and the Legg Inquiry had dominated UK/Sierra Leone relations at a time when there was so much that needed to be done in the country, in order to ensure that the gains achieved with the restoration of the legitimate democratic government were not to be lost. I hoped that we could now focus on these.

Chapter Seven

Treason Trials and Executions

Sierra Leone was struggling to get back to normality despite the fact that hostilities were continuing in the east of the country. But normality would not return unaided. It had to be given a push. By reopening the mission we had encouraged the opening of the British banks, Barclays and Standard Chartered. We had also encouraged the reopening of the British Council and other diplomatic missions. HMS *Cornwall* had paid a return visit in July. Her captain, Anthony Dymock, and chaplain, Garth Petzer, had now left the ship but, under the able command of Captain James Rapp she was warmly received by the people of Sierra Leone, who remembered with deep affection the sterling assistance she had rendered earlier in the year.

The next step was to bring Celia out. I was tired of living a bachelor existence. I had deliberately not taken down our Christmas decorations at the residence to await Celia's return. Various visitors were bemused to see a Christmas tree with all its decorations on display in the entrance hall in June. I had agreed with Celia that we would have our delayed Christmas celebrations when she had made it back to Freetown. If Celia came out, more wives would be encouraged to return to join their husbands and thus a little more 'normality' would be re-established. Colin also arranged for Ruth and the children to come out for the summer holidays, so at the end of July they all flew out together.

Celia's arrival marked the opportunity for our official crowning as Komrabai and Yabomposse Penfold. The coronation was to take place on a Saturday in the Freetown City Hall, but first we had to go to King Naimbana's home, a very modest house in the centre of Freetown. There Celia and I were dressed in long flowing robes made of colourful local cloth, predominantly blue. Leather sandals had also been specially made for us. The King's drum was beaten signifying that he was leaving his house and we all proceeded in our cars to the City Hall, where a large crowd had gathered.

As usual there were endless speeches. In his remarks King Naimbana noted that it had been his great-grandfather who had signed over the very land on which we were standing to a representative of Queen Victoria. At that time the family name was 'Bana', but when the British came they asked the King his name and he replied: 'Me name Bana.' The British misunderstood and henceforth the family were called 'Naimbana'. Who would have thought that some 150 years later his great-grandson would have been crowning a representative of Queen Victoria's great-grand-daughter as a paramount chief?

The speeches were interspersed with much dancing in which Celia and I joined, Celia demonstrating a natural rhythm that was loudly appreciated by the assembled crowd. We were then formally introduced to the King by Alfred Akibo-Betts, a former Mayor of Freetown, and we were crowned. On my head was placed a white hat with a long white tail running down the back. Celia's hat resembled more a straw sun hat with a white band around it. We were presented with certificates that read:

> To Chief Komrabai Penfold. In recognition of his remarkable international patriotic role in restoring constitutionality and democracy to our war-torn nation.

And:

> To Yabomposse Peter Penfold. In recognition of her unparalleled steadfast role behind the international successes of her husband.

All the chiefs and sub-chiefs joined us as we sang and danced in a circle. It was a very joyous occasion, all captured by the television cameras. Apparently it was the first time that the crowning of a paramount chief had ever been televised.

As Komrabai Penfold I was a paramount chief of the Western Area, but it had not stopped there. A couple of weeks previously I had paid another visit to Bo and there, not to be outdone by the chiefs of the Western Area, the Mende chiefs appointed me a paramount chief of the Southern Area. This time I was given the name 'Ndiamu', which in Mende means 'friend'. As a Mende Regent (sub) Chief, Sam Hinga Norman was at the ceremony and he delivered a very moving address to the hundreds assembled in the town hall. He noted that in Sierra Leone's history, two great British people had been sent to the country: in the previous century, 'Governor Clarkson who gave us a prayer' (Governor Clarkson's prayer for Sierra Leone was still read over the radio every morning); and in this century, 'we have been sent High Commissioner Penfold – who gave us hope.'

Soon after our coronation Celia and I paid a visit to Makeni. It was an early opportunity for the new close protection team, led by Dave Thomas, to get out of Freetown. On the drive north, as we passed through the villages and towns *en route*, we saw some evidence of the people picking themselves up and getting back to their 'normal' lives. There were people in the fields planting their crops and in the villages rebuilding their homes. There was still little traffic on the roads and the area around the Occra Hills looked fairly deserted. We were greeted on the outskirts of Makeni by a huge crowd, who had been waiting for us for several hours. They thronged around our vehicles as we got out to be greeted by Dr Koroma, the minister resident for the north, and Paramount Chief Bai Sebora Kasanga II. Dave and his team were somewhat wary of the milling crowds but, as usual, they handled it coolly and professionally.

One of the main purposes of the visit was to launch the northern branch of the Movement for the Restoration of Democracy (MRD), the body that we had helped in Conakry. A large crowd of several hundred was assembled inside and outside the town hall for the occasion. After the endless introductory remarks by various dignitaries I was invited to deliver a speech. I likened the development of democracy to making a soup – democracy soup. I outlined the ingredients that were required to make democracy soup – a democratic government elected in free and fair elections, a truly representative parliament looking after the interests of the people and including an active opposition, an independent judiciary, a well motivated and trained police force, a non-political and professional army, an honest and hard-working public service, an independent and responsible media, and an active civil society. Like cooking any soup over an open fire, sometimes things fell into the pot – such as coups or corruption – which (to great cheers from the audience), had to be lifted out and thrown away. Good democracies were like good soups, they did not have to be all the same – each would be flavoured in its own special way with the right herbs and spices, they did not all have to follow exactly the Westminster recipe. Sierra Leone's soup would take account of her culture and traditions, like the Chieftaincy system. I was confident that, given the resources and determination of the people, Sierra Leone could make a good democracy soup.

After the ceremony a large group of us retired for lunch to one of the few houses in Makeni that had not suffered too much damage. We waited until the chairs on which we had been sitting at the town hall were brought to the house and then we dined not on soup but on a meagre but appetising meal of scrawny chicken and rice. Dr Koroma, a leader of one of the northern political parties that had contested the previous election, gave an impromptu and impassioned speech. He proposed a toast to Her Majesty The Queen and then asked us all to rise to sing the national anthem. To my surprise all those present sang not the Sierra Leone anthem but *God Save The Queen*. Even more remarkably, the assembled gathering continued lustily with the second verse. I reflected whether even in Britain so many people would have known the words. Here was yet another manifestation of the love and respect that is held for The Queen throughout the world but especially in the Commonwealth. I was so proud to be her representative. The respect for The Queen in Sierra Leone was matched with the respect Sierra Leoneans felt for the late Queen Mother. The home for the elderly in Freetown was named after King George VI and the Queen Mother would send a cheque every year to help support it. On her ninety-ninth birthday I made a point of visiting the home and spending some time with the inmates, not one of whom was as old or as active as she was at the time.

We stayed with Bishop Biguzzi in Makeni. He had managed to replace some of the furniture that had been looted. Over supper that night, made from food that we had brought from Freetown, the Bishop reflected on what life had been like in Makeni when he had first arrived there in 1974. At that time there was constant electricity and water, a daily postal and newspaper service and the roads were tarmaced. In the supermarkets he could buy anything. Indeed, there was nothing that he missed from his days in Italy that he could not buy locally – even Italian ice-cream. All this had now gone. Listening to this devout and dedicated cleric, one realized just how far this beautiful country had fallen.

Zainab Bangura had told me how when growing up, a mobile library would visit her small village once a week and another elderly friend described a large department store in Freetown in the 1960s where one could even buy a grand piano. Now there was not even a bookshop in the whole of the country and people could barely find enough rice to eat.

Most of the population of Sierra Leone were too young to be aware of how developed their country had been. Their aspirations were much more fundamental – they just wanted peace and democracy.

Bishop Biguzzi took us to visit a centre for the poor being run by the 'Sisters of Charity', Mother Theresa's order of nuns. One could not help but admire these selfless Christian women who had given up everything to care for the sick and needy, following in the spirit of their remarkable leader. The five nuns from India and Kenya fed hundreds of the poor people of Makeni every day. They lived at the centre very simply. As we walked around talking to the people gathered there, the senior nun told me that Mother Theresa preferred the Sisters to live in single-storey buildings to ensure that the Sisters stayed on the same level as those who they were helping.

Before we left Makeni we also visited the HANCI orphanage on the outskirts of town. This was the home supported by the British charity, Hope and Homes, set up by Colonel Mark Cook. This too had suffered, but the children were now back with the dedicated Sierra Leone staff. Among the children was Tenneh Cole, the little deaf girl who had been shot through the jaw and had been sent to a hospital in Southampton in England for surgery and treatment. The story had attracted a great deal of publicity in the British press at the time prior to our arrival in Sierra Leone.

The case of Tenneh Cole raised the question of who should one help in the midst of widespread deprivation, how much should one do for one individual when there were so many who needed help? Some people felt that instead of spending so much money on flying one child to Britain, one could use the same money to bring help to many more locally. There was even the risk that the person helped might be treated with envy back home and ostracized. Even the HANCI orphanage itself was regarded by some of the people of Makeni in this light. They felt that too much was being done for the children there and not enough for the countless others in the town. It was sad, but understandable, to meet such reactions. However, in my view it was better to help a few than nobody and often by helping one person one might attract publicity and thereby encourage more help for others. I was to bump into Tenneh unexpectedly the following year. After the orphanage in Makeni was overrun again by rebels she was brought to the Deaf and Dumb School, alongside the Blind School, in Freetown.

Generally there was little need for orphanages and old folks homes in Africa because of the 'extended family' practice. An African considered it was his duty, no matter how poor he or she may be, to offer a home to any member of his or her family, no matter how distant the relationship. It was one of several African practices from which we in the West could learn. However, poor Sierra Leone had suffered so much killing and deprivation that even the extended family practice could not cope with the problems of the orphans and aged.

During the visit to Makeni I had met with the northern chiefs and presented a wind-up radio to each one of them. Not to be outdone by their western and southern colleagues they said that they wanted to make me an honorary paramount chief for the Northern Region. They would make arrangements for my next visit. I continued to stress that I saw these honours as an expression of the gratitude that the Sierra Leone people felt not towards me personally but towards the government and people of Britain whom I represented. Tony Lloyd was to announce to the House of Commons that there was probably nowhere on the planet more pro-British than Sierra Leone.

I am sure that he was right although my colleagues back in the Foreign Office appeared to be somewhat embarrassed by all this warmth and friendship. They continued to view the Kabbah government with suspicion and appeared to be always looking for something to criticize them about. This attitude was seen no more clearly than when a clip of film appeared on French television that showed soldiers in Sierra Leone army uniforms executing some civilians in the bush. The department in the Foreign Office immediately jumped to the conclusion that this was evidence that President Kabbah's government was also responsible for human rights violations. James Jonah, the Minister of Finance, was visiting Britain at the time and Tony Lloyd was briefed to confront him with these accusations and warn him that all British assistance to Sierra Leone would cease. I tried to point out to my colleagues that almost certainly the film must be covering some of the executions carried out by the army on the innocent civilians during the period of the junta rule. Indeed, the film sounded very similar to the footage that had been put together by Julius Spencer, the Minister of Information, to demonstrate to the international community just how evil the AFRC had been. The department was sceptical of my interpretation. James Jonah was summoned into the Office and shown the clip of film. Dr Jonah immediately recognized the clip from Julius Spencer's film, and told his interrogators so. There were a few red faces.

But there were to be further developments that would put a strain on the close relationship between Britain and Sierra Leone. For the previous few months members of the junta and their supporters had been appearing in court to face treason charges. When President Kabbah had returned a number of people around him had advised that he should carry out immediate executions of those members of the junta and their cronies who had been captured. Kabbah insisted that they should follow the rule of law and that they should face trial.

Treason Trials and Executions

Around 100 people were charged with treason in both civilian and military courts. Prosecuting so many people for treason would have been demanding for any country, let alone Sierra Leone given the state of the country, but nonetheless they went ahead under the supervision of the hardworking Attorney General, Solomon Berewa. Human Rights activists, including representatives from the International Bar Association, flew in to observe the trials, which were open to the public and televised. Every night one could tune into Sierra Leone television to watch the proceedings, which had an air of unreality about them. The setting was a British court with the lawyers dressed in gowns and wigs, but the scene was African.

The civilians were tried in three separate courts. Under the Sierra Leone Treason and State Offences Act merely accepting a position from or acting in support of the illegal junta constituted a treasonable offence, and the conviction for treason was death. Hence most of the civilians were found guilty and sentenced to death. This led to articles appearing in the British press saying in effect that Kabbah's government was no better than the junta. These were the supposed 'good guys', but they were carrying out mass executions. There were demands that British ministers should intercede with President Kabbah. I pointed out that the international observers had all noted that the trials had been free and fair and that there would still be a long drawn-out appeals process before the decision whether to go ahead with the executions could be brought to the Prerogative of Mercy Committee and the President.

Nevertheless, Tony Lloyd felt impelled to telephone President Kabbah to plea for clemency and followed this up with a letter. The Sierra Leone people reacted badly to what they saw as interference in their judicial process. They did not understand why the British Government should be so concerned for these people who had subjected them to such acts of brutality and misery, especially as the rebels were still continuing their atrocities in the bush. Demonstrations against Britain were planned but in the end they did not take place because, I was told, of the continued high esteem the people held for me. I explained to President Kabbah that it was not that we had any special feelings for these terrible people but that it was the policy of the new government in Britain to oppose the use of capital punishment anywhere in the world and to encourage all governments to abolish it. In response he pointed out that it was only in recent times that capital punishment had been abolished in Britain and in relative terms Sierra Leone developmentally was still a hundred years behind Britain. We could not expect a country like Sierra Leone to be as advanced socially and morally. What Kabbah failed to mention was that although capital punishment for murder had been abolished in Britain back in 1969, the death sentence for treason had only just been abolished in the UK through the passage of the Criminal Justice Bill on 31 July of that year.

The position with the convicted soldiers was different. The thirty-four soldiers who had been found guilty by the military courts martial did not have recourse to an appeal process. This had been removed from the statute books by President Stevens back in 1971. Therefore, on 19 October, within a week of their conviction, twenty-four of them were executed by firing squad.

They included several of those who had first appeared at the residence the day following the 25 May coup – Corporal Gborie, the first to announce the coup that Sunday morning over the radio, Sergeant Zagallo, who had been responsible for the worst of the looting, Squadron Leader Victor King, the helicopter gunship pilot, Captain Johnny Moore, who had been assisting Lincoln Jopp with our military training programme, and the AFRC's 'chaplain', the Reverend Josiah Pratt. Among the others executed were Brigadier Hassan Conteh, the Chief of Defence Staff, Colonel Max Kanga, the Chief of Army Staff, and Colonel A.K. Sesay, one of the senior officers who had taken over the negotiations at the residence and was to become the AFRC's Secretary General. Somewhat controversially there was one female officer executed, Major Kula Samba, who had been attached to the Triple R Commission.

The executions took place at the 7th Battalion's headquarters at Goderich, on the outskirts of Freetown. Although there had been no announcement, word soon spread around and a crowd of up to 5,000 people gathered to witness the executions, including the media, who carried graphic reports of the event. The condemned soldiers were brought down from the back of an army truck and led across to a line of stakes fixed in the ground. Each convicted soldier, as he was blindfolded and tied to a stake, had something to say. Gborie sang in Krio, '*Tell Papa God Tenki*' (Tell God Thank You). Sesay called out, 'Goodbye all of you. We are going to shed our blood for peace.' Kanga, recognizing someone in the crowd, asked him to tell his family to take care of his building materials. One of them said, laughing, 'I am going to die as a hero,' while another cried out, 'Please tell my people goodbye. Let them don't seek revenge, my soul will rest in peace.' As the Reverend Pratt was tied to his stake he sang, 'Unto Jesus I surrender.' Several others abused the Ecomog soldiers who were present – 'You live by coups in Nigeria. Did you kill any of them? Why kill us now?' Only Kula Samba remained silent throughout the entire events.

The warrants of execution were read out by the police officers overseeing the execution. Christian and Moslem prayers were said by a priest and an Imam, and then the firing squad of Sierra Leone soldiers, their faces blackened with charcoal, lined up in front of those tied to the stakes. At 4.22 pm the order rang out: 'Fire.' Ten minutes later the firing stopped as the bodies hung limply on the stakes. Some twitches of movement came from the bodies of Gborie and Conteh. Further shots were fired and all the bodies were still. The large crowd clapped and cheered as twenty-four coffins were brought forward and laid in front of the dead bodies. The female radio announcer covering the proceedings announced, 'A job well done.'

The President exercised clemency for the remaining ten so that we were able to claim that our demands for clemency had been acted upon to a certain extent. He told me that Britain had been the only country in the world to make representations about the executions. He clearly had suffered much personal anguish over the decisions but there was little doubt that if the executions had not been carried out there would have been riots on the streets and a real chance that President Kabbah might have been overthrown.

Aware of the deeply held views of the people and the risks of further instability, I had felt uncomfortable lobbying President Kabbah over the executions, even though I had done so. But I did wonder whether this was a policy pursued as energetically by HMG everywhere. About a week later I heard over the BBC *Focus on Africa* that someone had been convicted of murder and sentenced to death in the neighbouring West African state of Benin. I brought this to the attention of the department in London and said that I assumed that we would be making representations to the Benin government in line with our policy to condemn and seek clemency for anyone convicted for capital punishment anywhere in the world. The department were not aware of the case but a telegram was sent to our High Commission in Nigeria, who covered Benin, instructing them to raise the matter with the Benin government. The latter must have wondered what on earth was going on. There was very little substance to the UK's relations with this former French colony. Months could go by without any communication between the two governments. And then suddenly out of the blue they received a message from the British Foreign Office complaining about some obscure Benin criminal who had been convicted for murder! The High Commission carried out their instructions. They reported back that the person was unlikely to die as no capital punishment had been carried out in Benin for several years. I felt that the point had been made; an 'ethical foreign policy' should be applied even-handedly; though I did wonder whether Robin Cook telephoned the US Secretary of State each time someone in the United States was convicted of murder and executed.

Four days after the execution of the soldiers, Foday Sankoh's trial reached its conclusion. Sankoh had been returned to Freetown by the Nigerians in July and kept in detention in an undisclosed and closely guarded location away from the others in Pademba Road prison. His trial had got underway in early October and again the proceedings were televised. Sankoh displayed no remorse for the evil he had inflicted. He would taunt the police officers assigned to guard him in the court house: 'Have you been paid by the government? Have you been fed today?' On 23 October a jury found him guilty on seven out of nine counts of treason. High Court judge Samuel Ademosu sentenced him to death. Sankoh's lawyer lodged an appeal and Sankoh remained in jail pending his appeal.

Some have argued subsequently that if the appeal process had been completed and Sankoh had been executed, Sierra Leone may not have had to face the future disruptions and loss of lives; but this did not take account of the further 'interference' from the international community.

Foreign Affairs Select Committee Inquiry

Back in Britain MPs had returned from their summer break and the Foreign Affairs Select Committee of the House of Commons (FAC) was gearing itself up to continue its investigation of the scandal surrounding the Arms to Africa affair. Robin Cook's hope that the FAC would have got tired of the matter after their summer holidays had not materialized. The MPs still felt that there were opportunities to embarrass the government. I was summoned back to London to appear before the Committee.

Robin Cook and Sir John Kerr had already appeared before the FAC a couple of times before the summer recess and had been given a rough time. They had been reluctant to release papers on the Sandline affair or to allow other officials to be questioned, especially before the Legg Inquiry had been completed, but the committee continued to demand my presence. I wrote to Sir John saying that although I must be guided by him and the Secretary of State, personally I had no objection to appearing before the FAC. Robin Cook agreed that both Ann Grant and I should appear before the committee. Ann had been promoted and was now the Director for Africa, replacing Richard Dales, who had gone off to be Ambassador in Norway. All the other members of the African Department who had been dealing with Sierra Leone – Craig Murray, Tim Andrews and Lynda St Cooke – had been replaced. I was therefore the only one still doing the same job since the Sandline affair broke.

The hearing before the FAC was fixed for 3 November. Again I had the benefit of Stephen Pollard's advice. The meeting was held in the Grand Committee Room of the House of Commons. The committee comprised twelve representatives from both sides of the House under the chairmanship of Donald

Anderson MP. In the way that Sierra Leone had become a pawn in West African politics, so here in the UK she had become caught up in British politics. One felt that for some members of the committee the main purpose was not to establish exactly what had happened in Sierra Leone but what could be done to embarrass Robin Cook and the government. Some members of the committee had taken a lot of time and trouble to read the multitude of documents about the case that Robin Cook had finally agreed to make available to the committee. Others appeared to have only been guided by the findings of the Legg Inquiry and press comment. Each member of the committee was given an allotted time with the result that the questioning did not follow any logical path. One darted backwards and forwards in the sequence of events and often went over the same ground on more than one occasion. The whole event was televised and was open to the press and public.

Tim Spicer was to give evidence before me and I sat patiently behind him among the public audience with my solicitors and colleagues from the office listening to him give his version of events. He dealt competently with the variety of questions thrown at him for a couple of hours. He denied that Sandline was linked in any way with Branch Energy or Executive Outcomes. He insisted that he had kept HMG fully informed about what he was doing throughout his meetings with me and officials in the Foreign Office and that nobody had advised him that the supply of arms would be in breach of the sanctions. He admitted that he had known President Kabbah since the time the latter had been elected to office and had had a number of discussions with him and therefore did not need to use me as a conduit to the President. He was emphatic that Craig Murray and Tim Andrews could have been in no doubt following the meeting held in the Foreign Office on 19 January that Sandline would be supplying arms to President Kabbah and Ecomog as part of the contract and that he had received no warning from them that this would be in breach of sanctions. David Wilshire MP put it to Spicer that somebody was lying about what took place at the 19 January meeting, to which Spicer replied that this was an implication for the committee to make.

As the committee broke for a ten-minute break we exchanged hellos. This was the first time that we had met since the meeting in his office back in January. After all that had transpired I felt no animosity against Spicer. Here was a man who had served his country loyally. At one time he had been an aide to General Sir Peter Billière and was later British Army spokesman in Bosnia, for which he had been awarded the OBE. There was little significant difference in the accounts of the meetings we had had together. Both of us felt that we had been badly treated. His conscience was clear, and so was mine. Spicer would later record all these events in his book *An Unorthodox Soldier* and went on to establish Aegis Security, which was used extensively by the UK and US Governments in Iraq.

After the break I took my seat in front of the committee. The Chairman started by asking me what I personally regretted about the whole affair. To their obvious surprise I told the committee that I personally had no regrets and that I had no doubt at all that everything I had done was legal and in fulfilment of British policy. I was then subjected to a barrage of questions mainly arising from the Legg Inquiry findings. There were several attempts by members of the committee, particularly the Tory members, to get me to criticize Robin Cook. Earlier on Sir John Stanley MP, a former Tory minister and one of the better informed members of the committee, had asked a question that inferred criticism of the Foreign Secretary to which I had refrained from answering. Sir John noted, 'Diplomatic silence, fully understood,' at which point Sir Peter Emery MP interjected, 'Go on, criticize the Foreign Secretary.' Whatever my personal feelings about the Foreign Secretary's public remarks, I was not prepared to air them in public, particularly as part of a game to get at the government.

Labour MP Andrew MacKinlay asked about the recent executions, inferring that more could have been done to stop them. I took the opportunity to relate the story of the 86-year old woman whose son had been killed and his penis cut off in front of her. When she started to cry, the rebel had cut out the boy's heart and stuffed it into her mouth and then chopped his head off and gave to the woman to hold. The rebels then burned down the woman's home and threatened the rest of the villagers not to help her. She was found three days later by an Ecomog patrol sitting in the smouldering rubble of her home, still nursing her son's head. I told MacKinlay that the rebel in question was one of those who had been executed.

Towards the end I was asked by the Chairman if there was anything I wished to add. I noted that in Sierra Leone there was a genuine civilian democratically elected government, which was a phenomenon, compared to most of Africa. The people of Sierra Leone had courageously stood against the junta for ten months seeking its restoration, which had been achieved thanks in large part to the role played by Britain. What the people of Sierra Leone could not understand was why we in Britain seemed to be regarding what we had done as a scandal instead of a huge success.

After nearly four hours of questioning, the Chairman wrapped up proceedings. It had not been a pleasant experience. In later years I was to watch Dr David Kelly go through a similar experience with the same committee in connection with the Iraq Inquiry. I could see on his face the same puzzlement that I had felt, namely, what was I doing here?

Ann Grant appeared before the committee the following week. She was accompanied by Craig Murray, who stuck to his version of what had transpired at the meeting with Spicer and defended his decision not to pass my memo of 2 February to HM Customs and Excise. They both acquitted themselves well in the face of the often belligerent questioning; more importantly, they had defended their ministers.

The final session of the FAC on Sierra Leone was with Robin Cook on 16 December. He was accompanied by Tony Lloyd and two officials from the African Department. The two ministers were hauled over the coals by members of the committee for over two hours. Donald Anderson MP commented, 'Everything which could have gone wrong seems to have gone wrong in this sad affair,' and Ernie Ross MP suggested it was the longest running farce in Westminster.

The Foreign Affairs Committee tabled its 400-page report before the House of Commons at the beginning of February. It included a number of recommendations on the workings of the Foreign Office in dealing with arms sanctions and contact with private military companies. Although the senior officials in the Foreign Office, Sir John Kerr, Ann Grant and Richard Dales, were criticized in the report and, notwithstanding the fact that the committee accepted the ambiguities of the sanctions orders, I was the one who was singled out most for criticism. There had been an attempt by one member of the committee, Sir John Stanley MP, to include another conclusion which read:

> We conclude that Mr Penfold's consistent advice that a peaceful restoration of President Kabbah was only likely to be achieved if the junta faced a credible threat of military force was both realistic and in accord with the British Government's policy objective of a peaceful resolution.

However, this was rejected by the Labour members of the committee.

Although there was some criticism of Tony Lloyd, the ministers emerged virtually unscathed. It was perhaps best summed up in the 'La Bimba' cartoon that appeared in the *Sunday Times*, which showed a caricature of Robin Cook saying, in answer to the comment 'The Commons committee was highly critical of the Foreign Office on the arms to Sierra Leone affair', 'It was completely wrong to have unelected officials take the blame – but, better them than me!'

The tabling of the FAC report should have been the end of the whole sorry affair. In fact, it continued. It was revealed that a member of the committee, Ernie Ross MP, had passed a draft copy of the FAC report to Robin Cook before it was tabled in Parliament. For this, Mr Ross was suspended from the Commons for ten working days. Also, the Chairman of the committee, Donald Anderson MP, was forced to publicly apologize for leaking some of the contents of the report to an FCO official prior to publication.

With the FAC inquiry out of the way, I was permitted to return to Sierra Leone to resume my duties. But before doing so, I was given my annual report. This was conducted by the new head of the African Department, who had been brought in, together with a whole new team, to sweep away the cobwebs of the

Sandline Affair. As he had only been in his post for a couple of months, it was somewhat surprising that he felt able to report on my performance for the whole year. He gave me the worst report I had ever received in my thirty-five years of service. Out of a rating scale of 1–5, I was given a 'box 4' – an unsatisfactory performance requiring improvements to bring up to an acceptable level. I was criticized for not understanding HMG policy, for failing to provide timely and detailed reports and for failing to send the accounts back on time. I was given a low marking for 'adaptability and resilience'. The report concluded that I was not fit for promotion, that I should not be given another posting but instead should be sent off to some academic institution to write a paper.

As the countersigning officer, Ann Grant – who had been promoted to Director for Africa – endorsed all the findings of the report. (John Everard had been promoted and posted to Peking; Craig Murray had been promoted and posted to Accra.) It was a most damaging report and would effectively signal the end of my career. So much for Robin Cook's claims to the House of Commons that there would be no scapegoats and that no officials involved in the Sandline Affair would suffer.

The Arms to Africa affair had consumed a vast amount of time and effort on the part of Government, Parliament and the press. There had been three major investigations – by HM Customs and Excise, the Legg Inquiry, and the Foreign Affairs Select Committee – producing reams of documents and costing thousands of pounds. The actions and integrity of ministers and officials had been subjected to intense scrutiny and their careers put on the line. The story had dominated the UK media and press for months and months. And all for what? What had actually happened?

The democratic government of a minor African country had been overthrown in a military coup. In support of efforts to restore the legitimate government the United Nations had imposed a ban on the supply of arms to the country. A British firm had negotiated a contract with the deposed African President to supply arms and assistance. The British envoy to the deposed government got to learn of the proposed contract. Through the efforts of an African force the legitimate government was restored. Two weeks later a supply of arms and ammunition supplied by the British firm had arrived in the country and was locked away. Was it really worth all the fuss?

There was an ironic footnote. With the withdrawal of Sandline there was no one to fly the Ecomog troops around the country. To replace Sandline, an American private security company with the odd sounding name Pacific Architects and Engineers (PA&E) was engaged to operate a couple of helicopters and maintain a fleet of army vehicles for Ecomog. PA&E, who were based in Portland, Oregon, and had links with the Pentagon, had provided a similar service to Ecomog in Liberia. And who paid for some of the flying hours and provided the vehicles for PA&E? The British Government, with around £2 million of British tax-payers' money!

Although I was upset about my annual report, what concerned me most was the amount of time that had been taken up in dealing with all these inquiries. I had spent most of 1998 back in the UK instead of doing my job in Sierra Leone. The British Government's attention had been directed towards the various inquiries in the UK instead of helping to re-establish stability and democracy in Sierra Leone.

If we had done so I wonder if we could have avoided the terrible events to come, which would lead to further appalling loss of life, more awful atrocities, the establishment of the largest United Nations peace operation and the deployment of British troops?

Chapter Eight

Rebel Advances – 1999

I flew back to Sierra Leone on 15 December on a special charter flight that had been leased from Sabre Airways. This would be the first direct commercial passenger flight from London to Lungi for two years and was to be the forerunner of the renewed scheduled flights by Sierra Leone national airlines. Businessmen like Clive Dawson and Kevin McPhillips had been putting a great deal of effort into getting the flights up and running as a further sign of normality in Sierra Leone and to get business going again.

Deteriorating Situation
In the six weeks I had been away the situation in the country had deteriorated dramatically. The rebels had taken the town of Koidu, the diamond mining centre in the east of the country and the base for Branch Energy. The group of Lifeguard employees who had been providing security for the Branch Energy mine had been evacuated. There had been quite heavy fighting between Ecomog backed by a battalion of loyal ex-Sierra Leone army and the RUF. The tactical way that the rebels had taken the town and the manpower and equipment that they had used indicated a significant improvement in their capabilities. It became increasingly apparent that they had received substantial supplies of arms and ammunition and an influx of National Patriotic Front of Liberia (NPFL) fighters. There was even talk of white Ukrainian mercenaries fighting alongside the RUF. Charles Taylor had undoubtedly increased his interest in Sierra Leone.

President Charles Taylor of Liberia had long supported the RUF, dating back to the 1970s, when he and Foday Sankoh had been among a group of Africans who had gone to Libya to learn how to spread revolution and mayhem in their respective countries. Sankoh had reputedly spent most of his time in Libya in his comfortable hotel rather than at the terrorist training camp in the Libyan Desert. When Taylor returned to Liberia to form the NPFL, Sankoh went with him. Most of the other RUF members, who had been disaffected students and teachers and who had gone to Libya, did not return to Sierra Leone. They went on to the United States, Canada or South Africa. This left the way clear for

Sankoh to take over the leadership of the RUF by shooting the rivals to the leadership who had remained in the bush.

Sankoh fought alongside Taylor in Liberia in the latter's quest for power. Many observers felt that it was in Liberia that the RUF had learned the art of chopping off victims' arms and legs. Undoubtedly the Liberian civil war was a brutal war in which hundreds of thousands suffered and were killed. It had lasted seven years. Around a dozen peace agreements had been torn up by Taylor. At one time there were five concurrent Liberian presidents. Finally elections were held. Taylor made it widely known that if the people did not vote for him, he would go back to killing them, and so he was 'democratically elected'. Taylor was vicious and corrupt and could not throw off his roots as a 'warlord', but he was no fool. Unlike Sankoh, who had received only three years of formal education, Taylor had qualified as an economist in Boston and he continued to maintain very close links with the black caucus in the US Congress and with black US businessmen. At one time he had been arrested in the US and locked up but he had managed to escape. One of his close supporters was the Reverend Jesse Jackson, who was to involve himself in the affairs of Sierra Leone.

As a *quid pro quo* for Sankoh's support, Taylor continued to support the RUF, in return for which he benefited handsomely from the diamond wealth in Sierra Leone. Liberia had some diamonds but nothing on the scale of Sierra Leone. After Taylor's assumption of power, the export of 'Liberian' diamonds increased twentyfold. The country remained poor and impoverished but Taylor's personal bank account, according to press reports, grew to over $800 million.

President Kabbah's attempts to curb corruption and control the diamond industry did not sit well with Taylor's plans. On a personal level the two did not get on well. There could hardly have been two more different heads of state of neighbouring countries both theoretically democratically elected. Kabbah was an honest, sincere but somewhat weak UN bureaucrat; Taylor was a cunning, corrupt warlord. Although Sankoh could not match Taylor's guile and cunning, as another warlord he and Taylor made easy bedfellows. It suited Taylor much more to have Sankoh in power in Sierra Leone with him pulling the strings from Monrovia. Hence his decision to increase his support for Sankoh and the RUF.

Flushed with their success of taking the Kono diamond fields with this influx of support from Taylor the rebels moved westwards taking the towns of Masingbi and Magburaka, burning villages along the way and creating thousands of displaced civilians. They launched attacks on Makeni and although this was Ecomog's brigade headquarters for the north, its troops finally had to make what they described as 'a tactical withdrawal'.

Freetown remained peaceful and quiet as people started their preparations for Christmas. Both Ecomog and the Sierra Leone government continued to put out statements denying the rebel advances. There was nothing wrong in government trying publicly to stop people from panicking but in private they acted as if they believed their own propaganda. It did not help matters that Ecomog, and especially General Khobe, continued to either keep Kabbah in the dark or paint a rosy picture to him about the security situation. I had several frank meetings with the President and his ministers telling them that they should focus all their energies on stopping the fighting. They wanted to talk about development projects and arrange overseas ministerial visits. I told them that until there was peace and stability they were wasting their time discussing other issues. The civil society groups were also becoming increasingly disenchanted with the performance of government.

Soon after my return there were a couple of rebel incursions at Waterloo, the gateway to the peninsula. They were beaten off by Ecomog, but it showed that at least some of the rebels were close to Freetown. These rebels were AFRC as opposed to RUF under the command of SAJ Musa, the former leading member of the NPRC government, who had returned from the UK where he had been studying at Warwick University with a scholarship given by the British Government as a reward for having stepped down in 1996. Musa had enjoyed widespread support from both the army and the people when the NPRC were in power. It was he who had started the programme of 'cleaning day', one Saturday in every month when everybody had to stay at home for a couple of hours in the morning and clean up their homes and neighbourhoods. Kabbah's government had continued this practice.

In the High Commission we too were preparing for Christmas. While I had been away Celia had dug out our Christmas decorations and the residence was looking very festive. For most expatriates who work overseas in so-called developing countries and who are prepared to live without the daily pleasures enjoyed by people back home in UK, times like Christmas are especially important. It is one of the rare times when you make that extra special effort to recreate the memories of home. For those like Celia and me who try to practice Christianity in our daily lives, Christmas of course had an even deeper significance. It had occurred to me just days before flying back that because it was a direct charter flight I could try to bring out some traditional Christmas fare, which would have been difficult to purchase locally. I had contacted the firm of King's Barn in the UK, who provided a service for flying out frozen food to diplomatic missions. We normally could not use them in Freetown because by the time the consignment had been transhipped in Brussels or Paris and then left lying around in Conakry waiting for a flight, the food was far from frozen by the time it reached Freetown. However, the direct charter flight made it feasible and I arranged for a couple of turkeys, capons, gammon hams and ducklings on the flight, albeit at an exorbitant cost. We planned to use one of the turkeys and one of the hams at a Christmas reception at the residence on 22 December for all the staff and their families, members of government, the diplomatic corps, the British and the international community.

By now London was getting increasingly nervous about the security situation. The RUF commander, Sam Bockarie, alias 'Mosquito', had issued a public threat to attack Freetown on 25 December. Such threats were not unusual. To the irritation of many Sierra Leoneans the BBC was regularly contacting Bockarie on his satellite telephone and giving him air time on *Focus on Africa*. On a previous occasion he had announced his campaign to 'Spare no Soul', whereby he was going to kill everyone and everything 'down to the last chicken'. It was disturbing that the BBC World Service should carry interviews from people that by law would not be allowed to be broadcast in the UK.

London's fears were fuelled by the attacks on Waterloo and the claims that there were 'thousands' of rebels in the hills waiting to attack Freetown. London, especially the Ministry of Defence, did not use my rule of thumb when assessing Sierra Leone numbers to knock off the last nought. 'Thousands' usually meant 'hundreds' and 'hundreds' meant 'tens' when referring to the strength of the rebels, certainly in terms of the number of trained fighters carrying a weapon as opposed to the 'camp followers'.

This was not to say that I was unconcerned about the deterioration in the security situation and the threat to Freetown. It merited reducing our numbers within the High Commission and the British community. The Americans had already ordered the withdrawal of their community and the closure of their mission. But this too was not unusual. The Americans always tended to jump early. In Sierra Leone they only had about seventy in their community to get out and their position was nowhere near as important and influential as the British.

Most British diplomatic missions around the world had contingency plans to deal with deteriorations in the security situation leading, if necessary, to evacuation. They mostly followed a three phase plan:

1. Stay indoors, keep your head down, keep in contact with the British Embassy/High Commission (often through a 'wardens' network), and listen to the BBC.
2. Advise dependents, i.e. wives and children, plus those who can be considered 'non essential', to leave by commercial means.
3. Close the mission and advise all the community to leave.

For phase three there are usually plans to assist the evacuation, if necessary, using military resources if commercial means are no longer available.

Of course, it was not always possible to go through these three phases in an orderly way. A sudden coup, as we had experienced the previous year, could mean compressing the phases. But my assessment was that we had not reached this stage in the run-up to Christmas. These were always difficult decisions to make and one should always err on the safe side when it comes to protecting lives. But I wished to avoid exacerbating the situation by announcing the total evacuation of the community. Such a move would create panic in Freetown and might actually encourage the rebels to launch an attack. I had already been involved in six previous evacuations in St Vincent, Ethiopia, Uganda (twice), Montserrat and Sierra Leone. All of them had been successful and therefore I felt that I knew what I was doing. Indeed, I doubted that there was anyone in the Foreign Office who had had more first-hand experience of evacuations.

I recommended that we move towards phase 1 by advising the community not to move around the town unnecessarily and stay indoors after dark, and that we should consider going to phase 2, i.e. evacuation of dependents immediately after Christmas if the situation continued to deteriorate. However, I was overruled by London. They ordered the immediate and total evacuation of the entire community and were sending RAF Hercules aircraft out to facilitate it.

I tried to argue that not only was the decision wrong but it was also impractical. When arranging evacuations it was not only necessary to plan how people would leave, but it was also important to have a rough idea of numbers involved and the ability to communicate with them. Because I had spent so much of the year being dragged back to London to appear before the various inquiries, one area of my responsibilities as High Commissioner on which I had been unable to focus much attention during the year was our consular evacuation facilities. For most of the year I did not have a consular officer so that our consular section had remained closed. It had amused me to see Robin Cook proudly telling Parliament that he had increased the number of staff working on Sierra Leone. What he did not point out was that all the extra staff were in the Foreign Office in London and most of them were actually assigned to dealing with the Sandline affair, preparing reports and statements and answering parliamentary questions and MPs' letters on Sandline. In Freetown I was still waiting for a full complement of staff. As early as February I had alerted the office to our staffing needs. By December we still did not have an officer to deal with communications, filing or secretarial duties. An experienced officer, Alan Sutton, had been sent out temporarily for three months to help open the consular and immigration section. But he had just left and a young, keen but inexperienced officer, Alisdair Hamilton, had just arrived to take up the post.

The previous year's evacuations had gone well. At that time we had had some idea of the size of the British community and a semblance of a 'wardens' network'. The British community was large. The vast majority of them were what were known as British Overseas Citizens (BOCs) or British Protected Persons (BPPs). Many of them were Lebanese or Sierra Leonean. They had lived in Sierra Leone for years; some would have been born in the country. Most of them had never been to Britain. Their status as BOCs or BPPs did not give them right of abode in Britain. In fact, it gave them little else other than a British style passport and the right to register at the High Commission. However, when it came to evacuations, they were considered and treated as full members of the British community. During the previous evacuation many of them had left the country. Some had returned; others had stayed throughout. The wardens' network had not been fully re-established. We therefore had little idea of exactly how many were in the country.

There was a further complication over numbers. As we were the only European Union mission operating and, apart from the Nigerians, Ghanaians and Gambians, the only Commonwealth representation in the country, there were an undefined number of European and Commonwealth citizens who would turn to us for assistance in the event of an evacuation as we had done the previous year. Therefore, if we were going to mount a sudden evacuation we had no idea just how many people to evacuate.

The next problem was how to communicate with them. We could not rely upon telephones – many people did not have them and even fewer had telephones that actually worked. Through the wardens' network we had established a VHF radio network. However, during the coup many wardens had had their radios stolen by the looters, so it was necessary to establish a new radio network. We had been pressing London for this for some time and I had been pleased to hear that a communications team was flying out before Christmas with equipment to set up a system. When they arrived they did not have the equipment for the wardens' network and all they did was install some new radios in our vehicles and in the office.

On 23 December we received the instructions from London to evacuate most of the staff and their families and all the British community. The Foreign Office put out a message on the BBC World Service advising all the British community in Sierra Leone to leave immediately. Two RAF Hercules would be flying in the next day. Because, apart from Alisdair, the close protection team and me, the rest of the staff were being evacuated and therefore packing their suitcases, we were fully stretched to inform the community of the arrangements for the evacuation. This was not helped by the fact that I was still banned from talking to the BBC so that when their West African representative telephoned me from Abidjan to ask about the evacuation, I was unable to pass on the details. Instead we had to make announcements over some of the local radio stations, which of course only covered parts of Freetown.

The British, international and Sierra Leone communities were bemused by these events. Not a shot had been fired in anger in Freetown, not a rebel had appeared. They did not know what to make of the BBC announcement from London. Those who heard it contacted the High Commission to seek advice. 'On what is this based? Have the rebels entered Freetown? Has the government collapsed?' Such were the questions asked by people who had survived many coups and disturbances in the past. We told them that the advice was that they should leave immediately.

The word of our proposed evacuation spread around the international and Sierra Leone community. President Kabbah telephoned to express concern. He sounded very tired. As a practising Moslem he was fasting for Ramadan. Although I admired and respected his devout views, I did wonder whether he should be weakening his physical and mental capacities at a time when there was so much going on around him.

'So Britain, our closest friend, is abandoning us.' I told him that we were concerned about recent rebel attacks and that we had a responsibility for our community. We did not want to be in a position of waiting until it was too late to evacuate. Kabbah said that we were playing into the hands of the rebels to create tension and panic and to weaken support for his government and people. He claimed that Ecomog had the situation in Freetown under control. More troops had been flown in and the CDF had now been brought in to clear the bush areas around Freetown. He denied reports that Makeni in the north had been attacked. The attack on Waterloo had been partly pre-empted by Ecomog who had picked up reports of rebels in the area and had come under attack when they had gone after them. Some of the rebels had been captured and the others beaten back. He claimed that those captured were in a very sorry state without food, clothing and had little ammunition.

Julius Spencer added his concern about our decision to evacuate. 'If the British go then that's the end of our country, and our attempts to achieve democracy.'

With the RAF Hercules coming in for the evacuation I suggested to London that could they not at least pick up the Gambian contingent of troops waiting to come and join Ecomog in Sierra Leone? Setting off from Dakar they would have to over-fly Banjul. Nothing came of this suggestion so on Christmas Eve the UK staff and their families drove in convoy to the Mammy Yoko helipad to pick up the Paramount helicopter to whisk them off to the waiting RAF Hercules at Lungi. As they drove past the golf course, people were playing golf. All was peaceful and quiet.

Celia had been most reluctant to leave, especially as I was staying. She insisted that this time the parrots would not be left behind so she left clutching two wooden boxes with two bemused parrots inside.

We bade our farewells at the helipad. It was very difficult. Instead of wrapping Christmas gifts, checking the food for Christmas dinner or doing the countless other things we would normally be doing on the day before Christmas, here we were saying goodbye to one another with no clear idea when we would be seeing one another again. I said goodbye to the others – Colin and Ruth and their children, Andrew and Rachel, who had been so excited at the thought of spending Christmas one last time in Freetown. Now they did not even know where they would spend Christmas. Also, Alison and Graham, who had been looking forward to their first Christmas in Sierra Leone. I felt particularly sorry for Alisdair as he said goodbye to Erie, his new wife. This was to have been their first Christmas together and now she was going alone to Britain, where she had no family or friends. Alisdair and I and the close protection team drove back to the compound feeling very miserable as the helicopter took off.

Only fifty members of the community had heeded the advice to leave. Most were not prepared to believe that the situation warranted such a sudden departure; many others had not been contactable in the short time available or had not heard the announcements.

It was assumed that people would be evacuated to the UK, but at the last minute we were informed that the RAF flights would not be returning to the UK but would dump the passengers in Dakar, Senegal. Our colleagues in the embassy in Dakar had to turn out to look after the evacuees from Freetown, few of whom were prepared for a stay in Senegal. They had no friends there, no visas and little money. Most caught flights to Paris. When Celia arrived at Charles de Gaulle Airport on Christmas Day with two parrots, the French officials would not let her board the connecting flight to Heathrow with them. She refused to leave the parrots at the mercy of the French authorities. She flew on to New York.

Officials back in London were surprised at the low number of Brits who had taken part in the evacuation. We tried to explain that with no sign of any disturbances in Freetown, most people, including members of the community, felt that the decision to order the closing of the mission and the total evacuation of the community was an overreaction. They were used to threats from the rebels, which rarely came to fruition and never at the time indicated. This was West Africa, where everything took longer than expected.

London decided to send the two RAF planes back to Freetown the next day to pick up any more Brits who wished to leave. The planes flew into Lungi again on Christmas Day. There was no one to pick up. They flew back to Dakar empty.

While the people of Freetown celebrated Christmas, we spent the day in the office trying to bring some order to the chaos caused by the sudden departure of the staff and families. I told Osman at the residence to go ahead and cook the turkey and in the afternoon those of us who remained went up to the residence and tucked into a hasty Christmas dinner. It was a sombre Christmas celebration but at least we were getting one, which was more than those who had been flown out the previous day.

As I climbed into bed that night I had rarely felt so miserable. Celia's and my gifts remained under the Christmas tree. I had not felt like opening mine on my own. Christmas Day had come and gone without any sign of rebel attacks. I had no idea where my wife was. I had not even been able to ring my mother to wish her Merry Christmas. I had a strong impression that officials back in London had been determined to get the evacuation out of the way so that they could enjoy their Christmases with their families with little thought to the disruption

Presenting my credentials to President Kabbah.

The British High Commissioner's residence, Runnymede, in Freetown. In the foreground, Emmanuel Fillie, my driver, and Mal Scott, head of the RMP Close Protection Team.

All photographs are from the author's collection unless otherwise stated.

President Abacha of Nigeria 'introduces' President Kabbah to the crowds at the national stadium. On Abacha's right, the President of Niger, in the foreground, the late President Conte's aide – 'the ashtray carrier'.

The late General Maxwell Khobe, who commanded the Ecomog forces that drove the junta out of Freetown in 1998, enabling the return of President Kabbah. On his left is General Kpamber, who assumed command of Ecomog when Khobe was seconded as CDS of the Sierra Leone army.

10 DOWNING STREET
LONDON SW1A 2AA

THE PRIME MINISTER

6 June 1997

Dear Mr. Penfold,

I know that Robin Cook has already sent you a message of congratulation. I should like to add my personal thanks and best wishes to you, Colin Glass and Dai Harries for your exceptional work helping to evacuate British nationals from Sierra Leone in what were obviously appallingly confused and dangerous circumstances. I know that you also did your best to bring the various factions together and to avoid bloodshed. Your efforts do great credit to the Diplomatic Service.

I am very grateful also to Lieutenant Colonel David Gale and Major Lincoln Jopp for the outstanding job they did, in the finest traditions of our Services. I hope Major Jopp is making a speedy recovery from his injuries.

I know that you have all been working under the most arduous of conditions and am very pleased to hear that you are now safe.

Very well done

Yours sincerely

Tony Blair

Peter Penfold Esq CMG

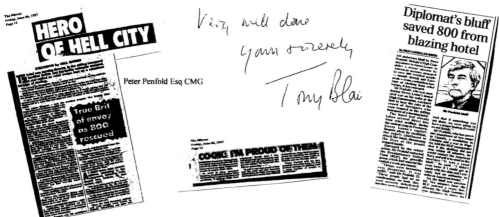

Following the coup and evacuation, we received many plaudits including a letter from Prime Minister Tony Blair and a centre-page spread in the *Daily Mirror* entitled 'Hero of Hell City'.

But a year later it was a very different story!

Demonstration in Freetown during the HM Customs Investigation and Commission of Inquiry into the 'Arms to Africa/Sandline Affair'. (*The* Mail on Sunday, *and back cover*)

Carried in a hammock through the streets of Freetown on my return from Britain and appointed as a paramount chief. (*Alimamy Kamara*)

Coronation of Paramount Chief Komrabai Peter Penfold and Yabomposse Penfold, seated either side of the late King Naimbana.

Atrocities in the bush. The rebels had no shame in displaying their savagery to the camera. These photos were given to me by another victim who was about to be murdered but miracleously an Ecomog jet appeared and in the resultant confusion he was able to escape. He has subsequently passed away.

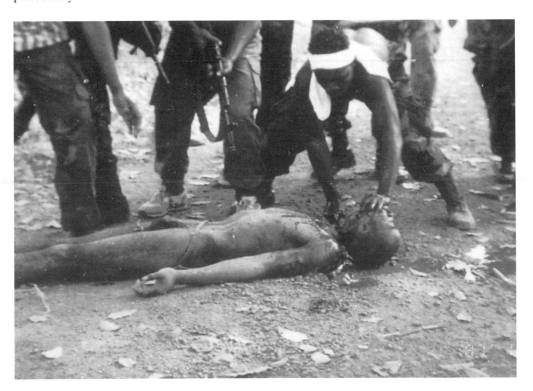

Scenes of destruction following the 6 January 1999 invasion of Freetown. In the foreground, *top*, Dave Thomas, head of the RMP Close Protection Team.

The victims – bodies burnt and left lying around following the 6 January invasion of Freetown.

Foday Sankoh, leader of the Revolutionary United Front (RUF), which committed most of the atrocities.

Street justice in Freetown against one of the rebels.

Members of the CDF who fought alongside Ecomog against the rebels.

With the Kamajors in Bo. (*Andrew Gale*)

Flying to Bo on board HMS *Cornwall*'s helicopter with Francis Okelo, UN Ambassador. (*Andrew Gale*)

Preparing to leave Bo by HMS *Cornwall*'s helicopter. *Extreme right:* The late Colonel Andrew Gale, the defence attaché who displayed outstanding bravery in the aftermath of the May 1977 coup. *Second from left:* The late Dr Mike Downham, ODA medical expert who saved the lives of many children in Bo by hiding them in the bush.

Peter Penfold Amara, born on the toilet floor of the football stadium in war-torn Sierra Leone.

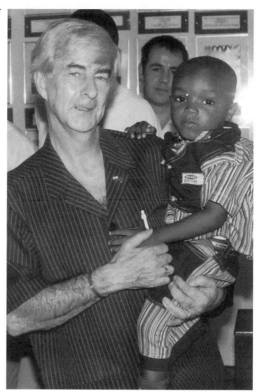

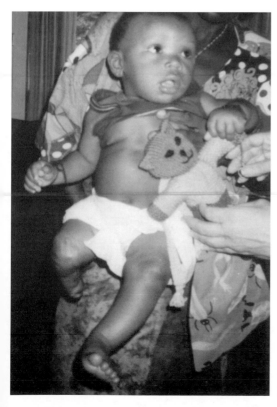

Little Abu Sesay. During the 6 January invasion of Freetown, when he was less than two months old, rebels hacked off his foot, having just killed his father.

British Minister Clare Short visiting war-torn Masiaka. On her left, Momodou Koroma, former Sierra Leone Foreign Minister.

On tour with President Kabbah. On his right, former Vice-President Dr Joe Demby. In the background, Keith Biddle, who was appointed head of the Sierra Leone Police Force.

On the Mabang Bridge heading for Moyamba with the late Chief Sam Hinga Norman, a true hero of Sierra Leone.

At the residence with Chief Norman and Bishop Biguzzi, another hero of the Sierra Leone conflict.

Saying farewell. President Kabbah and General Sir David Richards, who masterminded the British troop deployment and is now Chief of the Defence Staff.

Mammy Noah, Zainab Bangura and Celia Penfold – three remarkable women!

that they were causing to us in Freetown or to those who had been delegated to assist, such as our colleagues in Dakar or the military personnel. Clearly little thought was given in London to the spiritual significance of Christmas.

For the next few days there was a frenzy of activity in the office. As the word spread that the British High Commission staff had fled, people became increasingly nervous. Freetown was peaceful but the underlying tension had risen. Increasing numbers of the Sierra Leone and the international communities wanted to leave. The Sierra Leoneans flocked to the High Commission to acquire visas for the UK. One effect of the RAF planes having been flown to Lungi was that all commercial and charter flights had ceased operations. Airline companies took the view that if it had been necessary to use military aircraft to get people out then it was obviously unsafe for commercial aircraft to come in. Thus our hasty evacuation had actually made it more difficult for people to leave, including the hundreds of members of the British community who were still here. They received no comfort from our announcements that there would be no further assisted evacuations.

With the threat of further fighting increasing, Ecowas called an emergency meeting of foreign ministers in the Ivory Coast. The head of the African Department was going to fly out to Abidjan and it was agreed that I should also attend. Francis Okelo was going to fly up in his UN executive jet and I was able to hitch a ride. As I was going to be away for a few days, there seemed little point in the close protection team staying behind as there would be no one for them to closely protect. I suggested that they be given a break and fly off to Conakry for the weekend. They could come back when I returned from Abidjan. Dave, Batch, Craig and Paul flew by Paramount helicopter and I flew with Andy to Abidjan. I locked up the office and told Solomon I would be back in a couple of days. I could see the look of apprehension on his face. We had been through this before. Last time I had said that, it was nearly ten months before I saw him again in Freetown.

It was my first visit to Abidjan. It was such a contrast to Freetown. The Ivory Coast was considered to be one of Africa's success stories – a stable, well ordered and economically developed country, the jewel in the francophone African empire. There was a story, probably apocryphal, that as both Ghana and Ivory Coast had moved to independence their respective leaders, Nkrumah and Houphet-Boigny, argued about which would be the best way forward for their respective countries. Nkrumah's watchwords had been 'political freedom for the masses'; Houphet-Boigny had said 'economic development' should come first. They agreed to differ and would compare notes after ten years of independence to see who had been the most successful. The 'winds of change' blew in Africa, but Nkrumah only lasted a few years and was removed in a coup and poor Ghana went through years of turmoil. Meanwhile, Ivory Coast under Houphet-Boigny and with the close involvement of the French went from strength to strength and became one of the richest economies in Africa, based on cocoa and coffee.

The French had been very smart. As in their other former colonies they had carefully groomed the future leaders. Houphet–Boigny, for example, had been a minister in the French Cabinet in Paris. From the British point of view it would have been unthinkable to have seen someone like Nkrumah as a minister sitting in the Cabinet in London. Only Sékou Touré in Guinea refused to go along with the French controlled decolonisation plan, and poor Guinea suffered dramatically as a result of saying '*non*' to De Gaulle. Houphet–Boigny had died and his successor, Konan Bédié, had continued the same policies in Ivory Coast, but perhaps with a less sure touch. Nonetheless, Abidjan was like a successful thriving French city with sky-scraper buildings and smooth roads.

Andy and I checked into the plush Inter-Continental hotel where the meeting was to take place the next day. That evening Francis Okelo and I were invited round to the home of the Ivorian Foreign Minister, Amare Essy, for a quiet supper. Lansana Kouyaté, the Ecowas Secretary General and Joe Melrose, my new American colleague, were also there. The home was dotted with beautiful African paintings by Essy's wife.

Essy had been very much involved in the negotiations leading to the Abidjan Peace Accord. As a result he had spent a lot of time with Foday Sankoh, who throughout the negotiations had been living in luxury in Abidjan. It was when Sankoh had slipped away from Abidjan without telling Essy to go to Nigeria to clinch an arms deal that he had got himself arrested by the Nigerians. Essy claimed that he did not like Sankoh. Nonetheless, he had always been a strong propagandist for the RUF and a strong source of influence on the neighbouring Ghanaians. Essy appeared reluctant to accept that the RUF had no popular support in Sierra Leone and instead focused on the weakness of President Kabbah.

The meeting got underway the next day and it was clearly a Nigerian orchestrated show. The Sierra Leone delegation led by Sama Banya, their Foreign Minister, and Sheka Mansaray, the national security adviser, were seated opposite us. They remained silent most of the time. Any casual observer would not have realized that it was their country that was being discussed. The Nigerians made their usual late entry, keeping everyone waiting. They were there in force: the Ecomog generals led by Shelpidi, and the new Nigerian Foreign Minister, Olisemka. He did not have the charisma of the flamboyant Tom Ikimi, but here was a more serious and level-headed foreign minister. The Nigerians had been doing their lobbying behind the scenes to bring everyone to order. They wanted increased Ecowas support for Ecomog and public castigation of Charles Taylor for his support for the rebels. They got it. Although Africans, like others, argued amongst themselves in private, in public they would usually put on a united face and very rarely would they publicly criticize one of their fellow heads of state for acting out of order. But in the public communiqué issued at the end of the meeting Taylor was specifically named for supporting the rebels. When the Burkinabé Foreign Minister, who had arrived late, tried to defend Taylor and by implication, his own government, he was rounded on fiercely by the Guinean Foreign Minister, Lansana Kamara: 'Shut up, you don't have your troops dying for the cause of democracy.' Of course there were Burkinabés dying, but whilst fighting alongside the rebels. It was quite outrageous that Burkino Faso, the country holding the chairmanship of the OAU, a body committed to non-interference in other countries, should be actively supporting the destabilisation of the sub-region.

The head of the African Department in the Foreign Office had flown in, arriving after midnight, and flew out again before the end of the meeting. There was therefore very little time to exchange more than a few words between the sessions of the meeting. However, he told me that I was not to go back to Freetown. I should go and position myself in Conakry. I felt that I had been tricked into leaving Freetown. Andy and I flew to Conakry to join the other members of the team who had secured rooms at the Hotel Camayenne, but not room 503, which was unavailable. The team were disappointed to hear that we had been grounded and would not be going back to Freetown. Solomon and the staff back in Freetown were even more disappointed and apprehensive.

It was now New Year's Eve. Alisdair had flown back to the UK to be with his wife. The close protection team and I joined Val Treitlein for dinner at the hotel. But I was in no mood to celebrate. Somehow it seemed wrong to be enjoying ourselves with so many friends back in Sierra Leone who were so fearful of what the New Year might bring. I left the table early and went up to my room. I did not know where Celia was so I could not telephone her. I went to bed not even waiting to see in the New Year.

Chapter Nine

Atrocities

So 1999 began with me sitting in the Hotel Camayenne in Conakry. I was without Celia, the situation in Sierra Leone was confused and there was no indication when I would be back in Freetown. It all had a familiar ring.

I saw little point in sitting it out in Conakry this time. The government to which I was accredited was back in Freetown. If I was going to get back, I would have to exert pressure on those in London and I could do this more effectively face to face. I made plans to fly back to London.

Freetown itself remained quiet. There were indeterminate numbers of rebels close by and they had mounted an attack on Hastings, but Ecomog claimed to have driven them back. New Year celebrations had been subdued. Businesses and shops were open but there were not the usual crowds on Lumley Beach. More of the international community had arrived in Conakry, including the British officers attached to the UN force. Francis Okelo and General Joshi, head of the UNOMSIL forces, remained in Freetown to fly the international flag.

I spoke to Solomon in the High Commission and told him that I proposed to return to the UK to attend meetings there but I still hoped to be back in Freetown as soon as possible. He was somewhat discouraged by the news but confirmed that the staff, the compound and the residence were fine. The close protection team and I caught the Air France flight to Paris on 2 January and made a connection to Heathrow, but minus our baggage (WAWA in Paris!). I drove out to our empty house at Abingdon.

I went into the Foreign Office the next day to attend a Whitehall meeting to assess the situation. There was still much concern but now, with the High Commission closed, our information was sketchy. No decision could be made about our return; we would have to continue to monitor events but from afar.

I stayed at home the next day and went in again on the Wednesday the 6th. I telephoned the High Commission from the Foreign Office. Solomon had not got into the office and according to Christian, who was manning our switchboard, there were signs of fighting in Freetown. Other phone calls to friends in Freetown confirmed this. I decided to go back to Abingdon. Most people in Freetown, including the President, had my home telephone number and it seemed to me that it would be better if I were back there to receive any calls. The next four to five days were to be spent almost continuously on the telephone piecing together the dramatic events that were unfurling in Freetown.

January 6 Rebel Invasion of Freetown

The rebels struck Freetown on the morning of 6 January. Within a very quick time they had occupied large parts of the city. It later became clear that over the previous weeks they had infiltrated large numbers into Freetown, so that when the force moved in from the east there were substantial numbers already inside the city. Early on they took over one of the local radio stations, Radio 96.2 Voice of the Handicapped, and a Colonel Sesay announced that they had taken over State House in the centre of town. These announcements were short-lived. One of the Ecomog alpha jets dropped a bomb on the station and put it off the air. On Radio Democracy 98.1 Julius Spencer was announcing that Ecomog was in control but people should stay indoors. His was the only voice of government that people heard.

The rebels made their way through the eastern parts of the city, Wellington, Calaba Town and Kissy. They ordered people out of their homes and told them to tie white bands around their heads and sing and dance in support for them. The people were being used as human shields to prevent Ecomog from firing upon the rebels. This was how so many of the rebels had entered that morning, pushing the displaced civilians ahead of them. The Ecomog troops, though in good defensive positions, withdrew rather than fire upon the innocent civilians.

Most of the rebels were former members of the Sierra Leone army who had supported the AFRC rather than members of the RUF and initially they seemed to be content to merely encourage the people to sing and dance in support for them. But as more numbers arrived, including RUF supporters, the situation turned nastier and the awful atrocities started.

It was to be some time before a full picture would emerge of what happened during what was ten days of hell for the people of Freetown. Because of the numbers who had infiltrated the city during the previous weeks, the rebels had very quickly made their way through much of the city. Ecomog were in some disarray and government went to ground.

In the face of the Ecomog collapse and urged on by James Jonah and others, President Kabbah contacted General Abubakar in Abuja and requested that Maxwell Khobe, now promoted to general, be put in charge of the Ecomog forces. Abubakar agreed. As he had done in the February before, General Khobe led his men from the front. He stiffened the resistance and it was finally at the Congo Cross roundabout in the western end of the city that the rebels were halted by a combination of Ecomog and Civil Defence Forces. They started rolling the rebels back out of the city. The rebels continued to commit their atrocities on the civil population as they fled. Although the rebels had only occupied the centre of the city for less than one week, it took Ecomog and the CDF forces over three weeks to flush them out from the densely populated eastern suburbs of Kissy, Wellington and Calaba Town. It was in these three areas, particularly towards the end of the occupation, that the worst of the atrocities occurred.

Atrocities

The rebels' incursion into Freetown had been built around the use of civilian human shields. As they began their advance the rebels used gunfire to create panic and produce a mass civilian exodus towards the centre of the city. The rebels then mixed in and marched behind the thousands of civilians making up the human shield. These tactics were effective for the rebels, but proved frustrating for the Ecomog soldiers who were unable to identify and thus properly engage the enemy. It was deadly for the civilians who were in the line of fire once the shooting began.

Upon gaining control of an area the rebels carried out systematic looting raids in which families were hit by wave after wave of rebels demanding food, money and valuables. Those who didn't have what the rebels demanded would be killed and even those who gave up their meagre possessions were also often murdered. Just resisting rape or abduction, trying to escape or trying to protect a family member or friend, could lead to being butchered in the most horrific manner. Hundreds of dead bodies were left lying around the streets.

There were frequent accounts of people being burned alive in their houses. Children and the elderly were particularly vulnerable. Several organisations, but especially Human Rights Watch through the remarkable work of its representative, Corinne Dufka, were to record these gruesome acts in a report entitled 'Getting away with Murder, Mutilation and Rape'. Witnesses described to her scenes of rebels throwing children into burning houses and shooting at those who tried to escape. Family members trying to rescue their children or other relatives from a burning house were threatened with death and forced to abandon them to the fire. Another remarkable Sierra Leonean, Sorious Samura, a television cameraman, managed to film some of these atrocities and he was later to produce a graphic documentary, *Cry Freetown*, which won several international awards. Much of what he filmed was considered too gruesome to show on British television, even late at night.

One of the Kamajor leaders, who I knew, was heavily involved in pushing the rebels back. Leading a small group of Kamajor and Ecomog troops he was constantly making forays around parts of the city to try and halt the rebel advance. At one stage he came across a group of three rebels who were forcing a family out of their house. One of the rebels, dressed in army trousers and a stained T-shirt with a white bandana around his head, was holding up a baby by its legs in one hand and holding a machete in the other. As if he was slicing meat off a stick, the rebel swung the machete and decapitated the baby. My friend shot the rebel dead and another who was standing by watching this gruesome act with a grin on his face. The third rebel escaped.

The largest number of killings took place within the context of attacks on civilians gathered in houses, compounds and places of refuge such as churches and mosques. A study carried out by MSF (Médicins Sans Frontières) at the Connaught hospital found that some eighty per cent of all war wounded were survivors of mass killings and massacres. Human Rights Watch took testimonies from scores of witnesses to such atrocities including a 6 January attack on a family in which all but one of their seven children were killed, a 19 January attack on the church of the Brotherhood of the Cross and Star in Wellington, in which twelve people were gunned down, a 21 January attack on a compound in Kissy in which seventeen people were murdered and later burned, and a 22 January attack on the Rogbalan Mosque in Kissy in which sixty six people were massacred in cold blood.

Hundreds of people had hands, arms, legs and other parts of the body hacked off by the rebels. Many of the perpetrators of these atrocities were children, often high on drugs, some of them barely capable of carrying their AK47s, but still deadly in using them. In one incident over twenty people were lined up with their hands held out and a couple of rebels who could not have been older than sixteen went along the line and systematically hacked off the outstretched hands with rusty machetes. Other civilians were forced to plunge their hands in vats of boiling oil.

Throughout the occupation the rebels perpetrated organized and widespread acts of rape against girls and women. The sexual abuse was frequently characterized by extreme brutality and often committed right in front of husbands and parents. Young girls, especially virgins, were specifically targeted.

Countless hundreds of people, especially children, were abducted. They included Archbishop Ganda, the Roman Catholic archbishop of Freetown, along with six nuns (Sisters of Charity) and four priests. Four of the nuns were murdered and one of the priests wounded.

As the rebels withdrew from the capital they set entire city blocks and suburban streets on fire. Eighty per cent of Calaba Town was left in ashes and sixty-five per cent of the densely populated Kissy was totally destroyed. Many factories were put to the torch thus destroying thousands of jobs. Diplomatic premises such as the Nigerian and United Nations offices, government buildings, mosques, churches and several notable historical landmarks were all damaged, including Freetown's main market built in 1802, and the beautiful Holy Trinity Church on Kissy Street built in 1877.

In all, two thirds of the city was damaged, one in three of the population were displaced and made homeless, and it is reliably estimated that 5–7,000 people were killed in the orgy of death and destruction. And yet there was hardly a peep from the international community, who instead criticized the Ecomog and CDF forces for human rights violations.

Back in the UK I remained unaware of the full extent of the atrocities. For the first couple of days I was constantly on the telephone from Abingdon, talking to people in Freetown and to friends in the UK who were also talking to others in Freetown, as we struggled to keep abreast of events. None of the staff had made it to the compound, which meant that Christian was all on his own in the office, with just our local guards outside. I spoke to him every few hours. Each time he said that he was OK, though from time to time the shooting had come close. We were later to discover that the rebels got as close as Wilberforce village just around the corner from the compound and also half way up the hill leading to the residence.

After a couple of days the telephones went off. The rebels had attacked the Sierratel offices and shot two of the employees, which led to the others fleeing. Now we could only speak to a handful of people in Freetown who had satellite telephones. This meant that we were cut off from the office. I became increasingly concerned for our staff and other friends in Freetown.

No one was spared, young and old, rich and poor, but I was especially concerned about the members of staff who lived in the centre and eastern end of the city – Cecilia, my secretary, Osman and Alimamy, from the residence, Brima, our accountant, and several of the guards. I had long been a particular target for the rebels. We had intercepted several messages from people like Bockarie and other rebel leaders indicating that, whatever else they achieved, they should kill me and burn down the High Commission. I was not prepared to be intimidated by these threats but I was angry that they should extend to Sierra Leone members of my staff. Many of them had to burn their British High Commission identity cards and any other evidence of their links to the High Commission, such as photographs of me presenting them with their certificates for loyalty and service during the previous troubles.

When the rebels struck on 6 January, Francis Okelo, Subash Joshi and the few remaining members of the United Nations Observer Mission to Sierra Leone (UNOMSIL) team managed to get out to Conakry by helicopter; apart from one member of the team, Mike Booth, an American, who found himself trapped in the UNOMSIL offices, which were later burnt down by the rebels. He was to emerge in Conakry some time later, badly traumatized. Several expatriates were stuck such as Paddy Warren, the colourful owner of Paddy's Bar, to be featured in a BBC documentary, Chris Robertshaw, one of our wardens, Michael Moss, with the Methodist Church, and Hank and Catherine Meyer. Hank, a Dutch national, was the Honorary Belgian Consul.

One of my predecessors as British High Commissioner, Derek Partridge, had returned to Freetown for Christmas and had been staying with Hank and Catherine. Derek had been High Commissioner from 1976 to 1981. After Sierra

Leone, he had retired from the Diplomatic Service and had become a Liberal councillor in Rotherhithe, South London. Derek had developed a strong attachment to the country and stayed in touch with a number of friends, including Patrick, his driver at the time at the High Commission. Derek had given me much moral support during the Sandline enquiries, often writing to the UK newspapers to offer some words of experience. I had kept in close touch with Derek in the days before the evacuation at Christmas briefing him on everything we knew about the situation. He felt very strongly that London had overreacted in announcing an evacuation before Christmas. He recorded an interview with BBC *Focus on Africa* saying so. After my departure I had kept in touch with him from Conakry. As the warning signs began to increase after the New Year I told him that I really thought that it was now time for him to leave. Derek had flown out on the charter flight with me before Christmas and so, like all the others who had come out on that flight, he was now stranded because the charter company had refused to send their plane back. The company considered that if it was necessary to send in the RAF to evacuate people, then it was not safe to send back their civilian plane. Derek managed to get to Banjul and from there flew back to London just as the rebels were entering Freetown. We continued to keep in touch with one another back in the UK.

Some attempts were being made to call for a ceasefire. Moses Anafu of the Commonwealth Secretariat rang to say that he had been in touch with Bockarie, but the latter was defiant and confident of overthrowing the government. Both Sankoh, who had been whisked off to one of the Nigerian naval vessels as the rebels entered Freetown, and President Kabbah called for a ceasefire. Bockarie refused to adhere to it. We expressed concern about the situation and announced that HMS *Norfolk* was being sent to the area, though it was not clear what she was expected to do.

On 13 January I flew back to Conakry, arriving without my baggage. I met with Francis Okelo. He had just been into Freetown for the day to assess the situation and to meet with President Kabbah. The latter had also taken refuge with the Nigerians, but was now back in Hill Station Lodge. Looking down on the city from the veranda of the lodge, Francis described a scene like that in the Hollywood movie *Quo Vadis* where Peter Ustinov playing Nero looks down on Rome burning below. The Freetown version had a modern component – military Alpha Jets flying overhead. The situation was very grim, little power, no water, no telephones, food in short supply, hundreds of bodies lying around the streets and thousands of displaced people, many of them taking shelter in the Chinese-built national football stadium.

Sankoh had been flown to Conakry the day I had arrived there. With the UN's assistance he was put in touch with Bockarie by radio and they spoke for about an hour. Sankoh told him that the killings and burning of Freetown were not what he wanted and called for a ceasefire. The conversation came to an abrupt end when it appeared that the location from which Bockarie was talking, possibly around Port Loko some 70 miles from Freetown, came under attack from Nigerian jets. Sankoh was returned to Freetown.

A ceasefire was due to come into effect the coming Monday, but I warned London not to put too much faith in it.

HMS *Norfolk* had arrived in Conakry with Brigadier David Richards and a military team on board. Together with the commanding officer of the *Norfolk*, Bruce Williams, our Honorary Consul Val Treitlein and Patrick O'Brien, who had come down from the embassy in Dakar on board the *Norfolk*, we all called on President Conte of Guinea.

This was the first time I had seen the Guinean President since the return of President Kabbah in March of the previous year when I had sat just below him and shared his ashtray. I reminded him of this and he produced an ashtray for me while he chain-smoked his way through our meeting. President Conte was extremely concerned about events. Hitherto the Guineans had been somewhat ambivalent about the situation in Sierra Leone, for which they blamed the weakness of the Kabbah government as much as the rebels. But with the increased support for the rebels coming from Charles Taylor, President Conte now realized that we were dealing with the stability of the sub-region, and that if Sierra Leone fell to the rebels, then Guinea could be next. A number of multi-million dollar mining contracts were about to be signed by the Guinean government with some multi-national companies and the fighting in Sierra Leone was putting these in jeopardy. Conte urged more support for Ecomog and welcomed the assistance coming from Britain.

We were still out of contact with the High Commission but thanks to Francis Okelo's visit to Freetown, he was able to confirm that the buildings did not appear to have been damaged from the outside. London agreed that HMS *Norfolk* should enter Sierra Leone territorial waters. In the midst of all this chaos, we still had to follow diplomatic protocol. Formal diplomatic clearance from the Sierra Leone government was required. I typed up a letter and gave it to Francis to take in to give to President Kabbah. My letter came back with the President's agreement scrawled on the bottom. This was a marked change from the problems we had experienced the previous year getting permission for HMS *Monmouth* to go into Freetown, but then Tom Ikimi, the former Nigerian Foreign Minister, was no longer around.

I also arranged to get a satellite telephone into Solomon. When Francis Okelo went in to see President Kabbah with my letter seeking clearance for HMS *Norfolk*, he was accompanied by a couple of the British members of the UN Military Observer force, and they dropped off the telephone. It was therefore a great relief to receive a call in Conakry from Solomon Lebby.

He reported that the compound and residence were undamaged in spite of four days of intense fighting by the rebels to dislodge Ecomog from their

Wilberforce headquarters, situated between the office compound and the residence. The situation in the western end of the city had now eased. But it was still tense and there were still pockets of rebels in the central and eastern end of the city. I asked about the staff. As far as he knew none of them had been killed, but he still had not heard from everyone, especially those living in the centre or east, such as Cecilia or Osman. He said that the biggest problem was food. Many of the staff were starving. They had been stuck in their homes for so long. The price of rice had gone up from 200 to 1,200 leones per cup. I told him to requisition all the food in the houses on the compound and to take all the cash from the office safe and buy what more he could for them.

Electricity power had come back to parts of the western end of Freetown, but there was no water up the hills in the area around the compound and residence. This also affected the President's lodge and the Ecomog headquarters. The fire service tanker had been destroyed by the rebels, our water bowser was therefore being used to ferry water not just to our properties, but also to the President and to Ecomog.

The blanket curfew was being relaxed from 9.00 am to 3.00 pm in the west, during which time people scurried around trying to buy food. In the rest of the city it was relaxed for only two hours because of the presence of pockets of rebels. There was a heavy concentration of them still in Calaba Town. The Moslem holiday marking the end of Ramadan was coming up but people were advised to say their prayers around their homes rather than congregate in the mosques.

After the conversation with Solomon I went to see Patrick Buckley, the dour Irish World Food Programme (WFP) representative, to brief him on the food situation in Freetown. Buckley said that there should not be any food shortages because there had been plenty of food stocks in the warehouses before the rebel attack. However, we did not know whether the warehouses, which were mostly in the east, had been looted or destroyed by the rebels. He said that a freighter was on its way loaded with rice donated by the Italian government. I urged him to get it round to Freetown, but he was wary of doing so until he was sure that the port was secure. I undertook to ask HMS *Norfolk* to check.

James Jonah passed through Conakry from Freetown on his way to London, where he was hoping to see Tony Lloyd and Clare Short to seek more assistance from Britain. It was good to see him. Over a drink at the Camayenne he revealed more details of just how close the rebels had come to taking over completely.

It was also good to see again Dave Thomas and the rest of the close protection team, Andy, Craig, Batch and Paul, who arrived back in Conakry from London in good heart. They had been frustrated sitting in the UK and were worried that the team would be stood down and sent back to other units. I had pushed hard for their return. I realized that if I was going to get back in quickly, I would need them with me. It was just good to see them anyway. A close bond had developed between us all; they shared my commitment to what we were trying to do in Sierra Leone and it would have been awful if we had split up before getting back in. Unfortunately, with so many people still streaming out of Freetown, the hotel was full. All I could secure immediately was one extra room so the team spent their first night back in Conakry all squeezed into the one room. But as usual they put up with this inconvenience uncomplainingly. Over the coming days we gradually managed to acquire individual rooms for Dave, Andy, Batch, Craig and Paul, plus Peter Norman, the MILO, who had also flown out to join us. I was less happy to see him back. I still felt that it had been his somewhat coloured reports that had contributed to us being pulled out of Freetown so precipitously before Christmas.

In the meantime, HMS *Norfolk* had moved round to stay off the Freetown coast, and Brigadier Richards and Captain Williams had been able to fly into Freetown by the ship's helicopter, where they had a meeting with President Kabbah. David Richards' presence on the scene was good news. He went down to the national stadium from where he telephoned me in Conakry on his sat phone to report that there were 25,000 displaced people at the stadium. The most immediate needs were food and medicines. I informed Buckley. Frustratingly he would not advise the ship's owners to get the Italian rice ship round to Freetown. They remained concerned about the security situation despite the assurances of the *Norfolk* that the port had not been damaged. Instead Buckley had brought the ship into Conakry port, where they were going to unload the rice and hold on to it until the situation eased.

This attitude of some of the UN agencies and NGOs continued to annoy me. It was the very fact that the situation was unstable that led to the need for emergency and humanitarian assistance. Obviously one should not take unacceptable risks but if they were going to wait until the security situation was completely stable, we could wait forever. In the meantime people were dying. It seemed to me that the credibility of the international community to deliver assistance to people in conflict areas was on the line. They were good at sending in assistance after an earthquake or famine or flood but when it came to conflict areas, it required a higher acceptance of risk. To be fair to the agency and NGO representatives sitting in their hotels in Conakry and Abidjan, many of them shared my frustration but were overruled by their head offices sitting thousands of miles away in Western capitals.

By contrast DFID and Crown Agents flew in a plane load of food and medicines to Lungi, and an emergency DFID team flew in for a few days (staying on board HMS *Norfolk*). Once again we were the first to render assistance. Our medical supplies got the hospitals and clinics functioning and thanks to us some of the people had something to eat. Sierra Leoneans always appreciated our food assistance because we supplied rice, which they preferred to eat, instead of bulgar wheat, the food aid that was provided worldwide to

WFP and NGOs by the Americans. The US Government generously donated vast amounts of wheat to agencies such as WFP but one could not help but believe that this was partly to subsidize their Midwest wheat farmers.

With HMS *Norfolk* stationed off the coast and the close protection team back, now was the time to press London to let me go back in.

Initially London was only prepared to let me make a flying visit from Conakry using the *Norfolk* helicopter. Leaving one member of the close protection team at the Hotel Camayenne to man the satellite telephone/fax machine, which I had brought back from the UK, the other four members and I made our way to Conakry Airport, where we waited for the *Norfolk* helicopter. Val Treitlein had smoothed arrangements with the Guinean airport authorities and within minutes of the naval helicopter touching down we were airborne and heading for HMS *Norfolk*, which was positioned a couple of miles out to sea off the Freetown coast.

After a briefing on board the ship we set off again for Freetown, accompanied by David Richards and Bruce Williams. A team of Royal Marines had flown ahead to ensure that all was well. There were still pockets of rebels around Freetown and the helicopter flew fast and low, skimming the roof tops of the houses, many of them destroyed from the recent events. We landed at Hill Station Lodge, the President's house, on a flat piece of concrete alongside the swimming pool. Several Royal Marines were in position around the lodge.

We went straight into the large house. President Kabbah was in one of the reception rooms downstairs. He was alone and looked tired. We hugged each other warmly.

I asked Kabbah about the security situation but he could add nothing to the briefing I had already received from David Richards. He asked me how we could attract investment to Sierra Leone. I found this question bizarre. Here he was, having only narrowly survived being overthrown, with half his capital city destroyed and rebels still around, and he was asking about investment! I replied: 'Your Excellency, there is no way you are going to attract legitimate investors at this time. Your country has been half destroyed, the rebels are still around, factories have been burnt down, thousands of your people are displaced and starving. Sierra Leone has a reputation of being one of the most unstable countries in the world. Until that image changes, you will never attract investment.'

President Kabbah was upset by my frank words, and said so.

Inside the presidential lodge there was little indication of the perilous situation that the city was facing. The scene was eerily quiet and serene – no bustle of people, no telephones ringing. President Kabbah sat virtually alone on his hilltop while his capital burnt below. We spent about an hour with Kabbah partly trying to inject some dynamism in him but mainly comforting and consoling him. He had come so close to losing everything, perhaps it was not surprising that he should be subdued but I had not expected him to be so out of touch with reality.

I looked in on the residence and the office and then drove downtown to the national stadium. The contrast with the scene at the lodge could not have been starker. Thousands of people were gathered around the outside perimeter of the Chinese-built building. All were in a dishevelled state, their grim faces reflecting the torment they had gone through. Most of those present had fled to the stadium from the eastern end of the city, but there were also many there who had come in from Waterloo and Hastings on the outskirts of the city. As I walked around the outside they started cheering and crying out, 'Komrabai' and 'God bless the British.' Many others chanted, 'We want food, we want food.'

I went into the stadium where more had gathered in the passageways under the stands. I met Zainab Bangura. She was with Julius Spencer and Allie Bangura, the Minister of Trade and Industry. Both men, I noticed, were wearing army uniforms. They all looked tired, but were busy giving orders and instructions. Other civil society representatives were present including Hassan Barrie of the Sierra Leone Trade Union Council and Mr Freeman of the Civil Defence Unit. With the government all but collapsed, it was this group of dedicated Sierra Leoneans who had taken over the running of the capital. All the civil society groups had banded together to form the Civil Society Movement (CSM). They had divided the city into 106 zones. Every other day representatives from these zones would meet to report on the situation in each zone and to identify where assistance was required, where victims were assembling, where stocks of food were available or where food was urgently required and where bodies were lying around posing a health hazard. Several of the zones were still occupied by rebels and the CSM representatives from these zones would bravely slip through the rebel lines to come to the CSM meetings and return again. In this way an accurate picture of the rebels' whereabouts was built up and passed to Ecomog and the CDF forces. Members of the CDU mounted road blocks in their zones to help contain the movement of rebels. I was encouraged by the determination displayed by the CSM but it had few resources. Food was particularly scarce. Most of the warehouses where the stocks of rice were kept were in the eastern part of the city, to where it was still unsafe to go.

In the stadium the Christian Council of Churches (CCSL), under the leadership of its hardworking Secretary General, Alimamy Koroma, was distributing some meagre amounts of food and blankets. I went around talking to the people. I met the head man from Hastings village, who described how the rebels had attacked Hastings a few days before they entered Freetown, destroying most of the village, killing hundreds of its citizens and forcing all the others to flee. I promised him that I would do what I could for Hastings once it was safe for his people to return. Hastings would much later be twinned with its namesake in West Sussex and led to impressive efforts to help rebuild the devastated town.

One 'amusing' incident occurred as we walked around the stadium talking to the people in their wretched conditions. As well as the close protection team, we were accompanied by a couple of Ecomog soldiers. As I was kneeling down listening to an old woman clutching her eighteen-month old grandson (the mother had been killed by the rebels), I heard a 'clunk' behind me. I turned round and saw a hand grenade rolling towards me. It had fallen out of the Ecomog soldier's pocket. At first he did not realize but then he casually bent down, picked it up and put it back in his pocket. The close protection team and I held our breaths for a moment to see whether the pin had fallen out of the grenade. There was no explosion. The soldier appeared unconcerned and just walked on.

A maternity ward had been set up in one of the upstairs rooms of the stadium. It was full of women and children. Many of the women were heavily pregnant. A toilet off the large room was being used as the delivery room. The only piece of furniture was a wooden table, on which lay a woman who was giving birth to a baby as I entered. A midwife was assisting. The baby was born screaming. There was not even a rag to wrap the baby up in. What a way to enter the world! Born in the toilet of a football stadium in a warring city in West Africa.

I left the stadium feeling saddened and angry. I said that I would do what I could to help relieve the plight of those gathered there. I took Zainab, Julius and Allie back to the residence and gave them a meal. We discussed what the immediate priorities were. I went back up to the lodge, briefed President Kabbah on what I had seen at the stadium (he had not been there) and then climbed into the naval helicopter to start the laborious return trip to Conakry via HMS *Norfolk*.

On the next trip into Freetown I attended a CSM meeting at the Vine Memorial School at Congo Cross. I offered some words of hope and encouragement to these brave people and distributed some bags of rice, especially for the members of the CDU who were mounting the road blocks in order to ensure that the rebels did not manage to infiltrate back into the areas reclaimed by Ecomog. By sitting at a road block all day, the CDU personnel missed out on any food distributions taking place by NGOs such as CCSL; but the service that they were providing was vital for the security of the capital. DFID had also thoughtfully put gallons of disinfectant on board the first plane load of supplies to be flown in and we handed out a ten-gallon plastic container for every one of the 106 zones so that the areas could be sprayed to minimize the very real threat of a health epidemic.

The close protection team and I continued these trips from Conakry for the next few days. However, there was a problem. Each trip necessitated carrying a number of heavy diplomatic bags for the team's 'equipment'. This started to arouse the interest of the Guinean authorities as we flew in and out of the airport each day. They wanted to know what we were carrying. I assured them that it was merely diplomatic material but the size and weight increased their suspicions and delayed our departure and return each time. London would still not give the green light for us to stay in Freetown, so we decided to move on board HMS *Norfolk*.

Captain Bruce Williams and his crew made us very welcome on board but to say that conditions were cramped was an understatement. As a luxury I was given a cabin to myself alongside the captain's. It comprised a bunk-bed, which I had to climb up into by holding onto the various pipes running through the ship. Under the bunk was a desk top and cupboards and in a corner a sink hidden under another flat top. There was one chair, which had to be folded away when not in use as it took up most of the remaining floor space. A sign was put up on the sliding door of my cabin: 'British High Commission, Sierra Leone'. The hotel room in the Camayenne was a mansion compared to this. However, I was still far better off than the members of the close protection team. They were accommodated in odd corners of the bowels of the ship, some of them sleeping with their faces pressed to the pipes running around the ship.

We settled into a routine of commuting to the office by helicopter from the ship. Every morning the team and I would assemble on deck after breakfast and wait our turn to fly across after the Royal Marines. Although the ship was stationed off Freetown, she did not remain stationary. Because of the constant need to 'make water' with the desalination plants on board, she routinely sailed in a square formation. One morning as we were waiting there was some excitement as we peered into the water below and saw some dead bodies floating by. It was a gruesome sight. The bodies had obviously been in the water for some time and had become bloated, and had also lost their colour, which prompted some of the younger sailors to suggest that they were the bodies of some white mercenaries.

From the ship the helicopter flight only lasted five minutes but there was much hanging around, so that on some days it could still take nearly two hours to 'commute to the office'.

HMS *Norfolk* had to sail on to the Falklands and she was replaced by HMS *Westminster*. As she was the same class of frigate, the living conditions remained the same. She had sailed straight from Portsmouth, and her crew were more apprehensive about what they had come to. For some of the young sailors on board it was their first voyage. They watched in awe as the close protection team 'tooled up' each morning on the deck prior to flying into the war zone. An impressive collection of guns, grenades and smoke canisters were stuffed into the various pockets of their body armour. By contrast I just carried my briefcase. The young sailors waved off the team each morning and gathered in awe to see their 'heroes' return in the evening from the war front.

All the close protection team played up to the innocent adulation from the ship's young crew. One day one of them asked Craig: 'So would you really throw yourself into the line of a bullet for your boss?'

Craig casually answered: 'That's my job.'

The crew were puzzled by the close and informal relationship between the team and myself compared to the somewhat more formal and disciplined structure they were used to in the Navy. For example, initially we had left Paul behind in Conakry to maintain the office there but when it became apparent that it was no longer needed, he joined us on board ship. His reunion with us was like welcoming a lost member of the family.

There was not much to do of an evening, especially for the team. I would type up some reports and send them off using the ship's communications. This was a big help as I did not want to have to spend time sending and receiving telegrams in the office. Most evenings I would eat with the captain or in the senior officers' mess. The food was very good. The close protection team ate in the petty officers' mess. Sometimes there would be a film and one evening there was a quiz. The close protection team volunteered to enter as a British High Commission team. I was eating with the officers but I said that I would join them as soon as I could. By the time I made it to the petty officers' mess, the quiz was well underway and our team was not doing very well. Craig quipped: 'It's not surprising that the other teams are doing well. They have the same quiz with the same questions every week.'

When the scores were reckoned up, we were joint last with the team from the Royal Marines. A deciding question had to be answered to decide who would get the wooden spoon. For the close protection team this was a matter of honour. After all the adulation they did not want to face the infamy of coming last. The question was put: 'What is the name of the brewery that produces the beer Old Speckled Hen?'

I have never been much of a beer drinker, preferring to stick to gin and tonic. However, by good fortune one of the last private breweries in southern England in my home town of Abingdon was Morland, and they produced Old Speckled Hen. I passed the answer to Dave, our team captain. Our honour was saved. The Royal Marines had the wooden spoon but a couple of days later they deserved medals.

The helicopter had broken down so we decided to go in by using the rubber inflatable Zodiacs. Two of the boats were lowered into the water and we were gingerly lowered in after them. We started heading through the surprisingly choppy waters towards Freetown. We saw the outline of the Cape Sierra Hotel, which is where we had radioed ahead to Solomon in the High Commission that we would land. The other Zodiac with a team of marines on board and a couple of the close protection team was just ahead of us.

As we turned to head for the Aberdeen Bridge there was a commotion on the boat ahead, which had pulled up suddenly. It was not immediately clear what was going on. Then someone shouted, 'They're shooting at us.' At the same time I looked alongside our boat and could see spouts of water coming up in a line parallel to our boat. At first I thought it was a school of fishes swimming past, but then quickly realized that it was the path of tracer bullets skimming over the dark blue water. I dived into the bottom of the boat and felt Craig throw himself on top of me. The two boats spun around and headed at full speed back to the ship, which was some way off and oblivious to all the excitement.

We climbed back on board ship. It took a little while to piece together what had happened. There were some Ecomog soldiers guarding the Aberdeen Bridge and, although Ecomog HQ had been warned that we would be coming in by boat that day, clearly word had not filtered down to the men on the bridge. When they saw these two rubber boats speeding towards them with guys with guns and in uniforms, they immediately suspected that we were rebels. They panicked and opened fire. We decided to abandon attempts to go in that day.

The next day we went in, again by boat, as the helicopter was still not working. This time we were assured that everyone knew we were coming in but after the previous day's excitement there was a heightened anxiety about the trip. However, this time the journey was uneventful and we were greeted at the slipway round the back of the Cape Sierra by Solomon and Emmanuel and some Ecomog soldiers, who apologized profusely for the previous day's adventure.

I went up to see President Kabbah. I apologized for failing to make our meeting the previous day and asked him if he had been briefed on what had happened. He replied, 'Yes, I heard that there was a little difficulty. At least Ecomog were only shooting in the air.'

I told him that the shooting was much closer than that. Here was another example of Ecomog not giving him the full story. He needed to be told the truth and not just the upbeat version of events. If one of us had been injured it would have hit the headlines and could have had a dramatic impact on the UK's assistance.

We continued to live on board HMS *Westminster* for a while but after the excitement of being shot at by Ecomog, we decided that we would actually be safer staying at the High Commission rather than attempting the hazardous commuting from ship to shore each day. So with London's agreement the close protection team and I moved back on land. I moved into the residence and the team reoccupied their house on the compound. Some of the Royal Marines also moved onto the compound, which now more resembled army barracks than diplomatic premises.

Living back on land meant that we had more time to deal with the enormous tasks confronting us in attempting to help get Freetown back on its feet. It also brought us more into daily contact with the victims of the atrocities. Every single Sierra Leonean with whom we came into contact had suffered a personal tragedy – a member of the family killed, a home destroyed, a hand or leg amputated, a mother or daughter raped, possessions looted, jobs lost. And all in the most deliberate, brutal and barbaric manner. Most of these people were not involved in the politics or security of the country. They were just trying to eke out a living in this the poorest country in the world. But even in their poverty they had not been able to live in peace.

Our own local staff had been by no means immune. Those for whom we were particularly concerned, because they had been living in the east or centre of town, gradually reappeared at the High Commission. They recounted the terrible times they had gone through. Fortunately not one of them was killed. Cecilia, our receptionist, had had to flee on foot with her family, leaving all her possessions to be looted. Osman, the cook, kept his head down and survived. Emmanuel went into hiding and when the rebels came to his house he did not reveal to them that he was the British High Commissioner's driver, a fact that if discovered would have meant his instant death. Several of the staff had lost family members. One of the guards had his house burned down in front of him. It was too easy to think that such calamities do not affect Africans as much as they affect those who live in the West because the Africans are so poor to start with. But as the guard related his story I imagined what it would be like if my house in Abingdon was destroyed. That would be a major tragedy for me, the loss of all my prized possessions plus the destruction of the most expensive thing I owned, i.e. my home, but at least I had insurance and a job and friends with whom I could stay. What was it like for the thousands of Sierra Leoneans now made homeless? Maybe their homes were not much more than shacks, their possessions the sort of thing you give out to a jumble sale and the cars, for those who had them, rusting buckets on wheels, but they were all that they possessed in the world. They had no means of replacing them. The tragedy for them was infinitely worse. I raided my wardrobe and handed out clothes and belongings to those in need. I gave the guard some money to enable him to rent another house for him and his family for six months until he could get back on his feet.

It was harrowing listening to all these stories. Solomon related the story of his boyhood friend who had emigrated to the United States to make his fortune. He was always writing to Solomon trying to persuade him to join him in the US but Solomon had stubbornly refused saying that the place for all patriotic Sierra Leoneans was at home helping to rebuild their country. The friend had come back to Sierra Leone for Christmas to see whether he should return permanently. He did! He was caught up in the fighting and was killed. His body was put into a mortuary along with several others and then the rebels came back and burnt down the mortuary. Even in death there was no peace for the poor Sierra Leoneans.

Solomon's friend was just one of the thousands who were killed during this orgy of death and destruction. For most their passing was noticed by only their close relations and friends. Some deaths did attract more attention. Two

Western journalists, who were among the few to fly in to cover the story, were killed in an ambush when they were accompanying Julius Spencer and members of Ecomog in a so-called 'safe' part of the city. Two government ministers were killed. One of them was Dr Koroma, the resident minister in the north, who only months earlier had been singing *God Save The Queen* in Makeni. He had had to flee his home for the safety of Freetown. He and his colleague were visiting friends in the centre of the city when they came across some rebels. They were taken captive and later murdered.

Remarkably, as far as I could ascertain not one member of the British community had lost their lives in the fighting, though many had suffered. One of these was Mr Shankerdass, the Asian businessman, who was also the Japanese Honorary Consul. He had been in his factory in the eastern part of the city when the rebels struck on 6 January and was among the group with Archbishop Ganda and the nuns who had been abducted by the rebels. For days they had been forcibly walked around the eastern end of the city as the fighting continued. They finally managed to escape from their captors with the assistance of some of the local community. Mr Shankerdass reached his home in the west and came round to the High Commission to report his safe return. This was on one of those days when we had commuted in from the ship and I met him in my office.

On the previous occasion that I had seen Mr Shankerdass at the Christmas party at the residence, he had a full head of jet-black hair. The person who appeared at the office that morning, looking thin and tired, had white hair. I scarcely recognized him. One had heard of people going white overnight with fright. This was the first time that I had witnessed it. He recounted the awful events that he had experienced. There were over a dozen hostages in their group. They were kept on the move by the bunch of rebels who constantly threatened them. One of the nuns, who was not particularly old, had trouble keeping up with the group so one of the rebels, who could not have been more than twelve years old, swung his AK 47 round and shot her dead on the spot – merely for not walking fast enough. The young rebel gave no thought at all to the fact that she was a nun. They had no respect for anyone's position. For example, just for fun they would stub their cigarettes out on the arms of the Archbishop.

It was not widely known that, although he had been born in Sierra Leone of an Asian parent, Mr Shankerdass did in fact hold a British passport. I advised London to keep this information to ourselves. Although I had spoken to his wife, who was in London, to assure her that we were doing everything we could to get him released, I was worried that it would increase the danger to him if it became known to his captors that he was British. Mr Shankerdass told me he was very grateful for this. He had no doubt at all that the rebels would have killed him if they had found out that he was British. He told me that on several occasions the rebels had berated the British, and had said that one of the persons they intended to kill was me. Mr Shankerdass flew off to join his much relieved family in London. He was back a few weeks later to get his factories working again, sporting his black head of hair once more.

Every atrocity committed was a personal tragedy, but perhaps the most harrowing were those related to the amputees. They would remain a constant legacy of these terrible times for generations to come. Children would grow up not feeling the caress of their mother's hand. Others would grow up seeing their grandparents going around with no hands or legs.

With the assistance of CARE and Handicap International, a camp for the amputees had been set up at Murray Town, which I had visited. Two rival organizations had been established to represent the interests of the amputees. This did not make sense so I invited a group of amputees to the office. I hoped to persuade the two groups to combine their efforts. They filed into my office, five men, two women, a teenage boy and young girl, a couple on crutches with legs missing and others who had had their hands or arms amputated. Their spokesman, Mr Sillah, made a little speech. After the meeting as they were leaving, I presented some pens that had been provided as handouts during the UK's presidency of the European Union. I went to give one to one of the visitors who had had both his hands hacked off. I drew back and quickly put it in his jacket pocket. The scene haunted me for weeks thereafter. I kept thinking of this poor man without any hands. How would he survive in life if he could not even accept the gift of a tiny pen?

The most disturbing were the young children. A 4-year-old girl, whose hand had been hacked off, asked her mother, 'Mummy, will my hand grow back again?' The youngest amputee I came across was Abu Sesay. Abu was less than two months old when the rebels struck Freetown on 6 January. As the rebels went through Wellington, one of the poorest parts of the city, Abu's family fled. His mother, Kadi Attatouray, took his older two brothers, while his father grabbed him and ran. The rebels caught the father and killed him instantly. They picked up the two month old Abu and, without giving it a thought, hacked off his foot. They then dumped him on top of his dead father. The mother came back and found the two of them lying in the road. A couple of months later, Kadi Attatouray appeared at the gates of the residence with Abu. We brought them in. Abu was a beautiful bright-eyed baby boy with a lovely smile but he could not even crawl. Where his foot should have been was a stump looking like an elongated tent peg.

Sad as was Abu's case and others like him, it was perhaps worse for those who had already lived a considerable part of their lives and now had to get used to living without their limbs. The number of double amputees ran to hundreds, and for those who lived in the rural areas and subsisted by tilling their small plots, it was the end of their productive lives. Many of them pleaded with their torturers to kill them rather than leave them without any hands. One such person, a customs official, begged the person who had just hacked off both his hands to shoot him dead. Instead, the rebel came back and smashed all his teeth with the butt of a gun, so that he could not even use his mouth in place of his hands. Such people recounted the difficulties of living, the loss of dignity, the humiliation of not even being able to go to the toilet without the assistance of another.

I contacted the Mouth and Foot Painting Artists Association in the UK. For several years I had bought their Christmas cards and marvelled at the way these artists had overcome their handicap – many of them had been thalidomide children – by producing the most amazing paintings using a paintbrush in their mouths or between their toes. To them they were artists first. Often they would display their paintings without revealing that they were handicapped. The association sent out a video and some books and cards that their members had produced and I passed these on to the amputees in Freetown.

It was important to help them realize that their lives could still have a purpose. All the visitors to Sierra Leone used to be taken to visit the amputees. Although this always had a dramatic impact upon the visitors, I had certain reservations about this practice. For a start, it tended to be treating the amputees like exhibits in a zoo. Also, much as I sympathized with the amputees, it often meant that the thousands of other victims – the displaced and homeless, the raped and orphaned – tended to be ignored. In my view a far better way to deal with the amputees was to find jobs or other useful things for them to do, so that their dignity could be restored. I advocated that government should provide jobs for the amputees in every government ministry, and not just menial jobs. To show the way I persuaded DFID to employ an amputee in our aid section in the High Commission. We employed a bright individual whom I had got to know at my church, Desmond Bangura, as an administrative assistant.

Setting an even better example was Rudi Bruns, a German businessman who ran the local bottling plant. Rudi was the Honorary Swiss Consul and he had a particular reason for showing his compassion to the victims of the rebels. In 1995 he had been among a group of expatriates who had been kidnapped by the RUF whilst working at the Sieromoco mine. They were held in captivity for three months and subjected to a terrible time. Rudi took on half a dozen amputees as both skilled and semi-skilled employees at his bottling works.

The sheer barbarity of the atrocities was difficult to comprehend. The rebels used to devise 'games' to play with the innocent civilian population. A particular favourite was to guess the sex of a baby in a pregnant woman's womb. Having placed their bets with one another, they then would hack open the pregnant woman and withdraw the unborn child. A bottle of beer was won – the mother and baby of course died.

As a diplomat serving in a foreign country, one was expected to remain objective and not to get too involved, but for those of us who were living in

Freetown at that time, daily coming across the tales of horror and misery, we would not have been human if we had remained immune to the evidence of suffering and torment. It was especially difficult for those in the front line of dealing with the victims of the atrocities – the doctors and nurses, those working for NGOs and international organizations alongside the government's health authorities. Most of the international staff had pulled out during the January invasion, leaving a few dedicated Sierra Leone staff to deal with the problems. It was one thing to see a person whose hands had been brutally hacked off after medical staff had attended to them. By then all one saw were two stumps carefully wrapped in white bandages, but imagine what it was like when such victims first appeared. Often they would come to the hospitals and clinics clutching their severed limbs, or with bloody hands still connected precariously by tissues of skin and sinew, dangling uselessly from their arms.

During the worst of the fighting in Freetown the rebels occupied Connaught Hospital, the main hospital downtown. Fly and mosquito–infested dead bodies were piled up outside the main gates, rotting and decaying in the sun. Inside the staff were forced at gunpoint to treat the rebels. One of the dedicated doctors was forced to treat a rebel while his fellow rebels were raping the doctor's wife in an adjoining room. He listened to her screams while he operated on the rebel.

Médecins Sans Frontières (MSF) staff soon returned and were dealing with the daily horrors. I received a report from them that detailed just one month's surgical activities at the Connaught Hospital: 271 patients had been operated upon, 172 of whom were suffering war-related wounds. The report chronicled interviews with seventeen patients whom the MSF staff were treating. They made pitiful reading. One adult female reported how the rebels chopped off her hand and told her to take it to President Kabbah and ask him for another hand. Another case study of a middle-aged female suffering with lacerations on her head, shoulder and back, noted: 'Unable to interview the patient as she died just after arrival. Others said that her whole family was killed in front of her, and that she died of a broken heart.'

After a while one became almost immune to the barbarity of the situation and sometimes it was the less gruesome stories that had a bigger impact. Bruce Williams, the tough captain of HMS *Norfolk*, was brought to tears when I introduced him to Mammy Noah at the residence on one of our first trips into Freetown from the ship.

Mammy Noah was a legend in Sierra Leone. In her eighties, this determined Krio lady had already lived to over double the life expectancy in Sierra Leone. She had been married to one of the first Sierra Leoneans to qualify as a doctor and all her family were eminent in the medical field, featuring prominently in a book on the history of medicine in West Africa. Her husband, who had spoken out against the excesses of Siaka Stevens, had died some years earlier. Mammy Noah was a gifted botanist and gardener. She had introduced several varieties of shrubs and flowers to Sierra Leone. My predecessor had engaged her services to help with the garden at the residence and when I arrived I took her on full-time overseeing the work of the gardeners at the residence and producing beautiful floral displays at the residence and the office. At the time it had amused me that she expressed concern that she would not be able to do much digging in the garden.

Mammy Noah lived alongside the President at Hill Station, where she maintained her nursery of plants and seedlings. During the junta rule the rebels had tried to mount an anti-aircraft gun in her garden. She chased them away shouting, 'I don't want that gun in my garden and we don't want you in our country. Go away!' And they did.

This feisty, tiny lady related to Bruce Williams and me how she had coped during the mayhem of the January invasion. For days she had had nothing to eat and, already frail, she became so thin that the wedding ring that she had worn on her finger for over sixty years had kept slipping off. Listening to her brought tears to our eyes.

Throughout our tour in Sierra Leone Mammy Noah became very close to Celia and me. To Celia she reminded her of her mother, who had passed away a couple of years before Celia went to Sierra Leone. The two of them would sit together for hours discussing all manner of things. Mammy Noah was an avid reader and devoted listener to the BBC World Service and there was nothing on which she could not offer an informed view. Celia was devoted to her. Her friendship gave Mammy Noah a reason to live.

On one occasion she appeared at the residence in tears clutching an eviction notice in her frail hand. Those responsible for protecting President Kabbah at Hill Station claimed that she would have to be moved on the grounds of security. I went straight up to Hill Station to see President Kabbah. I told him that it was ridiculous to consider that Mammy Noah's presence alongside the lodge constituted a security threat and that to move her away from her garden at this stage of her life would kill her. I added that if this was the type of government he headed, which evicted an 87-year-old woman who had stood up against the junta then it was not the type of government to which I wished to be accredited and I would ask to be removed. The President was unaware of the eviction notice and picked up his telephone there and then and gave orders that Mammy Noah was not to be moved. She was not bothered again and was henceforth treated with respect until she passed away a few years later. On her death the President's security officer immediately moved into her house.

I had continued to visit the national stadium regularly and on each occasion I would always look in on the 'maternity ward'. Often I would arrive just as a baby was being born. Following my first visit when I had witnessed the baby being born without even a rag to wrap it up in, I had written to friends in Cardiff, Bernie and Jane Latham, describing the scene. Bernie was the star of the television series *Hollyoaks* and I had first met him and his wife Jane when they had visited Uganda as part of a British Council sponsored Shakespeare tour. We had remained very close friends, and I was proudly godfather to their son Jack. They copied my letter around to friends and three weeks later I received twenty-two sack loads of baby clothes donated by the people of Wales. I was able to distribute these to the babies at the stadium and the other displaced camps. It was also through Jane and Bernie, and another close friend in the UK, Keith Harris, that we received 800 teddy bears from the UK charity 'Teddies for Tragedies'. These too were distributed around the displaced camps and hospitals.

One of the mothers, the birth of whose baby I had witnessed on the day before my birthday, decided to name the child after me. A few weeks later I was invited to the christening ceremony of 'Peter Penfold Amara'. He was a beautiful baby boy but I felt somewhat sorry for him that he was going to have to go through life saddled with my name. The parents would bring him up to the residence from time to time. He was not the only one. Other offspring were given the name 'Peter', 'Penfold' or 'Komrabai' and when the police hospital opened a maternity wing, they named it 'The Peter Penfold Maternity Wing'. One of the amputees proudly displayed the name 'Peter Penfold' on the back of his wheelchair and even one of the local football teams named themselves 'The Penfold Eleven'.

There was so much to do in the immediate aftermath of the January invasion. DFID and Crown Agents responded magnificently to the grave situation. They were the first to fly in food and medicines. The medicines enabled the government to get the hospitals and clinics up and running. Even while there were still pockets of rebels around in the eastern end of the city, we distributed bags of rice to the needy, especially those vulnerable groups of people who were not covered by the larger distributions being set up by government and the NGOs, such as the old folks home, the amputees camp, the schools for the blind and the deaf and dumb and the child soldiers camp at Lakka along the peninsula.

For some time child soldiers had been rescued in the provinces and brought to Freetown. Initially there had been no facilities to look after them. They could not be kept with the older captured rebels, nor could they be put in prison. An elderly Catholic priest, Father Berton, had taken them under his wing at his compound in the east of the city. Drawing upon my experience of meeting the RUF at Magburaka soon after my arrival, I would occasionally visit Father Berton's compound to try to understand what made these children tick and how they might be rehabilitated back into society. Much of the time would be spent just reading to them or playing football. My visits were far too infrequent to really win their confidence but I learned much from Father Berton's experience of being with them all the time. They did not want to be placed in family environments. Even those who had families in Freetown did not want to be reunited initially. They felt more comfortable in the company of one another, with those who had shared in their awful experiences. Their main wish was to recommence their schooling and education, which had been so savagely interrupted. When the rebels had hit Freetown, they had to be moved with Father Berton to a disused house at Lakka. Later, UNICEF would take over the running of the camp.

The Royal Navy ships, firstly HMS *Norfolk* and then HMS *Westminster*, had helped provide a logistical base for the humanitarian relief effort and with their crews we were in all parts of the city helping where we could. The two ships were not able to repeat the amount of work that we had achieved with HMS *Cornwall* the previous year, because they did not have the same resources – smaller crews and smaller helicopters. Also, to our and her frustration, the Ministry of Defence would not give clearance for HMS *Westminster* to come alongside for most of the time she was in Sierra Leone waters. Even when clearance was given, she only came into port on alternate days, which affected the amount of assistance she could render.

The reason given by the Ministry of Defence for this decision was 'security'. They were frightened that she would come under attack from the rebels. I found it bizarre. Here was a floating war machine, whose firepower on board could have obliterated half of Freetown and yet was prevented from showing its face in case just one young kid high on drugs with a rifle took a pot shot at it. I also sensed that many of the crew, especially the younger ratings, were not that keen to come alongside. On one occasion when the ship was in port, a couple of shots could be heard at night. For the residents of Freetown this was commonplace but the incident clearly unnerved some of those on board. They were not familiar with the sound of gunfire. Nowadays naval warfare is conducted at a distance. The enemy is located, someone presses a button, and a missile is launched at the target hundreds of miles away. Those on board a ship rarely get to see, hear, or smell warfare at close range. The modern day Nelson sits behind a computer screen in a semi-lit operations room. It's the ultimate arcade games adventure.

This experience with the Navy was in contrast to the Army personnel who came to Sierra Leone, or to the Royal Marines on board the ships. The marines, under the command of an exceptional officer, Captain Rory Copinger-Symes, were out and about with us every day and made it easier for us to move around.

I was delighted to welcome back David Hill from DFID to help co-ordinate our humanitarian efforts. We were able to identify a number of small projects, which with a little injection of funds made a significant impact. We had been given £50,000 to spend by DFID, and this was later supplemented with a further £50,000. We used some of these funds to get the fire service working again. All the fire appliances in Freetown had been damaged or destroyed. For a long time the government's one new appliance lay burnt-out at the bottom of Hillcot Road as a permanent reminder of what had gone on in January. This meant that that there were no means to put out any fires in the city; a dangerous situation to be in given the state of the city and the fact that it was still the dry season. One 25-year-old tender was at the station. It had not been destroyed but its batteries had been looted. For a few leones we were able to purchase locally a couple of batteries and thus enable it to function again. Also, a Land Rover fire appliance had been reduced to a wreck but its pump was still working. We bought a second-hand Land Rover, and the fire service officers fitted its body onto the old appliance and got it working again.

Even though most of the rebels had now been driven out of Freetown and a degree of peace had been restored, there were still thousands in the national stadium because they had no homes to go back to. They had been destroyed. I continued to visit the stadium and give what help I could. The conditions were awful: no electricity, no running water, limited amounts of food either donated by NGOs or scavenged around the town, and appalling sanitary conditions. Families marked out their spots on the cold concrete floors underneath the stands and around the outside of the building. The grass in the middle of the stadium was left bare as this did not provide any protection from the hot sun. The football pitch, therefore, was in relatively good shape and it was this that led me to suggest what some initially considered a crazy idea.

On one of my visits I suggested that we should arrange a football match between those in the stadium and the British naval ship. It was common during a ship's visit to arrange a local football match and although there were clearly other things to do, why not? I said that I would kit out the team with the assistance of HMS *Westminster* and told the organising committee to select a team. This led to much excitement and the search to select their strongest team became as intense as if they were choosing a team to play in the World Cup. After all, this would be Sierra Leone versus England!

Decked out in their blue and white shirts (I deliberately chose Chelsea's colours), the 'Displaced Stars XI' took to the field to the cheers of the thousands gathered in the stadium. HMS *Westminster's* XI looked decidedly fitter and better nourished and they took an early lead. But, urged on by their supporters, the Displaced Stars team fought back and soon had equalized. As the game went on in the hot sun the sailors began to wilt and the Sierra Leonean team went on to win comfortably. The crowd were ecstatic. I looked around the thousands of smiling faces in the stadium. For just a couple of hours all the miseries that they had been facing were forgotten as they cheered their team on. It was a special moment.

With so many displaced people, shelter was a major problem. CARE had brought in some plastic sheeting provided by funds from the American government, which were used to help set up temporary camps for the displaced and homeless. But we needed to help the people repair and rebuild their homes. We tracked down one backstreet workshop, Duncan's, which was making block-making machines. These machines were ideal for Africa – unsophisticated, not expensive (about $250) and cost-effective. One poured some sand and a small amount of cement into a rectangular mould fashioned from iron plates, the mixture was then compressed by pulling down on a long iron lever, and out popped a block that was ten times firmer and more durable than the mud bricks that were usually used in poorer African countries. We commissioned Duncan to make machines for us, which we then distributed to local communities as part of self-help schemes to repair and rebuild their homes. We also made a bulk purchase of bags of cement from the local cement factory, which fortunately had not been destroyed in the fighting, and with each block-making machine we handed out half a dozen bags of cement.

Health and sanitation was another priority for government. When we had first returned there were hundreds of bodies still lying on the streets or buried superficially in makeshift graves around the city. We had distributed the disinfectant to every one of the 106 zones set up by the Civil Society Movement to spray around the city and thus prevent the outbreaks of disease. DFID now sent in a dozen tipper trucks, septic tank emptiers and water bowsers to help clear the bodies and debris and deliver water. They were handed over to a very grateful Minister of Health and Sanitation, Dr Tejan-Jalloh.

Getting the schools open again was a major task. Many of the schools were damaged, some were totally destroyed, and others were being used as centres for displaced people. All were bereft of essential teaching equipment. One of those totally destroyed was the Sierra Leone International Mission school (SLIM) at Old Wharf, Wellington. This school, which catered for 1,400 pupils, half of whom were orphans, had been one of the best schools in Freetown. The rebels had burned it down. We provided funds to build a temporary structure on the compound to allow the school to reopen. In just two weeks, the local community, under the guidance of an energetic Trinidadian building engineer, Joe Ramsahoi, had put up a very impressive building using equipment purchased with the DFID funds. 'Brother Joe', as he was known by all the local community, was about the biggest man I had ever met – a mountain of a man. I found it amusing that he should be associated with a project called 'SLIM'.

The amount of assistance required for the schools was enormous but it was very important to get the children back to school. This would be a further indication of normality returning. I discussed the enormity of the task facing him with the able Minister of Education, Dr Alpha Wurie. With the reaction of the people of Wales in mind to the need for baby clothes, I suggested to him that in addition to the efforts of his government and the official assistance from the international donor community and bodies like UNICEF, we should consider tapping into the generous goodwill of the ordinary people of Britain. The concept of the scheme 'Help a School in Sierra Leone' was born.

The aim of this scheme was to put individual schools in Britain in direct touch with individual schools in Sierra Leone. Initially schools in Britain would be able to render assistance through the provision, for example, of teaching materials, games equipment or clothing. But in time it would lead to an enduring relationship through which the pupils of the respective schools would get to know one another and learn more about each other's country and environment. I had long believed that the more you can put people in touch with one another then barriers of ignorance and mistrust are broken down and all problems become resolvable.

I again contacted Jane and Bernie Latham for their support at the UK end and we engaged the services of a number of friends and family in Britain to produce pamphlets advertising the scheme. Cardiff City Council helped by providing facilities and a UK office for the project was established. In Freetown I sought the support of the British Council and we established a committee comprising teachers, parents, and others whose task would be to identify which schools should be linked with which. We tried to match schools with similar interests. From the start we tried to keep bureaucracy and government involvement to a minimum.

We launched the scheme in Freetown in April at the Prince of Wales School and a week later, the first 'twinning' was arranged – the June Holst Roness Primary School in Freetown, named after a former mayor of the city, with the Severn Primary School in Cardiff, which just happened to be my godson Jack's school. President Kabbah joined me at the ceremony at the June Holst Roness School and, as we were videoing the ceremony to send to Cardiff, he surprised everyone by saying a few words in Welsh, which he had picked up when studying at Aberystwyth University.

All schools were invited to join the scheme on a voluntary basis, including handicapped or special needs schools. Several links were established, including the Milton Margai School for the Blind with the Dorton House School in Sevenoaks, Kent. Once the link was established, it was left to the individual schools to decide how they wished to continue. This could take several forms but often the children in their respective schools would write to one another. The blind children corresponded in Braille and Tim Hetherington, the renowned photojournalist and a close friend, acted as 'postman'. (Sadly, Tim was to die when covering the conflict in Misrata, Libya.) One of the teachers from a linked school in Nottingham spent part of her holidays teaching at her counterpart school in Freetown. The scheme eventually became part of DFID's Global Partnership Scheme.

This range of activities kept us very busy in the High Commission. David Hill returned to the UK. He had worked wonders but the constant demands for help had had an effect and he needed to have a break. We still did not have a full complement of staff. Colin Glass had joined me, minus family, soon after my return for a couple of months, but his tour had now come to an end. He was replaced by Steve Crossman, who was coming from Hanoi, where he had met his Vietnamese wife, Lan. Hanoi had been a tough post, so Steve had some idea of what he was coming to.

Getting staff to come to Sierra Leone was not easy. The Foreign Office had to rely upon volunteers. The system with which I had been familiar in the past of being told at short notice to pack a suitcase and go to 'Timbuktu' had long gone. This was a pity in my view, both from the Foreign Office's interests and for the officers concerned. I would never have dreamed of volunteering for Kaduna back in the 1960s, but it was this unexpected posting that had given me my first taste of Africa and had set me on a career that had been far more fulfilling than sitting in comfortable offices in Europe or North America.

While in the High Commission we were doing what we could at grass roots level to help the plight of the suffering Sierra Leoneans, we were also heavily engaged at a political and diplomatic level in the efforts to find a lasting solution to the problems of insecurity and instability.

Chapter Ten

The Lomé Peace Agreement

When the Ghanaian Kofi Anan had been appointed United Nations Secretary General at the end of 1996, many had hoped that this would be an opportunity for the UN to really focus on African issues. At first he appeared reluctant to do so. Perhaps it was because he did not want to be accused of bias towards his home continent, or he was still recovering from the abysmal failure of the UN peacekeeping efforts in Rwanda, which he had headed at the time. However, when the UN had to stand aside while NATO took the lead on Kosovo and people started asking why the protection of human rights was more important in Europe than Africa, Anan started to take a closer interest in Sierra Leone.

In February 1999, following the Freetown invasion, Kofi Anan announced a 'dual track' policy towards Sierra Leone – one track was to help the legitimate Government of Sierra Leone to reassert its authority over the country and the other track to establish dialogue with the rebels. We fully supported this policy. On 2 March Robin Cook announced in the House of Commons a further package of UK assistance of £10 million, which would be used to provide non-lethal assistance to Ecomog and to help train a new Sierra Leone army. This would help to 'roll back the rebels', he informed the Members of Parliament.

This seemed the right policy, though I was wary that the 'dialogue' should not move on too quickly to 'negotiations' and advised London so. At the time the Government of Sierra Leone controlled about thirty per cent of the country, mainly in the south and west, the rebels controlled about thirty per cent in the north and east, while about forty per cent was under no one's control, nor had been for some time. It was important that, before the negotiation stage was reached, the government had indeed reasserted its authority over a bigger stretch of the country, so that they could negotiate from a position of strength and not from a position of weakness. This would have meant having to make concessions that would inevitably lead to problems in the future. Our assistance to Ecomog gave the West African force a fillip after their dismal performance in January.

Also now playing a crucial role were two helicopter gunships, Mi-24s, which had been acquired in the Ukraine by the Sierra Leone government to form an air wing for Ecomog. Armed with S8 rockets and a 12.7 Gatling gun operated by Fred Marafono, they were flown by Juba and Neall Ellis. This awesome firepower began to inflict heavy losses on the rebels and allowed Ecomog to go back onto the offensive. They started making preparations to retake Lunsar and Makeni.

In establishing a dialogue with the rebels, the first question to be answered was with whom did one talk? Sankoh was still in detention in Freetown, but did he really control all of the RUF? It was now over four years since Sankoh had actually been in the bush with his boys. Bockarie, out in the east in Kailahun, had got used to running the show and was forever making statements on his own behalf. Even if the RUF were united, it was questionable how much the ex-AFRC/SLA recognized Sankoh's leadership. Johnny Paul Koroma was still being held hostage and tortured by Bockarie.

To demonstrate this disunity Sankoh said that he would need to speak face to face with his supporters before he could tell President Kabbah what the RUF wanted. It seemed strange that a revolutionary movement that had been fighting for eight years did not know what it wanted. However, it was also a reflection of how little contact Sankoh had had with his boys in the bush. He needed to find out just how much control he still had.

I warned London that we should be careful how far one went in negotiations. Peace at any price may be no peace at all. I also reminded the department that for any peace agreement to succeed, it must have the full support of the people of Sierra Leone. What did the people want?

To find out, a 'national consultative conference on the peace process' was organized by the National Commission for Democracy and Human Rights, under its chairman, the small but energetic Dr Kadi Sesay. The purpose of the conference was to give the Sierra Leone people a chance to voice their views on what they wanted from the peace process.

The conference was held from 7–9 April at the Sierra Leone Commercial Bank complex at Kingtom in Freetown under the chairmanship of Professor Strasser-King, Pro-Vice Chancellor of the University. Around 300 people took part, with representatives from all the civil society groups – students, teachers, women's groups, paramount chiefs, religious leaders, trade unions, ex and serving members of the army, civil defence forces, parliamentary parties, the amputees and the displaced – an impressive cross-section of society. Although mainly Freetown based, some groups were flown in from Bo, Kenema and Lungi. DFID agreed to part fund it, along with the United States Agency for International Development (USAID) and the United Nations Development Programme (UNDP). The President opened the conference and the Vice President closed it, but otherwise the government stood back and allowed the civil groups to make the running.

In his opening address President Kabbah noted that whilst achieving lasting peace was a process, it was not just a question of giving ministerial appointments to the disgruntled. He noted that he already headed a government of national unity; were the people prepared to reward those who invoked terror, and maimed and killed?

The most moving and best received of the addresses was made by Mrs Lottie Betts-Priddy speaking on behalf of all the civil society groups. She noted that it was the ordinary people who had suffered most from the continuing fighting and therefore they must have a say in the peace process. Peace should not mean merely the present crop of politicians keeping their jobs. She denounced the RUF for brutalizing the people and accused the international community of double standards – what price did they put on an African life, she asked.

Francis Okelo, Joe Melrose and I were asked to deliver statements on behalf of the international community. Francis called the conference a milestone on the path to lasting peace and noted that its pursuit must be irreversible. Joe quoted Abraham Lincoln and Bob Marley on the way to attain peace. I said that the international aid community was getting fed up with seeing so much of its tax payers' money being wasted in countries like Sierra Leone because of coups, instability and corruption. We all wanted to see lasting peace and not just a quick fix. We needed to analyse why the previous peace agreements had failed. I liberally spliced my remarks with quotes from Robin Cook's and Tony Lloyd's statements in the Commons and ended by quoting from Tony Blair's recent letter to President Kabbah, in which he had said that we wanted to see 'a Sierra Leone that stands on its own two feet as a prosperous, democratic and peaceful country'.

Foday Sankoh had been invited to the conference. He did not come, but he sent a message reaffirming the RUF's continuous commitment towards genuine and lasting peace. He described President Kabbah as 'genuine, sincere and committed to peace and development' and said that he was 'genuinely sorry for all the pain and grief that my revolution has caused you. Let us now put all our hurt behind us and forge ahead.' This was the first time that Sankoh had offered any sort of apology to the Sierra Leone people. He was clearly trying to curry favour in order to be released from detention so that he could go off and meet his followers.

After three days of debate and discussion the conference set out its various conditions for the start of negotiations. These included a cessation of hostilities, RUF recognition of the government, no demands by the RUF for the withdrawal of Ecomog, the unconditional release of abductees and, picking up the strongest theme throughout the conference, no power-sharing with the RUF.

President Eyadéma of Togo had assumed the chairmanship of Ecowas and he offered his capital as a venue for Sankoh to meet his supporters. It was ironic that Eyadéma was now helping in the struggle for democracy in Sierra Leone. He was hardly the most democratic of African presidents. He had shot his way to power in the 1970s and rigged every election since then. At the previous

Togolese election, when he had been defeated by his opponent, Sylvanus Olympio, he had declared the results null and void and just carried on in office.

President Kabbah agreed to the meeting and on 18 April Sankoh, still a condemned man but looking very dapper in a smart blue tailored jacket, flew off to Lomé. On arrival he was greeted at the airport by five Togolese ministers and driven in cavalcade to his five-star hotel, where he waited for his RUF commanders. They were being flown up to Lomé from Monrovia by the UN. Sankoh was ensconced in a suite in the hotel and indulged himself in an orgy of food, drink and sex. He was to run up a hotel bill of over $400,000 in the short time he was there. The UN was expected to pick up the tab.

The RUF immediately started demanding a ceasefire. They were aware that Ecomog were now preparing to advance on Lunsar and Makeni. The RUF were not well equipped to defend these strategic towns but they did not want to give up any of their territory. Eyadéma and Taylor supported Sankoh's call for a ceasefire and started putting pressure on Kabbah. On 27 April in his message to the nation for the thirty-eighth anniversary of independence, Kabbah challenged the RUF to renounce violence and terror and to meet in the polling booths in sixteen months time. Two days later he wrote to Eyadéma setting out his conditions for a ceasefire, namely the vacation of the highways and mining areas by the RUF, that the ceasefire be part of a comprehensive peace agreement and that it be monitored by an adequate number of UN personnel.

Another figure entered the stage – Reverend Jesse Jackson, the American civil rights campaigner, whom President Clinton had appointed as the US 'special ambassador for democracy in Africa'. He had flown to Accra to attend an Afro-American conference to which President Kabbah had also been invited. In Accra, Jackson persuaded Kabbah to fly with him to Lomé to talk to Sankoh. James Jonah and Julius Spencer had accompanied Kabbah to Accra, but the Americans told Kabbah that there was no room on the plane for them to Lomé. The Americans considered that both Jonah and Spencer were 'hawks' and did not want them around the President. So Kabbah arrived in Lomé on 17 May accompanied only by Solomon Berewa and Maxwell Khobe.

President Eyadéma had laid on a guard of honour for President Kabbah at the airport, but Jackson, the great showman, had leaped up onto the dais uninvited to inspect the guard of honour. Within an hour of arrival Kabbah was being handed a ceasefire agreement to sign. The Americans had clearly been working behind the scenes with Sankoh, and the first draft unashamedly talked of it being arranged under the auspices of Jackson without even mentioning Eyadéma or Ecowas. Both Berewa and Khobe advised Kabbah not to sign it without further consultation back in Freetown but, under intense pressure from Jackson and Eyadéma, he put his signature to the document the next day.

The reaction back in Freetown was muted. Not many Sierra Leoneans had known that the President had flown to Accra yet alone Lomé, and therefore they were taken by surprise. The opposition leader, Raymond Kamara, criticized Kabbah saying that his signing of the ceasefire was contrary to the undertakings he had given Parliament. As an indication of how rushed the ceasefire had been, Major General Felix Mujakpuero, the new and impressive Ecomog Force Commander, issued a statement saying that Ecomog had not been told about the ceasefire and that he was awaiting a directive from Ecowas. This was a subtle way of pointing out that Kabbah did not actually control the forces fighting for him.

Kabbah was convinced that Sankoh was sincere, a view not shared by some of his ministers. A number came round to the residence for a private chat. Each one of them said that they felt that they would have to resign, especially if the ceasefire led to a power-sharing arrangement with the RUF. In the event not one of them did resign.

The reaction from the international community to the ceasefire was more positive. Tony Blair was one of the first to send a message welcoming it. Addressing his remarks to the government, the people and the rebels, he said:

> There can be no military solution to your problems. Making peace means making hard choices. It means talking to the rebels. It means being ready to accept back into society those who fought against you. And, where they have genuine grievances, it means addressing these. We in Britain know how hard this is. The search for a lasting peace in Northern Ireland is demanding. We have to make tough decisions too. But it is worth it.

Tony Blair's message, though welcomed by Kabbah, did not go down too well with the people of Sierra Leone, not least because it fell short of promising real help other than platitudes. It invoked a response from the leading civil society group, the Campaign for Good Governance, who sent an impassioned and graphic letter back to the Prime Minister saying:

> We are asking you Mr Prime Minister where is that gentleman's agreement we signed [a reference to the support given for the 1996 elections] in which you promised to be there for us and with us? Our freedom is being snatched from us. Please do not let them do that to us. Help us before the flames of democracy which you helped to kindle are extinguished forever.

The letter went on:

> We watch with pride as your Foreign and Defence Secretaries speak for the Kosovo Albanians that there cannot be peace without justice. We want them to say the same for us – small poor Sierra Leone. Milosevic is now a war criminal, but he did not amputate hundreds or even thousands of limbs,

arms, heads etc, including those of eighteen–month–old babies. He did not force mothers to eat the hearts of their children raw. He did not slit the stomachs of pregnant women. He did not gang-rape children as young as thirteen and send them back home to die. He killed masses of people, but at least he had the decency to bury them in mass graves, ours were left in the streets to rot. Today he is a war criminal; ours is staying in a five–star hotel depriving us of peace. You and the British people stood up in Kosovo for the principles of truth, justice and respect for human rights. We are asking you and your people to do the same for us.

I had not been consulted about the Prime Minister's message, but I kept up my flow of reports, passing on the concerns of the Sierra Leone people and expressing my own concerns about the way that the peace process was going. I said that we could live with another 'non agreement' like Abidjan or Conakry, but that the wrong agreement now could actually exacerbate the fragile situation. I suggested that Sierra Leone was being pressured with a choice of either peace or with democracy and good government, but that they could not have both.

My reports were not well received by the department. The department told me that 'peace at any costs was better than no peace.' This attitude totally ignored the sacrifices that the Sierra Leone people had made in their struggle for democracy. For nine months they had bravely held out against the 'peace' offered by the AFRC junta because they knew that the AFRC/RUF did not offer a lasting peace.

The references to Kosovo were symptomatic of the growing anger among Sierra Leoneans and many other Africans about the uneven-handedness of the West's response to Kosovo as opposed to Sierra Leone and other African conflicts. To the department's obvious annoyance I also drew reference to the stark differences in our reactions to Kosovo and Sierra Leone. I said that compared to the atrocities in Sierra Leone, Kosovo was like a Sunday school picnic. Thirty people had been killed in Kosovo and all of NATO had been sent in; 7,000 people had been murdered in Freetown in January and there had been barely a bleat from the West. Robin Cook had recently visited Kosovo, where he had seen a house with twelve dead bodies. He was quoted as saying that he had seen 'a vision of hell'. If that was a vision of hell, then Freetown, where there were hundreds of dead bodies lying around, must be hell itself.

Over 150 years previously a naval captain visiting Sierra Leone had written:

I never knew and never heard mention of so villainous a place as Sierra Leone. I do not know where the Devil's Poste Restante is, but the place surely must be Sierra Leone.

Captain Chamier, Life of a Sailor, *1883*

This was now my post office box address, to which Robin Cook had sent me!

The rebels continued to attack villages and civilians, disregarding the ceasefire. One rebel leader was quoted as saying that the ceasefire only referred to 'shootings' and that it was still OK to maim, burn and loot. The original purpose for the meetings in Lomé had been to enable the RUF to get their act together and to allow the international community to apply pressure on them. This could then lead to 'dialogue' between the RUF and the Sierra Leone government. But with the 'ceasefire' imposed by outsiders the stage was now set for the negotiations between Kabbah's government and the rebels to start in Lomé. To my mind it was a big mistake to rush into negotiations, but my views were ignored.

President Kabbah selected Solomon Berewa to lead the government delegation to the negotiations. Many eyebrows were raised at this choice. Berewa undoubtedly had unlimited patience, which would stand him in good stead in dealing with Sankoh and the RUF, but was it wise to select the man who had prosecuted Sankoh for treason? Berewa was not really a politician. Like Kabbah he was a lawyer and the two of them approached the talks as if they were arguing a legal case in court.

Alongside Berewa, Kabbah selected Sahr Matturi, the Deputy Foreign Minister, an SLPP MP, to represent Parliament, and Kadi Sesay. Making up the delegation was Sheka Mansaray, the National Security Adviser. Mansaray was among the brightest and most capable of Kabbah's advisers. It was he who had been most closely involved in the negotiations leading to the Abidjan Peace Accord, experience that would be of enormous benefit in Lomé.

Sheka came round to the residence on the Sunday morning just before he flew off to Lomé. We went over what to expect in Lomé. I suggested that the first thing the government delegation should do would be to ask Sankoh for whom did he speak. Kabbah had missed a useful trick by not making Brigadier Mani, one of the leading AFRC/SLA commanders, a member of the government delegation. This would have exposed Sankoh to how little he could claim to speak for all the rebels but Kabbah, encouraged by the Americans, did not want to expose the different factions on the rebel side. They felt that it would be easier to secure an agreement if only one signature was required on behalf of all the rebels. We discussed what other precedents could be called upon to help with the negotiations. It was important to recognize that, unlike many other conflicts, in Sierra Leone there was a legitimate, democratic, internationally recognized government on one side. The nearest equivalent was Mozambique, where Renamo had waged a guerrilla war against the government. After years of fighting where awful atrocities were committed on a scale similar to what the RUF and AFRC had done in Sierra Leone, a peace agreement had finally been achieved. The UN had played an important role, indeed James Jonah had been the UN's representative. However, in that agreement there was an important difference. There had been no power-sharing. Renamo had accepted a cessation of fighting and democratic elections in which they took part. Their fighters were disarmed and demobilized in a World Bank programme. Renamo did well in the elections, but not well enough to form the government. They instead formed an active opposition in the Mozambique Parliament. It was also significant that the Renamo commanders had gone around the country apologizing for their past misdeeds. If such an agreement could be reached in Sierra Leone, there was a chance of lasting peace. Sheka went off to Lomé under no delusions of the difficulties they would face.

A number of representatives of the international community were attending the negotiations. Francis Okelo fielded a large UN team. The UN were effectively organizing the meeting, although the Togolese took the limelight. The Ecowas Secretary General, Kouyaté, was there, with delegations from Nigeria, Ghana, the Ivory Coast, Burkino Faso and Liberia, as well as the hosts, Togo. Gaddafi sent some Libyans. The OAU Secretariat was represented and the wily and experienced Moses Anafu flew out from London to represent the Commonwealth Secretariat. The Americans were there in force. My American colleague, Joe Melrose, who had scarcely spent more than a couple of months actually in Sierra Leone, was sent to Lomé, to be joined by a team of US lawyers to help with the drafting.

Surprisingly, I was not asked to go to Lomé. Instead, Paul Harvey, the deputy High Commissioner designate for Nairobi, was asked to attend. Paul, who had previously served in the African Department in the FCO, but not on the West African side, had been appointed the Secretary of State's Special representative for Sierra Leone, taking over from John Flynn. Paul was a very capable officer but, given the lead role that the UK played in Sierra Leone and the complexities of the background to the troubles, I was surprised that it was not felt in London that my experience would be useful in Lomé. When I raised this with the department, I was told that I was needed to stay alongside Kabbah in Freetown.

Without a resident embassy in Lomé, Paul was in a similar position to what I had been in Conakry with regard to reporting on developments. Most of his reporting to London was done over the telephone. The occasional written report managed to filter through to us in Freetown, but usually too late to offer any substantive comment. Sheka rang me from time to time. He said that the talks were going frustratingly slowly. The quality of the RUF team was very poor and they kept going back on matters that it was thought had been agreed in previous sessions. The Chairman, Koffigoh, the Togolese Foreign Minister, appeared to be biased towards the RUF. Omrie Golley had appeared, funded by the Americans, to act as the RUF's legal adviser and spokesman. Sankoh himself did not take part in the talks. He remained in his hotel suite. But all decisions had to be passed by him, which accounted for the slow and painful progress.

Notwithstanding the clear views of the Cabinet, Parliament and people that a power-sharing agreement would not be acceptable, Berewa's delegation found itself under enormous pressure to offer ministerial and other government positions to the RUF. The pressure was strongest from the Americans but others such as the Togolese, Nigerians and the UK added their weight. To his astonishment Sankoh was asked how many Cabinet positions he wanted. He was well aware of the strength of feeling from the Sierra Leone people and felt before the talks got underway that the most he could hope for was an amnesty for himself. As a sign of good faith President Kabbah had presented him with a passport, a diplomatic one, to assure him that his execution for treason would not be carried out. Faced with this attitude of the international community and playing on the weakness of Kabbah, Sankoh said he would settle for the vice presidency, ten Cabinet ministerial posts, five deputy ministers, six ambassadorships and the heads of eleven parastatals.

The RUF propaganda machine, which had always been more effective than the Sierra Leone government's, had created an image that they controlled seventy-five per cent of the country. To the uninformed, like the Americans and the Togolese, it therefore seemed quite reasonable of Sankoh to ask for only half the government. They therefore continued to apply pressure on the Sierra Leone government delegation to give Sankoh at least half a dozen ministerial posts.

Word of these shenanigans reached Sierra Leone. A demonstration was held in Bo attacking Kabbah and declaring that they would fight any power-sharing arrangement. In Freetown a twenty-four hour 'stay at home' was organized by the civil society groups on 17 June. It was a remarkable show of people power. With less than twelve hours' notice people were urged to stay at home to demonstrate their opposition to power-sharing. Freetown was effectively shut down for the day. The markets remained closed, the taxis stayed off the roads, offices and businesses were shut down. The British High Commission was open, but I chose to work from home that day.

The organizers of the 'stay at home' met with President Kabbah and warned him that the demonstration was just a taste of things to come if he entered a power-sharing agreement with the RUF. He gave them assurances that this would not happen. A group of them, including members of the influential Inter Religious Council, then flew to Lomé to talk to the negotiators.

Jackson telephoned Kabbah to put more pressure on him to accept the RUF proposals. Kabbah told him that he would be signing his own death warrant if he did so. Kabbah told his Cabinet that the maximum number of RUF ministers he was prepared to accept, as part of the policy of 'inclusion', not power-sharing, was two.

Although most attention was focused upon the number of ministerial positions for the RUF, there were other aspects of the negotiations that were of concern. A key to the implementation of any peace agreement would be the disarmament, demobilization and reintegration, or DDR, programme. A programme, devised by the World Bank and ourselves, was already in place and had been accepted by the international community. However, with so many people in Lomé who had no real knowledge of the situation on the ground in Sierra Leone, they started rewriting the DDR programme, including, controversially, the 'encampment' of the CDF. There was a proposal to establish a 'human rights commission', but one already existed; similarly a 'council of chiefs', which also existed. There were plans to establish a special position for Sankoh. The American team of lawyers produced a draft form of words, in effect putting Sankoh in charge of the diamonds, which was crazy.

My concerns were multiplied when I heard that Paul Harvey was going to have to leave Lomé for a while and his place as UK representative would be taken by Craig Murray – he of Sandline fame, who was now Deputy High Commissioner in Accra. It seemed to me that Murray had tried back in 1998 to sell out to the RUF. What damage could he do now?

A Lomé 'Facilitation Committee', headed by Koffigoh, the Togolese Foreign Minister, and including Kouyaté, the Ecowas Secretary General, and representatives of the UN, Commonwealth Secretariat, OAU, Nigeria, Ghana, Liberia, US, UK and Libya arrived on a four-hour visit to Freetown on 22 June to put more pressure on President Kabbah and his government. A meeting was arranged at Hill Station Lodge, where they met Kabbah, Cabinet ministers, leaders of political parties and representatives of the paramount chiefs and civil society.

Speaking in French, Koffigoh said that the talks in Lomé had reached deadlock over two issues – the withdrawal of Ecomog and the participation of the RUF in government. He noted that the RUF had lowered their demands and that the government had increased their offers, but there was still a gap to fill. He looked to Kabbah's government to make further concessions so that the peace agreement could be signed. All the Sierra Leoneans present questioned the sincerity of the RUF. The NUP leader noted that at the last count 2,756 innocent civilians had had their limbs amputated and that 531 cases of AIDS as a result of rape had been counted. He asked, 'Can we trust the RUF to behave like human beings?'

I listened carefully to all the comments being made. I found it somewhat bizarre that here was another African, who had never visited Sierra Leone before, lecturing to a group of distinguished Sierra Leoneans about the future of their country and doing it in French to the English-speaking assembly.

There was a dramatic moment during the meeting when President Kabbah read out a fax he had just received from Dr Peter Tucker, the distinguished Sierra Leonean who had been the architect of the 1991 Constitution and was a mentor and family relative of Kabbah's. He had also served as Chairman of the

UK's Commission for Racial Equality. Tucker, who had fled to London during the fighting in January, urged Kabbah to withdraw his offers of ministerial and other positions to Sankoh and the RUF. He said that this was Kabbah's 'last chance to honour his country.' Tucker's words had a deep impact upon the Sierra Leoneans present but they seemed to wash over the visitors. Kabbah was also somewhat dismissive of them. He told Koffigoh that he was prepared to increase his offer to three Cabinet ministerial positions and three deputy ministers. The delegation flew back to Lomé.

When they got back to Lomé, Sankoh issued a statement, probably drafted by Golley, rejecting the latest offers and saying that he was still demanding eight Cabinet posts, the dissolution of the government and of all political parties and a four-year transition government. The tension in Freetown heightened and the number of calls asking if our visa section would open increased.

There were two more important visits at this time. President designate Obasanjo of Nigeria flew in for the day. He spent most of his time with the Nigerian troops, but at a meeting with Kabbah he again exerted pressure to reach an agreement at Lomé.

The United Nations High Commissioner for Human Rights, Mrs Mary Robinson, also visited. Her visit coincided with the release of the detailed and graphic human rights report by Human Rights Watch, entitled 'Getting Away with Murder, Mutilation and Rape'. The former Irish President was taken around the amputees camp at Murray Town. Visibly moved, she described the atrocities carried out in Freetown in January as 'war crimes and crimes against humanity' and worse than those in Kosovo. Her words were covered widely by the international media.

Those of us living in Sierra Leone did not need Mary Robinson's visit, nor indeed the Human Rights Watch report, to reveal the extent of the atrocities. We continued to live with them daily. Just before the Robinson visit Celia and I received a visit at the residence from Yabomposse Kabba. She was the wife of a former paramount chief, whom we had befriended in the past. Since the death of her husband she had been running a *gara* (local cloth) dyeing and printing business from her home. As the wife of a paramount chief she had a certain standing in the community. When the junta had taken over in 1997 they had looted her business and publicly humiliated her. She was just getting back on her feet when the rebels entered Freetown in January. We had not seen her since then. Sitting in our living room she recounted her story of what had happened to her on 6 January.

Mrs Kabba, who was in her fifties, went to her mother's house where other family members and friends had gathered. A young rebel, aged around twelve, wielding an AK47, came into the house. He ordered Mrs Kabba's brother to rape their aged mother. The brother refused. The young boy pointed his gun at the brother and threatened to shoot him. The brother said, 'I will not rape my mother, you will have to kill me first.' Without a moment's hesitation, the boy shot the man dead in front of the family. He then threatened the rest of the family. He forced Mrs Kabba to strip naked down to her panties. Stuck inside her panties was her '*poshi*'; resembling a fly whisk made out of animal skin and hair, this signified her status as the wife of a paramount chief. When the young rebel discovered that she was the wife of a paramount chief, he said he would kill her first. She fell to her knees and, even though she was a Moslem, she started chanting the psalm *The Lord is my Shepherd*. Another rebel came in at this moment and told the boy to let her go. Bundling up her clothes, she ran out into the street in her panties

She ran back to her own house and found it burnt to the ground. Outside the house was the head of her brother-in-law. He had been found in the house by the rebels. They had chopped off his head and thrown it out of the window. They then set fire to the house. His burnt body was found in the embers. Mrs Kabba buried her brother-in-law's head under a nearby mango tree. The rebels had taken her three teenage children away with them. Mrs Kabba had not seen them up to the time she recounted her story.

Celia and I comforted the sobbing woman. She was appalled at the thought of the RUF being given any position in government. She said that if she saw Foday Sankoh on the street she would kill him or willingly die in the process of trying. I reported the story to London as yet another case history in the human tragedy of Sierra Leone, but it did not dilute the enthusiasm to reach an agreement in Lomé with the RUF.

The chairmanship of Ecowas was usually rotated among the member states every twelve months and President Eyadéma's tenure was coming to an end at the end of June. He was desperate to see a peace agreement signed in Lomé in order to help rehabilitate his image internationally. Several late night sessions ensued. The quest to agree a form of words took precedence over the wishes of the Sierra Leone people and the situation on the ground. The 30 June deadline came and went but, although President Konaré of Mali nominally became Ecowas Chairman, it was agreed that President Eyadéma should get the credit for hosting the peace talks.

On 5 July President Kabbah addressed the nation. He told his people that he had been invited to fly to Lomé by President Obasanjo to finalize a 'comprehensive peace agreement'. He said:

Even today, as I prepare to travel to Lomé, the RUF continues to make unreasonable demands. I am sure many of you believe that the government has given the RUF far too much already, and that the RUF has given very little or nothing at all. Yet, they continue to make demands, prolonging the suffering of our people and delaying the start of reconciliation and the healing process. However, I have no doubt you will agree with me that after so much pain and suffering, after so much destruction of life and property, we need to exercise patience and persevere in our search for lasting peace.

The die was cast and President Kabbah flew off to Lomé. He took with him an 8-year-old little girl called Mamounia, who had had her arm amputated by the rebels and whose mother had been murdered.

On 7 July, in front of the world's media, President Kabbah and Foday Sankoh signed the Lomé Peace Agreement. Both were dressed in flowing African robes. Kabbah held little Mamounia in his arms. She was clutching a teddy bear, one of those that had been sent out by the UK charity Teddies for Tragedies that we had been distributing around the displaced camps and children's hospitals.

The agreement gave the RUF four ministerial posts in an expanded Cabinet of eighteen, and four deputy minister slots, plus the promise of various ambassadorial and public service positions. All combatants and collaborators were granted absolute and free pardon for any actions up to the signing of the agreement. The constitution was to be reviewed and new mandates to be sought for Ecomog and UNOMSIL. All prisoners and abductees were to be released, and all mercenaries were to be withdrawn. Disarmament would commence immediately. Among the bodies to be established were a Commission for the Consolidation of Peace (CCP), a Council of Elders and Religious Leaders, a National Electoral Commission and a Human Rights Commission, all having RUF participation.

The RUF was also to be accorded every facility to transform itself into a political party. Sankoh and the RUF had achieved far more than anyone expected. But there was even more. As well as receiving a specific pardon, Sankoh was to be Chairman of a new Commission for the 'Management of Strategic Resources, National Reconstruction and Development'. This was a euphemism for putting him in charge of the diamonds; and the position was to have the same status as the Vice President.

There was a hitch at the last minute during the signing ceremony. Alongside the signatures of Kabbah and Sankoh were to be the signatures of the 'moral guarantors' – the United Nations, Ecowas, the OAU and the Commonwealth. However, in the light of the recent Human Rights Watch report and Mary Robinson's comments during her visit, there was growing concern over the 'blanket amnesty' in the agreement for all the combatants. Francis Okelo was told by his New York headquarters that the UN was not prepared to put its signature to the document. Having overseen the negotiations, this was a grave embarrassment to him. The issue was resolved by allowing Okelo to sign the document but only after adding a disclaimer to the terms of the amnesty.

The Sierra Leone reaction to the peace agreement was mixed. There was some rejoicing on the streets of Freetown but it was hardly euphoric. Many

Sierra Leoneans felt that they had been betrayed by their president and the international community.

The international community was more positive about the agreement and again, one of the first to issue a welcoming statement was Tony Blair:

> I believe that this agreement offers the people of Sierra Leone the prospect of an end to the terrible suffering they have endured over the past eight years of conflict. The people of Sierra Leone now have a chance to rebuild their lives and their country in peace and stability and in a spirit of national reconciliation. Britain will help them in their efforts to sustain and develop their democracy.

I found it difficult to share the Prime Minister's enthusiasm for the Lomé Peace Agreement. I felt that the international community, especially those bastions of democracy, Britain and the United States, had acted disgracefully in forcing through the Accord. Sierra Leone's infant democracy had been undermined. Against the publicly and privately expressed wishes of the people, a power-sharing agreement had been reached in Lomé. The barrel of the gun (combined with the most horrific atrocities and human rights violations) and not the ballot box had achieved positions of political power. After signing the Lomé Agreement it was expected that Kabbah and Sankoh would fly back to Freetown together. But Kabbah flew back alone, leaving 'Vice President Sankoh' to continue to enjoy the luxury of his hotel suite in Togo.

Chapter Eleven

No More Guns, No More Killing

In the immediate aftermath of the signing of the Lomé Peace Agreement there was an unreal period of inactivity in Sierra Leone. The agreement had called for the disarmament of all the combatants and had set a totally unrealistic deadline of two months for this to be fully completed. In fact, it became increasingly apparent that, notwithstanding Sankoh's signature, the RUF were not disarming. They told the various United Nations military observers who were in the country to observe the DDR programme that they had not received orders to disarm from Sankoh. He remained out of the country enjoying the hospitality of the Togolese. To help give things a push, Clare Short, the Secretary of State for International Development, paid a visit towards the end of July.

This would be the first official visit to Sierra Leone since the signing of the Lomé Agreement. It was the first British ministerial visit since Tony Lloyd's brief visit in March 1998 and the first visit by a British Cabinet minister for many years. After its success in the 1997 General Election the new Labour government had created the Department for International Development (DFID) as a separate ministry to replace the old ODA, which had been part of the Foreign and Commonwealth Office. Clare Short had replaced the Tory minister Baroness Lynda Chalker, who had established such a good relationship with so many African politicians. For those of us serving in the Diplomatic Service in Africa, the change had both advantages and disadvantages. As part of the FCO Lynda Chalker had been responsible both for Britain's overseas aid programme and for the UK's policy towards Africa and it was difficult to separate the two. However, as a separate minister, especially with Cabinet rank, Clare Short carried far more clout in government and she had quickly established her credentials as an energetic minister, even though she did not conform to the image of 'New Labour', much to the annoyance of the Labour spin doctors.

Soon after her appointment Clare Short announced that her major priority was the elimination of poverty in the world. She also recognized that the problems of poverty and security were intertwined. This was one of the clear lessons of Sierra Leone, which now two years on since I had first arrived, had slipped to the bottom of the UNDP's poverty chart for the world. I had told President Kabbah that perhaps it was now better to be the poorest country in the world instead of the second poorest because now there was only one way to go – upwards.

Clare Short had been the MP for Birmingham Ladywood since 1983. Prior to that, she had been a civil servant in the Home Office. She had a reputation as a tough, no-nonsense, sharp-talking minister. I was looking forward to meeting her. She arrived from Nigeria with a small team, which included Brian Thomson, the head of DFID's West and North African Department. I met them at Lungi Airport and we jumped into the Ukrainian-piloted helicopter across to Freetown.

In a packed programme lasting two days and nights she met President Kabbah three times, addressed meetings of Parliament and the paramount chiefs and visited DFID-supported community projects in the devastated parts of Freetown, plus the Connaught Hospital and the amputees camp at Murray Town. At a meeting in Freetown she addressed representatives of around a hundred civil societies. She also met with the Ecomog Force Commander, Felix Mujakpero, UNOMSIL officers and NGO representatives.

I was keen to take her out of Freetown so we drove up to Masiaka, 50 miles north of the capital. This once-thriving town of over 15,000 inhabitants had been totally destroyed by the rebels as they advanced on their way to Freetown. Hardly a building had been left standing and all of the population had fled either to Freetown or into the surrounding bush.

With the signing of the Lomé Accord some people had started drifting back. On the trip we took with us the Sierra Leone minister, Momodou Koroma, and Paramount Chief Kompa Bomboi of Masiaka. The latter was now displaced and living in Freetown and this was his first visit back to his chiefdom since the fighting. We walked around the town looking at all the destroyed buildings – the school, the church, the mosque. There were emotional scenes as the people saw their chief again. A large crowd gathered outside the remains of his burnt down house in the hot afternoon sun. There was little shade and not one chair in the whole of the town on which Clare Short could sit as the usual speeches of welcome were made. People related the terror that they had faced as the rebels had killed, looted and burned indiscriminately. There were thousands of the Masiaka population still unaccounted for, especially children. The people welcomed the Lomé Peace Agreement but voiced concern over the sincerity of the rebels. They were desperate for help in rebuilding their homes and their lives. No help was coming from government or the international community. Clare Short made no false promises but her visit gave them hope. It also helped demonstrate to her the importance of getting the paramount chiefs back to their chiefdoms as one of the keys to encouraging the people to return to their homes and villages and to promoting development and reconciliation. I had advocated a DFID programme to achieve this and shortly after her return to the UK she approved a £2 million programme to help rebuild the chiefs' houses and court barres – the traditional gathering places for the people.

We had met some of the displaced on the way up to Masiaka, at the makeshift camp at Waterloo on the outskirts of Freetown. Waterloo was at the gateway to the peninsula and therefore the gateway to Freetown. In the olden days it had been the site of a major train station, hence its name. Thousands had taken shelter in and around the old community building, which had been destroyed in the fighting. Inside the building pools of stagnant water formed by the rain that came through the roof were dotted around the floor, providing breeding grounds for mosquitoes. Some people had assembled dilapidated structures made of straw outside. David Hill and I had visited the camp back in March and had distributed some bags of rice. We had been one of the first outside agencies to do so. Little had been done to alleviate the plight of the people, whose numbers had trebled since our previous visit. Because there was still concern about the security situation at that time, the government had insisted that the people should come into the displaced camps in Freetown. However, many of the people had small plots of land in the Waterloo area where they cultivated their crops of cassava, onions and tomatoes. They did not want to lose them as they provided some food to eke out their miserable lives, whereas in the Freetown camps they would be totally dependent upon the uncertain delivery of food stocks from the NGOs.

Back in Freetown President Kabbah joined us for a quiet supper at the residence. Celia and I had taken to inviting him down to the residence of an evening from time to time. As usual, other than a couple of security guards whom the close protection team looked after, he came alone. Such occasions were virtually the only time he left his residence and I believe he much enjoyed the opportunity to get out and relax. We usually kept the conversation light-hearted. With Clare Short we were able to keep the conversation relaxed, though she was able to probe his thinking on the implementation of the Lomé Peace Agreement and on the other vast range of problems that his government faced. Without other government ministers and officials around, the conversation flowed more freely and frankly compared with the next day's formal meeting at which the Vice President and ministers were present. On a one-to-one basis one was always impressed by the basic sincerity and goodness of Kabbah, though his weakness and political inexperience sometimes showed through.

The meeting with the civil society groups was a much livelier affair. Clare Short kept her prepared text to a minimum and allowed for a free flow of comment, questions and answers. In the packed hall of the British Council she was questioned vigorously about the differences in the international reaction to Sierra Leone to that of Kosovo and Northern Ireland. With a manner that was neither patronizing nor condescending, she clearly demonstrated that she empathized with the people and she won them over. She was to remain a firm favourite of the Sierra Leone people.

As well as giving a push to the DDR programme and hence the Lomé Peace Agreement, we achieved another key decision during Clare Short's visit. For a long time I had been advocating strong support for the Sierra Leone Police. It was just as important to get the police in shape as it was to help restructure the army. In a democracy, law and order was a civilian responsibility, i.e. the police and, if we were to strengthen the infant democracy, we had to help the police force, which had suffered as much, if not more, than any other democratic institution. Unlike the army, which had to be rebuilt from scratch, there was still a semblance of order and discipline in the police force, but there was still much to be done.

We had already part-provided and funded a team of Commonwealth Police Advisers to work alongside the Sierra Leone Police but, with President Kabbah's support, I had argued that we should fund and provide a UK policeman to head the Sierra Leone Police. This was a difficult decision for DFID and HMG. There were concerns that Sierra Leone policemen could be responsible for human rights violations, for which the head of the force would be responsible. There were also the obvious dangers to the individual concerned. However, we argued that unless we effected changes from the top, any efforts to improve the police would be wasted and this could only be done by someone with executive authority, not as an adviser. Kabbah argued that he had no Sierra Leonean with the necessary experience who had the trust and confidence of the people. Clare Short accepted these arguments and during her visit she told the President that we would be supplying a UK officer to head the force. To ensure a speedy appointment, Keith Biddle, a former senior Manchester police officer who was presently heading the Commonwealth team of advisers, was appointed to the post, leaving Adrian Thorne, his deputy, to head the Commonwealth team. It proved to be a very wise decision. Within a short time people saw a marked change in the police under Keith Biddle's leadership. The police were paid regularly and they looked smart in their new uniforms. Discipline was improved and corruption was weeded out. The police had pride in themselves and the people's confidence in the force was restored.

Clare Short's visit was followed in October by two other important DFID visits. Dr Mukesh Kapila, the head of DFID's department responsible for conflict and humanitarian assistance, paid his tenth visit. I had known Mukesh since my days in the British Virgin Islands when he was one of the ODA's medical advisers. Mukesh made things happen and much of what we had achieved with Sierra Leone would not have happened without his involvement.

For example, it was a conversation with him when we were in Conakry that had led to the establishment of Radio Democracy and the Sierra Leone Government Office. Now his department was overseeing our inputs to the DDR programme. Mukesh was constantly jetting around the trouble spots of the world, from Bosnia to East Timor. His visits to Sierra Leone, often accompanied by Brian Thompson and Garth Glentworth, the governance institutions adviser, were always invigorating. Mukesh was later seconded to the UN to work in the Sudan.

Hard on the heels of Mukesh Kapila was the Permanent Secretary of DFID, Sir John Vereker. This wily, experienced top civil servant took a more measured view of DFID's activities, conscious of the fact that as Permanent Secretary he was responsible for its coffers and its mandate to Parliament. He was an ideal foil to Clare Short and the two of them worked well heading up the DFID team. In his quieter way, he was equally impressive to the Sierra Leone people with whom he met.

The commitment to Sierra Leone by DFID remained strong thanks to such visits. It meant that there was a wealth of experience and first-hand knowledge on Sierra Leone in the DFID headquarters in London, unlike, sadly, the Foreign Office. Robin Cook never visited Sierra Leone all the time I was there; Tony Lloyd's four-hour visit in 1998 was the only FCO ministerial visit until Peter Hain came for a couple of days in January 2000, just shortly before I left. The Foreign Office officials were not much better. Up to the end of 1999 the total time spent by visiting officials from the African Department was less than seven days, and this supposedly to a country that was taking up fifty per cent of the department's time. In a different situation this might have been welcome but the officials dealing with Sierra Leone back home seemed to have written their own agenda and did not want to hear views that contradicted their version of events. I was keen therefore to see them in Sierra Leone to expose them to the realities on the ground, so that they could form a more informed view with which to recommend policy to ministers. It was noticeable that even when they came out, they only wanted to see certain people and only sought answers to questions that would support the views they had formulated in London. For example, when the head of the department paid his one and only short visit over a weekend, I could not persuade him to accompany me to a church where he would have gained a good feel for what was going on. One other member of the department was clearly worried about meeting Sierra Leoneans. He brought with him a supply of hand wipes, which he methodically took out and used every time he shook hands with a Sierra Leonean.

A strong message coming out from London post-Lomé, as evidenced by the Prime Minister's message, was the need for reconciliation – the people should bury their differences, forgive and forget. This was easier said than done with the memories of January still so vivid, with people walking around without hands and arms and so many still homeless.

Celia was in church one day when she noticed the young man sitting across from her. His shirt sleeve appeared to be flapping around. She then realized that the man's arm had been amputated at the elbow. His shirt sleeve was flapping because he was trying to make the sign of the cross at the appropriate time in the service, but with a hand that was no longer there. His memory was telling his body to do something to which his body could no longer respond. Celia watched him as he awkwardly made the sign of the cross with his left hand after years of making it with his right. The horrors of what he had gone through were still alive in him.

Encouraged by the Inter-Religious Council the religious leaders in the community were very active in preaching reconciliation within the spirit of the Lomé Peace Agreement. On Sundays and Fridays in churches and mosques around Freetown the message would be preached. On one occasion when the priest had just finished his sermon explaining Lomé and preaching reconciliation, an elderly lady somewhat hesitantly walked up to the front of the church. She turned embarrassingly to face the congregation and said: 'Please excuse me, I have never done this before, but I feel that I must say something in response to what our priest has just said.'

The packed church went silent as every face turned towards the woman. She went on: 'I am the headmistress of a school. I have been a teacher for thirty years. In all that time, I have been teaching my children about right and wrong, good and bad. If a child is good, he or she is rewarded; if a child is bad or misbehaves, he or she is punished. But now it seems that if a child misbehaves, he should not be punished, he should be rewarded, indeed, taking the analogy of the ministerial positions under the Lomé Agreement, I should make him a prefect. How can I reverse all that I have been teaching and practising all my life?'

She went back to her pew while the whole congregation sat there stunned.

In a simple but very clear way she was voicing the concerns of so many Sierra Leoneans. They did not want vengeance. They did not want retribution for what they had suffered. They were prepared to forgive, though not forget. But it seemed to them that 'rewarding the RUF' was wrong. Sankoh and the RUF did not accept that they had done anything wrong. They either denied committing atrocities, or said it was necessary for the common good.

To Sankoh the Lomé Agreement was not a peace treaty, it was a surrender document. It was the document by which he and the RUF were accepting the surrender of the government, Ecomog, the UN and the international community. They had won and therefore it was right that they should be rewarded with ministerial positions, with control of the diamonds, with houses and cars and with money from DDR. The old schoolteacher was right. If this attitude prevailed among the rebels, there would never be lasting peace.

The blanket amnesty in the Lomé Agreement had encouraged this attitude. To counter the bitter taste of the amnesty the drafters of the agreement had put in a clause setting up a Truth and Reconciliation Commission. The TRC, as it was called, had been very successful in South Africa under the chairmanship of Archbishop Desmond Tutu and people felt that this was what was needed to help reconciliation in Sierra Leone. But there were faults in this logic. For a start there had been no amnesty initially in South Africa. It was putting the cart before the horse to grant a blanket amnesty and then establish a Truth and Reconciliation Commission. At first many Sierra Leoneans did not understand the purpose of a TRC and even when it was explained to them, some questioned the need for it. Sierra Leoneans were very fatalistic. They adopted the attitude that if someone had done wrong, then God or Allah would punish them. They cited how bad people like Siaka Stevens had died in misery. Exposing again so soon the details of the atrocities in public forums, they said, would only re-open the wounds when they needed time to heal.

The UN had disassociated itself from the amnesty at the signing of the Lomé Agreement. This would subsequently lead to the establishment of a war crimes court, which would have far-reaching developments.

While the people of Sierra Leone were being persuaded to forgive and forget and efforts were made by us to establish camps for the DDR programme, the rebels continued to breach the Lomé ceasefire by attacking and looting villages. The divisions among the rebels also became more and more self-evident. This was starkly illustrated when a group of the ex-Sierra Leone army, who were hiding out in the Occra Hills just south of Masiaka, took some UN military observers hostage.

The group of UN military, which included five British officers, had gone into the Occra Hills, along with Bishop Biguzzi, some Nigerian Ecomog soldiers and local press reporters, to arrange the disarmament of this rebel group. Having set up the meeting one day, when the UN officers went back the next day, instead of disarming and coming back to Freetown, the rebels surrounded the UN group, disarmed them, trashed their vehicles and marched them back to their camp in the hills. Bishop Biguzzi was released but the rest were detained as hostages. What had started as a positive sign that the Lomé Agreement was working, turned into a disaster. This would be a foretaste of an even more serious event in the following year when British troops were deployed and attracted the attention of the whole world.

The rebel group, who later were to become known as the 'West Side Boys', were a particularly nasty bunch. These were the ones who had been closely involved in the attack on Freetown in January. They had names like 'Junior Lion', 'Captain Cut Hand', 'Major No Surrender', and 'Colonel Leatherboots'. They claimed that they had not signed up to the Lomé Agreement, which offered nothing for them. They said that they did not answer to Foday Sankoh, that their leader was Johnny Paul Koroma, who was still being held hostage by Bockarie in the east of the country.

A team of experienced hostage negotiators were sent out from the UK. Working day and night alongside the UN, Ecomog and the Sierra Leone government, our professional team finally secured the release of all the hostages who, as a bonus, brought out with them some of the abducted children. I met the released hostages when they reached Freetown after dark. They looked drawn and haggard. They had been badly treated by the thugs, many of whom were young kids high on drugs. It was a good end result to what had been an extremely dangerous situation.

Not only did this incident reveal the extent of the divisions among the rebels, it brought back into the picture Johnny Paul Koroma. As part of the negotiations to secure the release of the hostages, Bockarie had been persuaded by Charles Taylor to release Koroma and allow him to go to Monrovia. Sankoh flew from Lomé to Monrovia, and there the two of them had their very first meeting. It was somewhat frosty but led to the return of both of them to Sierra Leone.

Almost three months to the day of the signing of the Lomé Peace Agreement Sankoh and Koroma flew back to Freetown to be given a fanfare greeting by the world's press. A group of us were assembled at the Hill Station Lodge to meet them.

Koroma must have wondered what was going on. His footnote in Sierra Leone's history had been written as the leader of the ill-fated AFRC. In Kailahun his life was literally hanging by a thread at the whim of the psychopathic Sam Bockarie. Koroma later admitted to me that he was not sure whether each and every day with the RUF might be his last. And then he was plucked out of obscurity to share centre stage with Sankoh in front of the world's media. The experience had a profound effect on Koroma, and this showed immediately when he returned with Sankoh.

The two of them were invited to say something to the press on the steps outside the presidential lodge with the assembled group of dignitaries in the background. Sankoh spoke first. Dressed in African robes and looking somewhat dishevelled, he stumbled hesitantly through a written prepared text. He said that he supported peace and looked for the full implementation of the Lomé Peace Agreement. Reacting in a hostile way to a question from the press about when he would release the abducted children, he denied that the RUF were holding any 'adoptees'.

By contrast, Koroma stepped forward, dressed in a natty Western suit, and speaking off the cuff he said he was pleased to be back. He regretted what had happened in the past and committed himself to peace in his country. Koroma spoke clearly and positively. Everyone was impressed. Sankoh had not wanted to share the stage with Koroma. The Occra Hills incident had forced this upon him and he must have already started to regret it.

With the return of Sankoh and Koroma, hopes were renewed that at long last the peace process, especially the DDR programme, could get underway. Both men became members of the national committee chaired by the President to oversee the programme, of which I was also a member representing the international donor community. The committee met once a week. Sometimes the meetings dragged on for over four hours. Although President Kabbah went out of his way to flatter and cajole Sankoh at these meetings, the latter was clearly uncomfortable in such a setting. He could not debate and discuss in committee. He was used to either being treated as a Messiah by his boys in the bush, or to receiving dignitaries in suites of five-star hotels. To hide his discomfort he would either slouch on a sofa and pretend to fall asleep, or deliver a noisy diatribe against all those present. Kabbah just sat there and took it, as did most of the other ministers present. The only people who spoke up against Sankoh were Joe Demby, the Vice President, and Sam Hinga Norman, the Deputy Minister of Defence.

At one meeting at the end of the year Sankoh launched into an attack complaining that no one was helping him and the RUF as set out in the Lomé Accord. The international community was equally castigated. He said that the only thing that he had received from the community was a satellite telephone from the British, and even that did not work. I stopped him in full flow and pointed out, 'You seem to forget that £20,000 of British tax payers' money has been used to furnish the house you are living in.'

Sankoh retorted: 'That's a waste of money. The bed is not even comfortable.'

I shouted back at him: 'Then give it back!'

President Kabbah tried to calm things down but he was ignored as the attack switched to Norman and then Demby, who both shouted back at Sankoh. Sankoh shut up and switched back to his sleeping mode. It was interesting that at the end of the meeting he made a point of coming up to Sam Norman and me to mend fences with us. It was the classic case of the school yard bully. The more you try to appease them, the more they demand and intimidate. The way to deal with a bully is to punch him on the nose, not to offer him sweets. Sankoh only showed any respect to those whom he could not bully. He had no respect for the President or for any of his ministers.

Despite this, many people continued to flatter Sankoh, who revelled in this attention. My American colleague would go round to his house and lamely sit outside for hours waiting to be received. The endless succession of visitors to Sierra Leone all wanted to go and call on him. Sankoh treated them all with much disdain. He was particularly insulting to Madeleine Albright, the US Secretary of State. She flew in for the day and a meeting was set up. However, Sankoh ignored her and flew off to Kailahun to see his boys. He said that if Albright wanted to see him, she should come to Kailahun. The Americans sent a special helicopter to pick him up, and then gave him $1 million for his Minerals Commission.

Soon after Sankoh and Koroma's return a symbolic weapons destruction ceremony took place on the hockey field at Wilberforce barracks in front of a large public crowd. Groups of Sierra Leone army, CDF and RUF marched onto the field and handed over a motley collection of guns and rifles to the UN and Ecomog representatives. All the key players were there – Kabbah, Sankoh, Koroma and Norman. I sat next to Koroma in the stands overlooking the field. He was dressed in flowing white African robes, to symbolize, he told me, that he was now demobilized and no longer a soldier, though he still supported the army. I noted that what the army was presently demanding had changed little from what we had discussed back in May 1997. I asked Koroma whether he regretted that those negotiations had not been more successful. Candidly he admitted that it had been his biggest mistake to invite the RUF to join him.

'They were the problem then, and they are still the problem,' he said.

In my speech at the ceremony I had referred to previous speeches I had made, when I had described the dance of Sierra Leone as 'one step forward, two steps back', and said that hopefully the day's ceremony would mark the change in direction. As important as the DDR programme was and the need to help the ex-combatants, I warned that we should not forget the thousands of innocent victims of the fighting who remained in the displaced camps. There was no DDR programme for them. They just wanted to return to their homes and get on with their lives. All they asked for was to live in peace and security in a gun-free environment.

The symbolic destruction ceremony raised the public's hopes that the peace agreement was at last underway. But it was just a gesture. The very members of the RUF who had disarmed at the ceremony were later seen carrying weapons again around Sankoh's house, which was situated close to the High Commission offices. Taxi drivers used to sarcastically refer to the track leading up to Sankoh's house from the main road as 'Cut-hand Junction'.

The day after the symbolic ceremony there were further clashes in the bush between the RUF and ex-SLA, puncturing the euphoria of the previous day's disarmament. It epitomized the mood swings that one experienced in Sierra Leone – one day up, next day down.

Sankoh continued to prevaricate over the implementation of the Lomé Accord. He continued to pick and choose which bits of the Accord he would follow. He went ahead with the appointment of his ministers, though it was a struggle to find members of the RUF who were capable of performing the duties of a minister. In the RUF anyone who could do 'joined up writing' was considered an intellectual. He selected Mike Lamin to be the Minister of Trade and Industry, Peter Vandi, the Minister of Lands and Housing, and Paulo Bangura, the Minister of Energy, and, on the recommendation of Johnny Paul Koroma, Jomo-Jalloh to be the Minister of Culture and Tourism. They were a sorry bunch and hardly improved the quality of what was already a rather weak cabinet.

At a ceremony at State House attended by all the Cabinet and members of the diplomatic corps, and eventually Sankoh, Lamin made a short speech of acceptance on behalf of all the new members of government. Mike Lamin had been one of Sankoh's most senior field commanders and was obviously a person he trusted. But Lamin was scarcely someone who would encourage bona fide international businessmen to trade or invest in the country. As with so many of the RUF he looked emaciated in his ill-fitting suit and dark sunglasses. Lamin had been sent to negotiate with the SLA rebels in the Occra Hills, where they had buried him up to his neck in the ground and injected him with dirty water. There were doubts whether he would survive this punishment. Before the end of the year he went to the United States to represent Sierra Leone at the World Trade Organisation (WTO) conference in Seattle. Other delegates were amazed to see such a person representing Sierra Leone. At a meeting in Washington with the Sierra Leone community organized by the Sierra Leone Embassy he was nearly lynched by the angry Sierra Leoneans.

The other new ministers were no better.

Following the Lomé Accord the United Nations had passed a further resolution allowing for an expanded UN presence with an enhanced mandate to implement the Accord. The small team of UN military observers, UNOMSIL, was to become a 6,000-strong UN force, UNAMSIL. There was much discussion over how Ecomog and UNAMSIL would operate side by side. President Obasanjo of Nigeria had told Kofi Anan that his government could no longer afford to bear the financial costs of the Ecomog force. The UN Security Council took this to mean that the UN should bring in other troops to help out. What Obasanjo really wanted was for the UN to pick up the tab of the Ecomog operation. The UN was seen as a 'gravy train' to subsidize the West African troops. There were heated debates over who should contribute the extra UN forces. Finally it was decided that three of the Nigerian Ecomog battalions should be 're-hatted' – i.e. they should become part of the UNAMSIL force and wear the famous blue berets of the UN. Both Ghana and Guinea also insisted on getting a share of the UN coffers. The remainder of the UN force would be made up of two Indian battalions and a Kenyan battalion. Next came an argument over who should command the force. The Nigerians argued that it should be one of their generals as they were contributing so many of the force. The UN insisted that it should be an Indian general. A compromise was struck by accepting an Indian commander, Major General V.K. Jetley, but by replacing Francis Okelo, the UN Secretary General's representative with a Nigerian, Ambassador Olu Adeniji, who had successfully completed a similar assignment for the UN in the Central African Republic. Adeniji proved to be an experienced and shrewd operator. After distinguishing himself with the UN in Sierra Leone, he would return to Nigeria as Foreign Minister and later was appointed Ecowas Secretary General.

The relationship on the ground between the UN and Ecomog became strained. Obasanjo had replaced the impressive Mujakpero as Ecomog Force Commander with Major-General Kpamber. Mujakpero had been Director of the Nigerian Army Legal Services at the time when Obasanjo had been arrested and tried by the Abacha government. Some felt that Obasanjo was harbouring a grudge and, although Mujakpero had only been in the job for a few months, he was sent back to Nigeria. In the short time he had been in charge of Ecomog he had displayed a welcome firmness in dealing with Sankoh and the RUF, and many regretted his departure.

Kpamber had previously served as the number two of the Ecomog force in Sierra Leone and had also served with Ecomog in Liberia, where he had reportedly struck up a friendship with Charles Taylor. As Taylor was seen as the architect of Sierra Leone's problems, Kpamber's appointment was viewed with concern by many Sierra Leoneans. Many of the Ecomog troops had not been home to Nigeria for over three years and some of the officers were now engaged in commercial deals in Sierra Leone. There were mixed views over whether Ecomog should pull out. I had much sympathy for the Ecomog position. Nigeria had carried the burden to help restore democracy in Sierra Leone for too long, and practically on her own. Many of their troops had lost their lives in the cause. However, I also shared the concerns of many, including President Kabbah, that the continued Nigerian presence would not help his ambition to root out corruption in his country. Corruption was rife throughout Africa, but Nigeria had made it into an art form.

The rift between Ecomog and the UN was not helped by the withdrawal of my colleague, Mohammed Abubakar, the Nigerian High Commissioner. I had grown to like Mohammed very much. We had gone through a great deal together from the negotiations in my residence in 1997 to the endless upheavals since then. He had served in Sierra Leone since 1991, so his knowledge of the situation was second to none. I much valued his wise, realistic, but usually pessimistic advice. Although his influence on President Kabbah and the government was overshadowed by the Nigerian military officers serving in Sierra Leone, especially Maxwell Khobe, he was much liked by the people and in appreciation before he left he was appointed an honorary paramount chief. Celia and I dressed up in our chiefly robes one Saturday morning to attend the colourful ceremony in front of the law courts.

The international bickering over Ecomog and the UN was exploited by Sankoh, who switched his allegiances from one day to the next and it did nothing to calm the fears of the Sierra Leone people. Despite the shortcomings of Ecomog they had faith in them as opposed to the UN troops, who displayed a marked reluctance to keep the rebels in their place. This was further fuelled when Bockarie impounded a UN helicopter and detained some UN personnel in Kailahun. This led to Sankoh being pilloried both internally and on the international stage for the behaviour of Bockarie. For a long time Bockarie had been testing Sankoh's leadership, and for the latter this latest incident was the last straw. He despatched some loyal RUF fighters to Kailahun to eliminate Bockarie. Bockarie got wind of this and fled to Monrovia to seek sanctuary with Charles Taylor. Bockarie's departure was greeted enthusiastically by the Sierra Leone people. To them he personified the evil of the RUF and removing him from the scene would be a positive step forward. Many Sierra Leoneans would ideally have hoped that his removal could have been permanent.

And so we headed towards the end of the year and the dawn of a new millennium. In that there was no major fighting taking place, the peace appeared to be holding. The UN were deploying more troops and there was some disarmament taking place, albeit too slowly; Ecomog was withdrawing, but hopefully not too quickly. The Sierra Leone government remained weak and ineffective, but was still there. A third of the population remained displaced. Britain's standing in the country was as high as ever and some of the DFID-funded projects were making a positive impact.

I attempted to reflect this cautious optimism in a song that I composed for the choir of the Milton Margai School for the Blind to help raise funds for the school:

> *My West African Home*
> *No more guns, no more killing,*
> *No more crying and fear of living.*
> *No more hunger, no more pain,*
> *No more hiding in the rain.*
> *Peace and democracy,*
> *That is what we want to see.*
> *Here in Salone … my West African Home.*

In the face of alarmist predictions that computers would crash all around the world with the advent of the new millennium, the Foreign Office's attention was more concerned with the effects of 'Y2K' than the plight of poor Sierra Leone. There was a deluge of instructions from London of what we had to do to prepare for the potentially imminent disaster. All our embassies and high commissions around the world were told to send signals back to London at two minutes past midnight as we entered the new millennium to make sure that our communications were functioning. In response I told London that as we already lived in a country where for days we could go without electricity or water, where telephones or faxes rarely worked and e-mails did not reach, and where even the diplomatic bag service could take weeks to arrive, it seemed rather meaningless to us to get worked up about the possible effects of Y2K. In any event, I added, as this was Sierra Leone we did not expect the New Year to reach us until the end of February.

Thankfully Christmas passed peacefully. My daughter Catherine and her boyfriend had flown out for Christmas and New Year, so for once we enjoyed a family Christmas, attending Christmas services at both the Catholic and Anglican churches. To see in the millennium a group of us went down to Toke, about one and a half hours' drive along the peninsula, where we danced around the camp fire under the African night sky to see the dawn of the new millennium, before collapsing under our mosquito nets on the beach.

Welcome to the new century. What would it bring for poor Sierra Leone?

Chapter Twelve

Farewell Sierra Leone – 2000

Diplomatic postings overseas generally last three years. Some are longer but it is rare for them to be shorter. As I had spent so much time out of the country, I argued that I should be entitled to complete a full three-year tour in Freetown, which would mean that my tour would end towards the end of 2001. But London insisted that I should leave at the end of April. My successor had already been selected – Alan Jones, who had been serving as the Deputy High Commissioner in Tanzania. So early in the New Year I went up to Hill Station Lodge to give President Kabbah the news. He was, to quote his own words, 'shocked and horrified'. He had expected me to stay in Sierra Leone for at least another year and said that he would take the matter up with ministers in London. The opportunity for him to raise the matter came very soon with the arrival of Peter Hain, the new Minister for Africa in the Foreign Office, who was paying his first visit to Sierra Leone in the middle of January.

Peter Hain had succeeded Tony Lloyd in a reshuffle in 1999. Poor Tony Lloyd had been made to carry some of the can for Sandline. I felt much sympathy for him. He had been a sincere, well-meaning minister, who had been let down by officials in the office. Many had felt that if a ministerial head had to fall, it should have been Robin Cook's, and not one of his junior ministers – but such was political life.

Notwithstanding Tony Lloyd's departure, there was much excitement about Peter Hain's appointment. This was the man who had made his mark in Britain in the 1960s as a leading campaigner in the anti-apartheid struggle. Born in Kenya and brought up in South Africa, he made a point of saying that he was 'a son of Africa'. He had proved to be an energetic minister in the Welsh Office and his move to the Foreign Office appeared to indicate that he was going places. He was welcomed in the Foreign Office, especially by those like me dealing with Africa. Prior to his arrival in Sierra Leone, he had made an impact by describing Savimbi, the Angolan rebel leader, as a thug who had no place in Angola's future. If he felt that way about Savimbi, what would he think of Sankoh? The omens for some realistic thinking on Sierra Leone looked good.

Peter Hain flew in from Nigeria accompanied by Ann Grant, the Director for Africa, and as usual we accommodated them and Hain's Private Secretary at the residence. Again we invited President Kabbah for a quiet supper to enable the minister to get the feel of the President in a relaxed and informal setting. However, the chemistry was not as good as it had been with Clare Short. Maybe the two of them were tired, but it seemed to me that the experience of growing up as a 'son of Africa' in Kenya and South Africa was not very relevant to the situation in West Africa, where there had been far fewer white settlers. Peter Hain was not that much impressed with President Kabbah, whom he felt was more like an old style African chief than an African politician. At the end of their official meeting the next day when the two of them were alone, President Kabbah raised with Peter Hain the question of my departure. The latter said that he was aware that I had done a good job and would be missed and assured the President that I was being replaced by a good man. However, he said that he would take note of the President's comments. Kabbah took this to mean that the decision to replace me was still open to change.

A meeting had also been sought with Sankoh. I advised against going to Sankoh's home and the close protection team advised against using the High Commission office. So instead the meeting took place in one of the meeting rooms at the presidential lodge. We went to great pains to ensure that the British TV team who were accompanying the minister did not get a picture of the two men shaking hands. Sankoh was on his best behaviour, and constantly used a word that he had obviously just learned – 'marginalized'. He was 'marginalized from the peace process', he was 'marginalized from the government', his supporters were 'marginalized from the DDR programme', etc. Peter Hain sought a firm assurance from Sankoh that he was committed to peace. Sankoh gave it. Peter Hain was not impressed by Sankoh, whom he considered a bully, but he still wanted to keep alongside him. He felt that it was important to help him in order to lock him into the political process. This meant providing assistance for the establishment of the RUF as a political party.

Peter Hain was more impressed with Johnny Paul Koroma; and he had some useful meetings about the UN's role with Ambassador Adeniji and General Jetley. In a public speech at the British Council, attended by parliamentarians and civil society leaders, he outlined what Britain was doing for Sierra Leone, including military training and support for DDR. He announced a contribution of £250,000 for the Truth and Reconciliation Commission. He concluded:

I believe that Sierra Leone is now turning the corner. You can make this beautiful country a free country, a democratic country, a prosperous country, and a safe country for its people. Britain wants to help you make this vision a reality.

There would be one more British ministerial visit before our departure – Clare Short again, her second within the space of eight months, which was a clear demonstration of her personal commitment to the problems of Sierra Leone. As a double bonus, Sir Jeremy Greenstock, 'our man at the UN in New York', was also visiting at the same time. Jeremy was one of our most senior diplomats, a class act. As Britain's representative on the UN Security Council he had a key role to play in all of the UK's international relations and was closely involved in the developments in Sierra Leone. We had never met but I had followed his reports from New York with keen interest and much admired the consummate skill with which he helped steer HMG's policies through the complex and bureaucratic machinery of the UN. He, of course, would go on to feature prominently in events in Iraq before finally retiring to become Director of Ditchley Park.

Africa featured heavily in all of the UN's deliberations and Jeremy had chosen to visit some of the key African countries with which the UN was grappling, e.g. Angola, South Africa, Zaire and Zimbabwe. Sierra Leone certainly merited inclusion in the travel itinerary. He arrived one day ahead of Clare Short so Steve Crossman and Rob Symonds, our military liaison officer, were able to take him on a trip to the DDR camp in Port Loko.

When Clare Short arrived we immediately took her back up to Masiaka. I was keen to show her the changes since her last visit. For a start we were able to travel there without an armed Ecomog escort. Instead, the police, whom DFID were assisting, supplemented the security of the close protection team. Over half the population had returned and were busy rebuilding or repairing their broken homes. Unfortunately, Paramount Chief Kompa was not with us. He had gone off to Mecca on the Haj but the sub-chiefs were there and they arranged a welcoming reception. This time there were plenty of chairs for us to sit on as we gathered under an awning in the hot sun. Sitting in the audience was Sheka Mansaray. Masiaka was his home town, and in my brief remarks I made a point of praising all he had done and was doing for the peace and security of the country.

I again had invited President Kabbah to come to supper at Runnymede with Clare Short but he insisted that this time he should host a banquet in her honour, so instead we invited James Jonah, Momodou Koroma and Zainab Bangura to join us. The occasion was marked by a remarkable display by the residence staff. During the dinner while we were still eating, all four of them, Osman, John, Alimamy and Toma, dressed in their crisp white uniforms, suddenly came in from the kitchen and stood at the end of the table. Celia and I initially thought that Osman had come to apologize for forgetting to cook the vegetables for the dinner (none had appeared – oh dear!). Osman started to speak, looking directly at Clare Short, who had broken off from talking to James Jonah and turned her chair to face the staff.

'Madam Minister, there is something we wish to say to you. It is about the announcement that the High Commissioner is leaving. We are not happy about that. We need him here. Our ship is just coming to land, but we fear without him it will sink before it reaches.'

John, shaking with emotion, continued: 'We were in church last Sunday together when the priest announced our chief is going. Everyone was shocked and started crying. We do not understand why he has to go now. This is another blow for our country.'

The next to speak was Toma. 'I represent the village of Juba. The people there want me to say that they are not happy. Why can't the High Commissioner stay until the elections?'

Alimamy, as shy as ever, hung back behind the others. Clare Short asked him if he had anything he wished to add. Clutching his testicles for comfort, he said: 'Yes please, I agree with everything that has been said. We do not want our High Commissioner to leave us right now.'

It was a very emotional and dramatic moment, which took us completely by surprise. Clare Short had handled it beautifully. She was the first amongst us to immediately realize what was coming when the staff had walked in. Zainab openly cried. James Jonah and Momodou Koroma dropped their faces and wiped away a tear. Jeremy Greenstock broke the tension by clapping them. I was embarrassed but full of admiration for the guts they had displayed. It was like a messenger walking into a meeting at No. 10 Downing Street unannounced and addressing the Cabinet. No wonder Osman had forgotten to cook the vegetables! Clare Short told them that she was aware of the strong feelings about my departure. It was not her decision but she knew that I was needed back in London.

As with all her meetings, Clare Short displayed an uncanny ability to read the moment and make the appropriate response. Unlike so many other politicians, she never tried to flannel people. She always gave whoever was present an opportunity to say something. She was both a good talker and a good listener. She was not bothered with the spin, she saw the substance.

The next day she was again in good form in meeting the Sierra Leone market women's association. The meeting was arranged in one of the downtown markets. It was very colourful, full of the sights, sounds and smells of Freetown. The women were gathered in their blue, white and green outfits, surrounded by their market produce – the dried fish, onions, tomatoes and cassava leaves set out on the dry stone slabs. As we disembarked from our vehicles the women started singing and dancing. Many of them were carrying placards saying, 'Don't let Penfold Go' and 'We Want Komrabai to Stay'. A petition was handed over to Clare Short to pass on to the Prime Minister.

It always amazed me to see the energy and dynamism of the market women. These, tough, hard working, semi-literate women were the backbone of the community. As women, they were the driving force behind the grass roots economy. As mothers and daughters, they bore the brunt of the problems. Thanks to the efforts of people like Zainab Bangura, these women had grasped the fundamentals of democracy. *En masse* they were a formidable force and yet the government still tended to treat women as second-class citizens. For example, it was very difficult for women to obtain bank loans for homes and businesses. With DFID's assistance we set up a loans scheme to help the women, which was launched by Clare Short at the meeting.

Just prior to Clare Short's visit the 'new' DFID-funded ferry had arrived. This had been a long drawn-out saga. The previous ferry, which had plied its route between Freetown and Tagrin providing the lifeline between the capital and the international airport at Lungi, had gone aground in February of 1999, thanks mainly to the vessel being overloaded with Ecomog military vehicles. This had had a serious effect on both the economy and security. We had informed the President at the time that the British Government through DFID was prepared to fund an immediate temporary replacement to the tune of £1 million, the largest single gift to Sierra Leone. Finding a second-hand ferry was not easy. It was not exactly the sort of thing you see advertised in *Exchange and Mart*. DFID officials scoured the world looking for a suitable vessel. A few possibilities were located in various corners of the world, but for one reason or another they turned out to be unsuitable. When Clare Short had visited in July of 1999 she had informed President Kabbah that the new ferry would arrive shortly, but nothing had happened. Finally, a ferry was located in Greece and in November, after lengthy negotiations and some refitting, she started her journey through the Mediterranean and towards West Africa. However, she broke down *en route* and had to limp into Tenerife for further repairs. She finally arrived in Freetown in February. I had suggested that Clare Short might wish to hand her over during her visit, but the minister said she preferred that I do it. So almost a year to the day when her predecessor had gone aground, I handed over to President Kabbah the MV *Mahera*. At the handing over ceremony at the Freetown Docks, I suggested that perhaps a better name for the ferry might have been *Pretty Soon*, as this was the reply I had always given the President every time he had asked me, 'When will the ferry arrive?' Even after her arrival we continued to be plagued by running problems and it was thanks mainly to the efforts of Clive Dawson that the ferry continued to operate. Its timely arrival was to provide us with a good way to leave Sierra Leone.

Farewell visits were made to various places around the country. I accompanied the President to Pujehun, Bo and Kenema, where we witnessed the encouraging sign of large numbers of the CDF handing in their weapons under the DDR programme.

Early on in my tour I had recognized the value to Sierra Leone of the wind-up radio and had written to the inventor, Trevor Baylis, to tell him so. By ordering from Argos, we had been able to keep the costs down so that every paramount chief had received one. I had also discovered a wind-up tape recorder, less sophisticated but in some ways even more useful, which we also distributed during these visits. When handing out the clockwork radios I had already established a set patter along the following lines:

'It is to you, the chiefs, to whom the people turn for advice and information about what is going on in your country. It is therefore important that you are kept well informed, and one of the best ways to do this is through the radio. Therefore we are presenting to each chief a radio to help achieve this. But these are not ordinary radios. They do not need to be plugged into an electricity supply so that they can be used in the rural areas where there is no electricity. Nor do they need batteries, which are so expensive to buy.'

By now the chiefs and the rest of the audience would be in rapt attention as I pulled the radio out of the box. 'They get their power from the sun through this solar panel here.' There would be murmurs of approval from the assembled gathering, but also one or two nods of scepticism.

'Now some of you may be saying to yourself, now that's OK, but what about when the sun is not shining? When that's the case, you simply wind up this handle here a few times, turn the radio around and start winding, and then you flick on this switch here.' The strains of the local FM station, already carefully tuned in ahead of the demonstration, would come blasting out of the radio to howls of amazement and delight from the assembled gathering. It was a delight to see the reaction on the faces.

I followed a similar patter when handing out the wind-up tape recorders. This time the reaction was fused with the sensation of hearing the President's voice coming out of the machine while he was sitting alongside me. With these tape recorders it meant that one could hike into the remotest villages and, for the people living there, it might be the first time that they had ever heard their president. All sorts of organizations could use the machines – ministries, NGOs, civil society groups – to disseminate their messages with pre-recorded tapes on health, education, sanitation, environmental protection and human rights, and in local languages. They would be particularly useful in spreading the word about the DDR programme and peace and reconciliation.

In the outside world people communicated by e-mail or gathered their information on the Internet, CNN or through newspapers and books, but such innovations were too advanced for a country like Sierra Leone at that time, where there was no national radio, TV or press and the illiteracy rate was ninety per cent. In Sierra Leone, in order to go forward one went 'back to the future'. As in all societies, information was power and the dissemination of information a major challenge. But in Sierra Leone we did not use spin doctors. In their place we needed people to wind up the radios and tape recorders. Indeed, the role of the paramount chief's 'chief winder' became a respected position in the community.

In Bo I attended the prize-giving and annual reunion of the Old Bo Boys' Association (OBBA). Bo School was arguably Sierra Leone's premier school. It had been founded nearly a hundred years previously by the colonial administration to educate the sons of the chiefs. Its doors were now opened to a wider group of pupils but it still retained a very high standard of education. Over half the Cabinet had gone there. All members of OBBA were required to wear their school caps during the Bo School Week and on other specific occasions. Several times during my tour in Sierra Leone I would attend official meetings and see seated around the table grown – often quite elderly – men sitting with their blue and gold school caps perched on their heads. Each boy who entered Bo School was given a number, like joining the army or prison, and this number stayed with him for the rest of his life. Therefore, throughout the ceremonies in Bo, people were introduced by their school number. Pride of place was given to one very old gentleman, number forty-two, signifying that he had been one of the earliest pupils at this famous school. Sama Banya, the Foreign Minister, was number seventy-two.

My final trip up-country was with Sam Hinga Norman to Moyamba, a strategically important town halfway between Freetown and Bo. Moyamba District was where the north, south and west came together. No one tribe dominated. For example, although it was a Kamajor stronghold, it was also the home of Siaka Stevens, the former northern president. Moyamba set the pulse of the country but because of its strategic importance it had suffered a great deal in all the upheavals. The local paramount chief, a feisty lady, Chief Ellie Kobala, had been the first female Member of Parliament. She was a close friend of Sam's; they had been thrown into jail together in the 1970s.

Sam Hinga Norman was a very remarkable person. I had always felt that he was the opposite side of the same coin as Foday Sankoh. Both men had started from humble beginnings, both had become signals corporals in the army and both had felt grievances against the systems in place in their country. However, Sam Norman had taken pains to better his education and had developed a sense of decency and a strong commitment to democracy. He was also very tough. A few weeks prior to our trip to Moyamba, he was supposed to have been joining us at the residence for a dinner with one of our visitors from the UK. However, I learned the day before that he had had to go into hospital for an emergency hernia operation so I had not expected him to come. Lo and behold, the next evening he duly appeared at the residence looking remarkably fit and well. He had driven all the way from the hospital at Moyamba, where he had been operated on. It had taken me six weeks to get over my hernia operation. For Sam Norman it took six hours – a remarkable man and one on whom the future of Sierra Leone much depended.

It was a great pity that President Kabbah had never fully trusted Sam Norman. There were people around Kabbah who were envious of Norman's standing in the country, especially within the Kamajors, and they would tell Kabbah that Norman was after power for himself. Undoubtedly during the time of Kabbah's exile and return from Conakry, Norman, with the support of the CDF, was the most powerful man in the country and if he had wanted to seize power, he could have. This was a view shared by many, including David Richards. In his testimony before the Sierra Leone Special Court, in answer to a question about overthrowing the government, he said: 'In my professional judgement both in 1999 and 2000, if that [i.e. the overthrow of the government] is what they wanted to do, they could very easily have done so.'

But Sam Norman didn't. He was truly committed to the democratic process and thereby loyal to President Kabbah. During my time in Conakry several of Kabbah's close supporters approached me with a plan to remove Kabbah because they felt that he was not doing enough to get back to Freetown. At no time did Sam Norman ever suggest such a course of action.

Although Sam was from Mongeri, a village close to Bo, he clearly had a special affection for Moyamba and so, out of my respect for him, I agreed to accompany him on the quick visit to Moyamba. He and I set off with Emmanuel and the close protection team in the Land Rovers. The usual way to get to Moyamba was via Masiaka and Mile 91. But this route was still subject to attack from the rebels, so we went the back way via Songo and the Mabang Bridge. This was the route that the Kamajors had fought their way along to open up the road to Bo and Kenema. The signs of the heavy fighting and destruction were in evidence all the way. The bridge itself over the Kandiga River was the second longest bridge in Sierra Leone. The rebels had destroyed it by setting fire to the wooden planking. However, the iron girder structure was still in place and the local people had chopped down whole trees and used them to replace the planking, thus permitting vehicles to cross. We all got out of our vehicles and walked across while the vehicles gingerly drove over the tree trunks – not something to attempt in the dark. Sam gave a pep talk to the villagers living either side of the bridge telling them of the importance of keeping the bridge open until such time as it was properly repaired – something that a team of British Royal Engineers could have done in their sleep.

The journey to Moyamba took just under two hours and the people were out in force to greet us. Visits by dignitaries from Freetown were very rare. A large assembly was gathered in the community centre – chiefs, elders, religious leaders, schoolchildren, market women and Kamajors. As elsewhere the Kamajors were a force unto themselves. Throughout the proceedings, dressed in their colourful patchwork outfits with their dangling magic charms and mirrors, they would get up and start dancing and singing. No one told them to sit down and shut up. You didn't quarrel with the Kamajors. After all, they were the ones who had kept the rebels at bay.

I told the assembled gathering that sadly there were only a few days remaining before I would leave Sierra Leone, but they had used two powerful pieces of magic to persuade me to visit Moyamba – Paramount Chief Ellie and Chief Norman. It was my respect for these two important people that had brought me, and I was glad that I had. I encouraged them in their pursuit of peace and democracy in the rebuilding of their country. I handed over some block-making machines and bags of cement and presented some exercise books to the local school. I performed a magic trick with the exercise books, which brought howls of astonishment from all those present.

Sam Norman gave an address, which included the remarks that he had made previously in Bo when I had been crowned Paramount Chief Ndiamu, and then at the end he said that the Kamajors had one more function to perform. I was asked to stand up. A white headband was tied around my head and then a charm wrapped up in white muslin was hung around my neck. To loud chants and dancing I was proclaimed 'Grand Chief Kamajor' – yet another totally unexpected honour. I later suggested to the close protection team that now that I was 'bullet proof', perhaps I no longer required their services.

Back in Freetown more honours were to come. Again I was carried in a hammock through the streets of Freetown and in a colourful ceremony in the Victoria Park all the paramount chiefs gathered to appoint me a 'warrior chief'. I was presented with a replica of Bai Bureh's sword, which had been used in his struggle against the colonial administration.

President Kabbah had written to Robin Cook seeking the British Government's agreement to give me an award from the Sierra Leone government. Robin Cook had written back turning down the request, saying that it was not appropriate to give outgoing ambassadors or High Commissioners awards. (This was rather strange given that the British Government had often presented awards to outgoing diplomats in London. For example, Ray Seitz, the recent US Ambassador, had been given an honorary knighthood, and at the time that Robin Cook was writing to President Kabbah it was being announced that Chief Anyaoku, the outgoing Commonwealth Secretary General in London, was receiving a similar award.)

When the Freetown City Council announced that they intended to make me a Freeman of the City, I had expected the Foreign Office to similarly refuse their permission but to my surprise they said that they had no objection, although they pointed out that if I was given a medal, I could only wear it during the ceremony and at no other time in the future. In fact, I received a key. The ceremony took place on a Saturday morning. It was a very grand affair. The Chairman of the City Council, Mr Henry Nathaniel Ferguson, the equivalent of the mayor, presided over the ceremony in cocked hat and resplendent in his vivid red robes lined with ermine. The Town Clerk, bedecked in his wig and black robes, read out the citation proclaiming me an Honorary Freeman of Freetown to the large assembly, which included the Vice President, ministers, paramount chiefs and members of the diplomatic corps. To one side was the police band, with my old friend Sub-Inspector Mambu playing his cornet.

There were to be three more important visitors from the UK before our departure – Brigadier David Richards, Dr Garth Glentworth and Dr Lillian Wong. Each one of them in their different ways was a special friend to us and to Sierra Leone, and Celia and I were delighted that they would be our last houseguests at Runnymede. David Richards was coming out on a short visit to assess aspects of our proposed military training programme. He had not been back to Sierra Leone since the dramatic days of January and February of the previous year. Since then he had been heavily engaged in East Timor. Garth was paying something like his tenth visit on behalf of DFID. As Governance Institutions Adviser he was overseeing many of the key DFID projects such as the paramount chiefs, the public service, the law reform, the media and the forthcoming elections. I had known this softly-spoken, delightful Scot over several years. A man of immense experience in Africa, Garth could always be relied upon to bring out some food for the parrots, a fact which of course completely won over Celia. I had known Lillian for even longer, going back to my time in Ethiopia, but this was her first visit to Sierra Leone. Working in the Research Department she was the FCO's memory on Africa. There was no one in the Foreign Office with more experience and knowledge of Africa and I had been trying to get her to visit Sierra Leone ever since I had arrived. All three visitors were able to share in some of the various farewells.

David Richard's visit was to coincide with a sad event that was to cast a shadow over my final days and, more especially, to affect the dramatic events that were to follow our departure. The first person to host one of the several farewell receptions for us in Freetown was Kan Azad, the Honorary Consul for India. This quietly-spoken, charming, local businessman had become one of my closest friends. At the reception that he hosted at one of the local restaurants, word came through that General Khobe, the Chief of Defence Staff, had been taken ill and rushed to the Choithram Memorial Hospital, the private hospital that had been established thanks to the efforts of Kan Azad. Together with David Richards, Celia and I had returned from the reception to the residence and we had already prepared for bed when I was told by the close protection team member on duty that there were some Nigerian military officers at the gate wishing to see me urgently. By now it was nearly midnight and one was always somewhat cautious when people in uniform appeared at the gates so late. One of them was Commander Medani, Khobe's ADC. I invited him and his fellow officer into my study, where I received them in my dressing gown. The other officer turned out to be the Nigerian military doctor attached to Ecomog. The doctor said that General Khobe was very ill; indeed, they thought he was dying.

They had come straight from the hospital, where the President, Vice President, Ambassador Adeniji, General Jetley and the Nigerian High Commissioner were all gathered around Khobe's bedside.

There were neither the drugs nor the facilities to deal with Khobe in Sierra Leone, so my assistance was sought to get him out of the country. The doctor thought that the best thing to do would be to fly him to Britain. With assistance from the FCO and MOD duty officers I contacted an air ambulance firm in the UK and started to make the arrangements for a plane to come in and pick up Khobe. I had to emphasize that the British Government could not be responsible for any of the costs involved but short of that I told Medani and the doctor that I would do everything in my power to help. Although we were not on intimate terms, I had much respect for Khobe and Sierra Leone could ill afford to be without the services of this brave officer, particularly at that time. They went back up to the hospital to pursue the arrangements that we had set in train.

David Richards witnessed these events. He found it surprising that with all the resources of the Sierra Leone government, the United Nations and the Nigerian government to hand, they had turned to us for help – a far cry from the frosty days of Anglo/Nigerian relations. Medani himself had been one of the officers in Defence Headquarters who had been giving so many problems to our UK team of advisers in the Ministry of Defence. They considered him to be anti-British. It was a further example of how relationships in Sierra Leone transcended national interests.

Khobe's condition continued to deteriorate and by morning we were told that he was too ill to travel. The UK air ambulance was stood down. Instead the Nigerian government sent in a plane with some medicines on board the following day. With these drugs his condition stabilized and he was able to be flown back to Nigeria. This was a more sensible solution than flying him to the UK.

Back in Nigeria, Khobe's condition continued to stabilize but it was obvious that he was going to be out of commission for some time. This was very worrying. News of Khobe's departure raised the tension in Freetown. To Sierra Leoneans Khobe was the only soldier capable of standing up to the rebels. President Kabbah appointed one of the senior Sierra Leone officers, Colonel Tommy Carew, to act as Chief of Defence Staff in Khobe's absence. Carew was a nice man whom I had got to know in Conakry. He had been one of the first Sierra Leone officers to remain loyal to Kabbah when the AFRC had taken over. But he had little operational experience and hardly inspired confidence among the Sierra Leone public. In addition Carew had presided over the military courts martial that had tried the AFRC junta officers for treason. This was hardly likely to be well received by Sankoh and the rebels.

I telephoned the head of the African Department and made three suggestions to help calm the fears and ease the tension caused by Khobe's removal and

Carew's temporary appointment. Firstly, that we move across Colonel Mike Dent into the Defence Headquarters from the Sierra Leone Ministry of Defence, where he was working on a UK-funded reorganization project. Secondly, we advance the arrival of Brigadier Hughes, the UK officer coming out to head the UK military assistance team and act as a 'shadow' to the CDS, and thirdly, we ask David Richards to stay on for a few days to help calm fears and give confidence and provide military advice to President Kabbah. David's reputation was already high in Sierra Leone and he enjoyed the confidence of the President. The head of the African Department turned down all three suggestions on the spot without giving any of them any real thought. David reluctantly went on his way but fortunately the Ministry of Defence back in London told Mike Dent to move across to Defence HQ and arranged to advance Brigadier Hughes' arrival.

A short time later, despite the apparent stabilization in Khobe's condition, word came through that he had died in a Lagos hospital. The President declared seven days of national mourning. News of Khobe's death sent a shockwave around the country. I sent a report to London eulogising Maxwell Khobe and his contribution to Sierra Leone's struggle for peace and democracy, and warned of the heightened tension in the country. My warnings were somewhat dismissed. Although the Foreign Office recognized the potential dangers over a precipitable withdrawal of the Ecomog forces before the full deployment of the UN, they found it difficult to accept that individual personalities could have such an impact upon the situation.

We thus prepared for our departure against the backcloth of the heightened tension in the country. The UNAMSIL deployment was still going slowly, as was the disarmament programme. Sankoh continued to prevaricate. Many people feared a security vacuum would be created between Ecomog's withdrawal and UNAMSIL's full deployment, which would be exploited by the rebels. Khobe's death and my departure contributed to these fears. The Sierra Leone people were nervous but felt powerless to do anything themselves.

During the final week a special session of the Sierra Leone Parliament was convened, to which I was invited. I was led into the body of the chamber behind Hon Speaker Justice Kutiba and the Sergeant at Arms carrying the mace and was seated below the Speaker's dais. To one side of the Speaker sat Celia and up in the gallery were members of the diplomatic corps and other friends. The Leader of the Opposition, the Hon Raymond Kamara, rose to propose a motion lauding my efforts to promote and sustain democracy in Sierra Leone. Other Honorary Members spoke in support of the motion. Ramadan Dumbuya, leader of one of the minority parties, spoke of my efforts to teach the people of Sierra Leone what democracy meant. He quoted from my speeches on how to make 'democracy soup'. The acting Leader of the House wound up the debate and the motion was passed. As I left the chamber the strains of my song rang out over the Tannoy system – *No more guns, no more killing.... Peace and Democracy, that is what we want to see, here in Salone.*

I reflected that I had now been summoned twice to appear before a parliament. In Britain it was to answer charges against me of breaking UN sanctions. Here in Sierra Leone it was to be lauded for my efforts to bring peace and democracy to a poor African country. What a topsy-turvy world!

During the final week I had effectively left the running of the mission in the hands of Steve Crossman but I continued to look in each day to check the telegrams and speak to Steve and the other members of staff. I completed my valedictory despatch to the Secretary of State, which I entitled (with apologies to Graham Greene) 'Sierra Leone: The Heart of the Matter – The Struggle for Democracy'. In it I reviewed the events of the previous three years. I noted how of little relevance Sandline had been to events in Sierra Leone, although it had sadly dominated HMG's actions towards the country for so long.

Sadly, the practice of outgoing ambassadors and High Commissioners sending valedictory despatches was brought to an end by the Foreign Office under Margaret Beckett in 2006. Too many were being leaked to the press and embarrassing the government but Matthew Parris was later able to make a BBC radio series and write a book entitled *Parting Shots* by making use of the Freedom of Information Act to obtain copies of the more colourful despatches.

I also issued a farewell message to the people of Sierra Leone:

The past three years have been very eventful. I have much admired the fortitude and resilience shown by the Sierra Leone people, and through adversity, my wife and I have developed so many close friends among you. We will leave with many memories, both happy and sad. To have shared in your struggle for peace and democracy will forever remain in our hearts and minds. Celia and I wish each and every one of you the peace and happiness you have suffered so much for. You will remain in our thoughts and prayers, until we meet again.

Our last reception at the residence had been The Queen's Birthday Party, which we had held just days previously. This had provided an opportunity to say farewell to the staff in a social setting but there was one final ceremony to perform in the office. I had suggested that we should have one last parade of the local guard force. These were our 'unsung heroes'. It was they who, through all weathers, day and night, turned up for work to protect our offices and personnel. On many an occasion their lives had been threatened during the dark days of the junta and the events of January 1999. If it had not been for them, under the direction of Solomon, we would not have had our offices and homes still standing. It would have been so easy for them to have just abandoned their posts but they did not. I wanted to show that their loyalty had not gone unnoticed. With the assistance of the close protection team I arranged for individual certificates of service to be printed. On the final Friday in front of the steps of the High Commission offices the guards mounted a parade, and each one proudly stepped forward and was presented with his or her certificate. The local television was on hand to film the ceremony.

My very last duty was to say farewell to President Kabbah. I picked Celia up from the residence and together we drove up to Hill Station Lodge. The TV cameras were on hand to record the meeting, which was somewhat more stiff and formal compared to the endless meetings we had had together. For the benefit of the cameras the President thanked me for all that I had done for his country and the people of Sierra Leone, and for himself personally. He said that he hoped it would not be too long before I returned and that he would even donate a piece of his land in Freetown on which I could build a retirement home (an offer soon forgotten). As a parting gift I presented him with a book of pictures painted by members of the Association of Mouth and Foot Painting Artists in Britain. I suggested that this was a reminder that even in adversity when people lose their limbs there is still hope, and that they can still perform useful and talented lives.

The next morning, after Zainab Bangura had joined us for breakfast, we said our fond farewells to Osman and the rest of the residence staff and drove through the gates for the last time. To my surprise forty or more cars were waiting for us outside. As we drove in a cavalcade to the ferry terminal, people lined the route, which had been announced over Radio 98.1. They waved and we waved back. At the ferry there were hundreds more waiting to say goodbye, including Chief Soluku, head of the Council of Chiefs. He said, 'You arrived by car and you are leaving by ferry. That shows that you are truly a man of the people.'

Clutching Zainab's and Mammy Noah's hands, Celia was followed to the ferry by all the market women singing and dancing. I danced too, going backwards down the slope. Symbolically I did not want to turn my back on Sierra Leone. *My West African Home* was playing over the ferry's Tannoy system.

The ferry pulled away and Celia and I held one another as we looked down on the crowds waving from the ferry terminal. We gazed at the green hills overlooking Freetown. The sun was shining and the water was sparkling. Paddy Warren used to say that it was this sight, which he had seen thirty years previously when he had first arrived, that made him decide to stay and make Sierra Leone his home. I could see why. It was an inspiring sight, one to remember forever.

Farewell Sierra Leone.

Chapter Thirteen

British Forces and Blood Diamonds

Three days after we had left Sierra Leone the RUF launched attacks on the UN peacekeeping forces in the northern towns of Makeni and Magburaka. Four Kenyan soldiers were killed and several others injured. Dozens of UN personnel were held hostage, including three British and one New Zealand officers. They managed to escape and one of the officers, Major Phil Ashby, wrote about his exploits in his book *Unscathed – Escape from Sierra Leone*. The DDR camps in these towns, set up and funded by Britain, were completely vandalized and destroyed. A battalion of Zambian troops, which had been arriving at Lungi Airport to join UNAMSIL the day that we had left, was stopped in two separate incidents by young RUF rebels and relieved of all their weapons and transport, including a number of armoured personnel carriers (APCs). In Kailahun, in the east, RUF rebels surrounded the Indian peacekeepers stationed there, which included another British officer, Major Andy Harrison. It would be several months before his release was secured.

From his house in Freetown Foday Sankoh denied that his men were responsible for launching the attacks or that they were holding UN hostages. Hundreds of Sierra Leoneans marched on Sankoh's house to protest at the RUF actions. The RUF guarding Sankoh opened fire on the crowds, while the UN forces guarding the house withdrew. The crowds ransacked the house destroying or looting all the furniture provided by the British Government. In the mayhem Sankoh escaped and went into hiding.

From our hotel in Tunisia, where we were spending some leave *en route* back to the UK, we tried to follow events on the television and in the Tunisian newspapers. It was very worrying and frustrating. We telephoned several friends in Freetown who were clearly nervous about the developments. Some expressed the view that our departure, linked with the untimely death of Maxwell Khobe and set against the vacuum between the Ecomog withdrawal and the UNAMSIL deployment, had precipitated the attacks by the RUF – a fact allegedly confirmed later by Sankoh to some of his followers. I telephoned

President Kabbah. He tried to play down the seriousness of the situation saying that it was just 'a personality clash' between Sankoh and General Jetley, the UNAMSIL commander.

The latter had been vilified for suggesting in a leaked document that some of the Nigerian soldiers were engaged in illicit diamond mining in connivance with Sankoh. The Nigerians demanded Jetley's removal and the UN later acquiesced, which led to the Indian government withdrawing its contribution to the UNAMSIL force. None of this helped the increasing friction between Ecomog and the UN.

Five days after our departure, my successor, Alan Jones, arrived with his wife Daphne and presented his credentials. The next day, before Alan had even unpacked, Robin Cook ordered the evacuation of the British community. One thousand British Paratroopers under the command of David Richards were flown out to assist the evacuation, which went by the name of Operation Palliser.

Operation Palliser

The objectives of Operation Palliser were to secure Lungi Airport and to assist UNAMSIL in defending parts of Freetown, including the Mammy Yoko Hotel and the British High Commission offices and residence. Twenty-nine RAF Hercules and four Tristar aircraft were deployed along with HMS *Ocean* and her ten helicopters. HMS *Ocean* was later joined by the aircraft carrier HMS *Illustrious*, with her thirteen Harrier jets and five helicopters, and five more Royal Navy ships. It was one of the largest British naval flotillas deployed since the liberation of the Falklands back in 1982.

In all, 353 people were evacuated, mostly British and European nationals. The Defence Secretary, Geoff Hoon, informed the House of Commons that the cost of Operation Palliser had been some £8 million. It was interesting to reflect that three years previously we had effected the evacuation of ten times this number of evacuees without the assistance of British troops and at far less cost.

It was extremely fortunate that Operation Palliser was under the command of an officer of the calibre of David Richards, with his knowledge of the situation and his experience and commitment. David Richards knew that with the resources available he could do more than just assist an evacuation. As he later told the Sierra Leone Special Court, he realized that he could actively stabilize the situation and, after ten uneasy days, he obtained London's permission to do so. He moved the British troops into key positions to the east of Freetown and to the east of Lungi Airport and conducted an offensive operation against the rebels, assisted by Ecomog, the CDF and those elements of the Sierra Leone army, who, at the urging of Johnny Paul Koroma, had declared their loyalty to the government. Just co-ordinating such a disparate group of forces entailed using both immense military and diplomatic skills.

David Richards' actions through Operation Palliser eased the tensions in the country and the spirits of the Sierra Leone people were further lifted when Sankoh was captured, beaten up and put into detention.

By mid-June, when David Richards had returned to the UK, he and the British forces had bought enough time for the UN to start its operation again effectively. The UN increased the size of its forces to over 16,000, including a contingent of Jordanian troops – the largest deployment of a UN peacekeeping force in the world. UNAMSIL launched Operation Thunderbolt to clear the road leading to Lungi and retook Masiaka. Elements of the rebel Sierra Leone soldiers, the West Side Boys, took to the Occra Hills.

Robin Cook visited Sierra Leone, staying on board HMS *Ocean* alongside a contingent of Royal Marines who had replaced the Paras. It was almost laughable that he had waited until I had left before paying his first visit to the country with which he had become so involved. Robin Cook's visit was quickly followed by visits by Geoff Hoon and John Prescott, the Deputy Prime Minister.

Operation Barras

At the end of August a group of eleven soldiers from the Royal Irish Regiment and one Sierra Leone army soldier had gone into the Occra Hills to disarm the group of renegade Sierra Leone soldiers hiding there. Instead, the West Side Boys disarmed the British soldiers, tortured them and held them hostage. Alarm bells were rung back in London. Attempts were made to negotiate but although five of the hostages were released in exchange for a satellite phone and medical supplies, the West Side Boys, flattered by the international attention they were receiving, continued to increase their unrealistic demands and threatened to kill the remaining hostages. The decision was made to secure their release by force. Operation Barras was launched.

The hostages were being held in a small village, Gberi Bana, on the north side of the Rokel Creek. Surrounded by swamp and jungle, the rebel camp was well fortified by the rebel group under the command of the 22-year-old 'Brigadier' Kallay and numbered around 200, well armed and 'well high' on drugs.

On 10 September, in a well prepared and professionally executed operation, a team of SAS, backed by a contingent from the 1st Battalion of the Parachute Regiment and RAF Lynx Attack and Chinook helicopters, attacked the rebel force, which fought back fiercely. Sadly, one member of the SAS was killed in the action. At least twenty-five, probably more, of the West Side Boys were killed.

Fred Marafono, now under contract to the Sierra Leone government as part of the government's Air Wing, comprising two Mi-24 helicopters flown by Juba and another South African pilot, Neall Ellis, was on hand to help the members of his former regiment.

All the hostages were released safely in what the Ministry of Defence described as 'a very challenging operation ... of great complexity'. Tony Blair said, 'I cannot pay high enough tribute to the skill, the professionalism and the courage of the armed forces involved.' Rightly so. A book written by William Fowler, entitled *Operation Barras, the SAS Rescue Mission: Sierra Leone 2000*, would chronicle all the events.

Blood Diamonds

Much was also happening on the international front. At the beginning of July the UN Security Council adopted Resolution 1306, which imposed an embargo on the sale of rough Sierra Leone diamonds. Several observers had argued that the Sierra Leone rebel war was solely a fight for control of the diamond wealth of Sierra Leone. This was a gross misrepresentation and basically wrong. However, there was no doubt that diamonds had helped fuel and prolong the conflict. The RUF had been able to purchase its arms and ammunition with the diamonds, which had attracted a nefarious group of arms dealers and shady businessmen from around the world. Charles Taylor, in particular, had benefitted from the barter of Sierra Leone diamonds in exchange for military equipment and personnel, and for his political support. Much later he would be accused of giving the supermodel Naomi Campbell some diamonds ('dirty-looking stones') when they met in South Africa.

The British-sponsored UN resolution made it illegal to buy Sierra Leone diamonds unless they were accompanied by a certificate of origin issued by the government. This became known as the 'Kimberley Process' and would be expanded to cover other countries in Africa such as Angola and Zimbabwe. The international diamond industry, which for so long had turned a blind eye to 'conflict diamonds', was forced to adhere to the internationally regulated practice. President Kabbah was keen to use the diamond wealth to boost the development of the country and, with the tacit approval of the British Government, he had meetings with private security companies to talk about protecting the diamond mining areas once they had been retaken from the rebels.

The enforcement of the ban on 'conflict diamonds' played a significant role in ending the eleven-year rebel war. However, it would take a further show of force from the British military to secure the final end to the fighting. David Richards and his team returned to Sierra Leone in the autumn of 2000, forcing the RUF to agree to a ceasefire in late October. He would later say: 'What transpired ... was a fascinating example of modern-day intervention operations in an uncertain environment. It started as a NEO (Non-combatant Evacuation Order) but developed into something that has characteristics between counter-insurgency and small-scale war-fighting operations.'

Elsewhere on the international stage, as had happened the previous year with Kosovo, events in Yugoslavia overshadowed events in Sierra Leone as Milosevic was overthrown by his people.

Throughout all these events I sat on the river bank at Abingdon and contemplated my future. At no time were my views or experience sought by the Foreign Office. In the absence of any prospect of a further overseas posting, I was seconded for a year to DFID, at Clare Short's request, as a conflict adviser.

Chapter Fourteen

Di Wor Don Don – 2001

The year 2001 began with yet another capital of a West African country having added its name to the list of Sierra Leone peace plans. The Abuja ceasefire had been signed. This time Sankoh had been kept out of the picture. President Kabbah, under pressure from the international community and on the advice of Ambassador Adeniji, appointed Issa Sesay as 'interim leader' of the RUF in order to help push through the disarmament process. Sesay, in his twenties and one of the RUF's more intelligent commanders, was fearful of taking on this role in case other RUF commanders considered him a traitor to the RUF cause and killed him. He was assured by Kabbah and Adeniji that his efforts would not go unrewarded if the disarmament went ahead.

UNAMSIL remained in the country, at the time the largest UN operation in the world, but it often appeared powerless and it was only the British troop presence that provided the muscle and a degree of security that gave confidence to the people. The British military training programme continued.

With Sankoh out of the way and the British military presence dampening the enthusiasm of the rebels to recommence fighting, there remained one final piece of the jigsaw puzzle to finally achieve an end to the hostilities – the removal of Charles Taylor in Liberia. The RUF had continued to mine the diamonds that had ensured the continued support of Taylor but under intense pressure from the regional and international community, including the imposition of the sanctions against blood diamonds, and under threat from Liberian opposition forces (LURD), Taylor became increasingly isolated. His support for the RUF dissipated and, with the co-operation of Issa Sesay, the disarmament of the RUF was completed.

By the beginning of 2002 I had finally yielded to the pressures to take early retirement. In January, whilst attending a parliamentarian's conference on democracy in Ghana as a consultant for DFID, I decided to pay a visit to Sierra Leone, the first since the completion of my tour as High Commissioner. The BBC chose to send a TV team, comprising Isobel Eaton and Becky Milligan, to film my return for a *Newsnight* documentary.

Using the powers under the State of Emergency Act, President Kabbah had deferred the elections due in February 2001 until the following year. He invited us to join him on a trip to the east of the country, including Kailahun and Kono, two places that I had never been able to visit during my tour because of the fighting. The scale of the destruction in the east was enormous. We visited Mobi, Kabbah's mother's home town where he had spent his early years. The family home was a burnt-out shell and several of Kabbah's relatives had been murdered. The trip was clearly part of the campaign for the forthcoming elections and Kabbah sought assurances that he should stand again. He was facing a problem over whom to choose as his running mate from a number of candidates. I suggested that he lock them all in one room and not let them out until they had agreed amongst themselves who should be the candidate.

The visit, which lasted three weeks, was very emotional, with the added poignancy of attending the funeral of Dr Mike Downham, who had passed away in Bo just prior to my arrival. I met up with so many friends and colleagues, though my successor, Alan Jones, was 'too busy' to see me. Tony Blair had flown out on a brief visit. He remained at Lungi, where he was made a paramount chief of one of the local villages. I was kept away, much to the embarrassment of my fellow paramount chiefs.

After the Blair visit President Kabbah finally declared '*di wor don don*' – the war is over – to much relief and rejoicing. Praise was heaped upon Britain for the role she had played and Sierra Leone was seen as one of Tony Blair's foreign policy successes.

The US Government, having been criticized in the US press for its role in Sierra Leone, demanded that Sankoh should be put on trial for war crimes, barely a couple of years after it had been demanding that Sankoh be made Vice President. A United Nations administered but judicially independent War Crimes Court was established in Freetown at vast expense. The Sierra Leone Special Court, a hybrid of Sierra Leone and international law, tore up the amnesties provided for in all of the various Sierra Leone peace treaties and its American military Chief Prosecutor, David Crane, proceeded to issue indictments against Foday Sankoh, plus Sam Bockarie, Morris Kallon and Issa Sesay of the RUF. So much for the assurances given to Sesay if he helped with the disarmament process. Ambassador Adeniji felt especially aggrieved. Bockarie did not face the Court. He was killed fighting in Liberia, reputedly on the orders of Charles Taylor. Another RUF commander, Augustine Gbao, was later indicted.

Along with the Sierra Leone Special Court, a Truth and Reconciliation Commission was established – the first time that a country coming out of conflict was subjected to both a war crimes court and a TRC. With a budget of just $6.5 million, as opposed to the SLSC's budget in excess of $250 million, the TRC produced a 5,000-page report that detailed the scale of the atrocities throughout the country. It concluded that the RUF had been responsible for over sixty per cent of the atrocities, the AFRC and SLA thirty per cent and the CDF six per cent. It also noted that Ecomog had been responsible for one per cent though they were exempted from being charged with war crimes by the Special Court. The TRC report was critical of the SLSC, noting that the relationship between the two bodies 'could have been immeasurably stronger had the two institutions shared something of a common vision of the basic goals of post-conflict transitional justice.'

By the time that the TRC report was published, the Special Court's purpose-built courtroom and detention centre had been completed in the centre of Freetown and the trials started. However, Sankoh was no longer there. He had died in detention on 30 July 2003 and his indictment, along with Bockarie's, was withdrawn. Following the deaths of Sankoh and Bockarie, the two persons who were indisputably the most responsible for the worst of the atrocities, there were calls for the Special Court to be disbanded, but they were ignored.

Pursuing his duties with messianic fervour, Crane had not stopped at indicting just members of the RUF. Notwithstanding the positive role Johnny Paul Koroma had played in the peace and disarmament process, he was indicted for war crimes, but he managed to flee the country, never to be seen again. It was suspected that he died in the Ivory Coast. Other ex-AFRC/SLA members were indicted – Alex Brima, Bazzy Kamara and Santigie Koroma.

The biggest shock had come when Crane announced the indictments of Sam Hinga Norman and two other members of the CDF, Moinina Fofana and Allieu Kondewa. Norman, serving as Kabbah's Minister for Internal Affairs at the time, was unceremoniously dragged out of his office in handcuffs by the police acting on behalf of the court, bundled into the back of a truck and driven away. This angered many, including myself, who regarded Norman as one of the heroes who, with the CDF, had helped restore peace and democracy to Sierra Leone.

Norman and the other indictees had been incarcerated originally in an old slave dungeon in Bonthe, miles away from the capital and out of touch with their families and lawyers until the new courthouse and detention centre were built in the centre of Freetown. I visited Norman in the depressing conditions in Bonthe and kept in close touch with him by telephone from the UK. I would continue to visit him regularly in Freetown during my frequent visits to Sierra Leone in my retirement.

I had questioned Crane why he had felt it necessary to indict Norman and members of the CDF – these were the 'good guys', the ones who had fought bravely for the restoration of the legitimate government. Crane told me that he felt that he had to be seen to be 'even-handed'. I found his reasoning bizarre. It was rather like a referee, having red-carded a footballer for a brutal tackle, then sending off a member of the opposing team to keep the sides even. I did not necessarily dispute that some members of the CDF may have committed savage acts when defending their homes and families against the rebels. When a bunch of thugs and killers came to your village and started killing your family, chopping off arms and legs and burning down your homes, waving your finger at them and saying that it was against human rights was unlikely to have much effect. But if there were to be indictments against the CDF, then why stop at Norman? The chain of command in the CDF, such as it was, went all the way up to the President.

David Crane had claimed that no one was above the law and that it was equal justice for all. But, in addition to members of Ecomog being exempted, it is worth noting that before the SLSC was set up in Sierra Leone, the US Government had concluded a bilateral agreement with the Sierra Leone government that prevented any US national being brought before the court – shades of *Animal Farm*, where all are equal but some are more equal than others.

In February 2006 I flew out to Freetown to testify before the court on behalf of Norman, along with General David Richards and former Vice President Joe Demby. I was criticized by the judges of the Court for describing Norman as 'a national hero'. David Richards and Joe Demby also defended Norman and I admired them both for doing so. Demby was no longer Vice President; he had been ditched by President Kabbah at the previous election in favour of Solomon Berewa. David Richards' voluntary appearance was perhaps more telling as he was still a senior serving officer in the British Army. President Kabbah, who claimed that he had been unaware that Norman would be indicted, refused to testify in defence of his former minister.

The trials dragged on for several years eating up vast millions of dollars. Just as the CDF trial had reached its conclusion, Sam Norman died in peculiar circumstances following a routine medical operation in Senegal whilst still in detention in February 2007. Thousands took part in his funeral services in Freetown and Bo, which the Norman family asked me to arrange with Joe Demby.

All the other indictees were found guilty of war crimes and sent to serve their long sentences in Rwanda.

The highest profile indictee was Charles Taylor. He had finally been persuaded to step down by the Nigerians and Ghanaians. His indictment was unveiled in June 2003 when Taylor was in Accra during the delicate negotiations to end the renewed fighting in Liberia. It nearly derailed the whole peace process there. Clearly embarrassed by the action of the court's Chief Prosecutor in Freetown, the Ghanaians ignored the indictment and handed Taylor over to President Obasanjo in Nigeria as part of the deal to end the fighting. Obasanjo came under intense pressure, especially from the Americans, to hand Taylor over to the court. Obasanjo refused, announcing that he would only hand Taylor over to an elected government in Liberia. Elections duly took place in Liberia in October 2005 and Ellen Johnson-Sirleaf was elected President, Africa's first elected female president. Taylor was flown to Monrovia and immediately on to Freetown into the custody of the court. Taylor's trial was transferred to the premises of the International Criminal Court in The Hague for security reasons. At the time of writing this book, he is awaiting the results of his trial. If he is found guilty the British Government has agreed that he can serve his sentence in a British prison.

Several questions remain over the legacy of the Sierra Leone Special Court. Supporters of the court, citing the example of Charles Taylor's indictment, say that it demonstrates that no one can get away with such barbarous acts with impunity, not even heads of state. However, Sam Norman's indictment and subsequent death is a stain on the Special Court's legacy. Who else will come forward to fight for the cause of peace and democracy in the future if they face the threat of being treated as a war criminal?

Resolving conflicts diplomatically elsewhere has become more difficult as a result of the Sierra Leone Special Court's antics. When resolving conflicts it is usually necessary to persuade both sides of the conflict to cease fighting and killing, lay down their weapons and negotiate a peaceful agreement. Often this will require not only understanding, patience and skilful diplomacy but also some form of concessions such as pardons and/or amnesties. The Special Court demonstrated that such provisions and assurances negotiated on the ground in good faith become meaningless once the juggernaut of international justice comes on the scene. What incentive, therefore, will there be for some of those involved to stop fighting?

These are difficult issues and there is no easy answer but I suggest that if the international community is to get involved, it is better left to the International Criminal Court (ICC) to ponder rather than ad hoc courts like the SLSC. It is perhaps no coincidence that the United States was the major supporter of the SLSC. The US remains one of the very few major countries in the world to continue to boycott the ICC, claiming that ad hoc courts like the SLSC can pursue the cause of international justice more effectively.

However, the ICC also needs to take more account of indigenous forms of justice. My former American colleague, John Hirsch, has written that 'the decision to grant an amnesty or invoke "the duty to prosecute" is best taken by the citizens of the country rather than the international community through the Security Council or other instrument.' This theme of local supremacy has also been emphasized by the eminent British Africanist Richard Dowden, Director of the Royal African Society. He has written: 'The ICC cannot hand out justice in Sudan as if it were Surrey ... the Western-inspired Universalist idea of justice might come into conflict with local forms of law, jeopardizing the process of reconciliation. If the ICC is going to step into Africa's complex wars, it must understand the local contexts and think through the effects of its actions. Local input and outcomes must be as close to the heart of the ICC's mission as justice.'

These are views that I fully share.

Epilogue

The Sierra Leone conflict has become a benchmark for dealing with subsequent conflicts by the British Government. It is now given as a positive example of how direct military involvement can save lives and end conflicts. Tony Blair cited the example of Sierra Leone as part of his reasoning for Britain's involvement in Iraq and Afghanistan. David Cameron may well have had Sierra Leone partly in mind in justifying Britain's involvement in Libya. But, as will be seen in the events described in this book, the path followed leading to Britain deploying its military forces in Operation Palliser and Operation Barras was tortuous and by no means straightforward. The end of the Sierra Leone conflict came at a huge cost, some of which might have been avoided if different decisions had been taken at the time.

For those involved at the time, the Sierra Leone conflict will have long-lasting memories. Most have now moved on.

In 2003 Robin Cook resigned from the Cabinet over the Iraq war, as did Clare Short. He died unexpectedly in 2005 whilst out walking. Clare Short stood down at the last election as the Labour MP for Birmingham Ladywood.

Tony Blair has continued to visit the country regularly whilst pursuing his interests through his African governance programmes and the Tony Blair Faith Foundation.

David Richards has continued his successful career in the military and as General Sir David Richards is now the Chief of the Defence Staff.

Lincoln Jopp is now a colonel in the Scots Guards and recently took the parade at the Trooping of the Colour ceremony in London. Colonel Andrew Gale sadly passed away in 2008. Colin Glass and Dai Harries remain in the Diplomatic Service.

Having won the elections in 2002, President Kabbah stood down in 2007 and his SLPP party, led by Solomon Berewa, was defeated in the subsequent elections by Ernest Koroma's APC party. Kabbah's treatment of Sam Norman was given as one reason for the SLPP loss. President Koroma's government, including Zainab Bangura initially as Foreign Minister and later Health

Minister, now continues the struggle to maintain the peace and democracy and develop the prosperity that the courageous people of Sierra Leone deserve, but in the face of continuing corruption and a growing drugs problem.

On my retirement I was invited to become a member of a United Nations team of experts looking at lessons learned from the UN peace operations in Sierra Leone and we submitted our report to Kofi Anan at the end of 2002. I was offered the post of African Director by the International Crisis Group, the influential and widely respected think tank based in Brussels, but the offer was withdrawn 'on the advice of senior figures in the Foreign Office'.

Through various activities, such as the establishment of a charity for the school for the blind and patron of the Dorothy Springer Trust assisting the disabled, I maintain my close links and commitment to Sierra Leone. On two occasions, in 2003 and 2007, we brought the Blind School Choir to the UK to give a series of concerts in different venues around the country, including Westminster Abbey, where we sang *My West African Home*.

I visit the country frequently. On every visit I receive a warm welcome.

Glossary

AFRC	Armed Forces Revolutionary Council (later changed to Armed Forces Ruling Council)
APC	All People's Congress
AU	African Union
BHC	British High Commission
BOC	British overseas citizen
BPP	British protected person
CCP	Commission for the Consolidation of Peace
CCSL	Christian Council of Churches Sierra Leone
CDF	Civil Defence Forces
CDS	Chief Defence Staff
CDU	Civil Defence Units
CHOGM	Commonwealth Heads of Government Meeting
CMG	Companion of the Order of St Michael and St George
CPT	Close protection team
CSM	Civil society movement
DDR	Disarmament, demobilization and reintegration
DFID	Department for International Development
EC	European Commission
Ecomog	Ecowas military force in West Africa
Ecowas	Economic Community of West African States
EU	European Union
FAC	Foreign Affairs Committee
FCO	Foreign and Commonwealth Office
HE	'His Excellency'
HMG	Her Majesty's Government
ICC	International Criminal Court
ICRC	International Committee of the Red Cross
MBE	Member of the Order of the British Empire
MILO	Military Liaison Officer

MRD	Movement for the Restoration of Democracy
MSF	Médecins Sans Frontières
NGO	Non-governmental organization
NPFL	National Patriotic Front of Liberia
NPRC	National Provisional Ruling Council
ODA	Overseas Development Organization (later changed to DFID)
OAU	Organization of African Unity (later became AU)
OBE	Officer of the Order of the British Empire
PDP	People's Democratic Party
PUS	Permanent Under-Secretary
QBP	Queen's Birthday Party
RMP	Royal Military Police
RPG	Rocket-propelled grenade
RRR	Reconstruction, rehabilitation and resettlement
RUF	Revolutionary United Front
SAS	Special Air Service
SLBS	Sierra Leone Broadcasting Service
SLPP	Sierra Leone People's Party
SLSC	Sierra Leone Special Court
SSD	Special Security Division
TRC	Truth and Reconciliation Commission
UN	United Nations
UNCHR	United Nations Commission for Human Rights
UND	United Nations Department
UNDP	United Nations Development Programme
UNHCR	United Nations High Commission for Refugees
UNICEF	United Nations Children's Fund
UNOMSIL	United Nations Observer Mission to Sierra Leone (later changed to UNAMSIL – United National Mission in Sierra Leone)
UNPP	United National People's Party
USAID	United States Agency for International Development
WAWA	'West Africa Wins Again'
WFP	World Food Programme
WNAD	West and North Africa Department (DFID)

Bibliography

Ashby, Phil, *Unscathed – Escape from Sierra Leone*, Macmillan, 2002.

Dowden, Richard, *ICC in the Dock*, Prospect, May 2007.

Foreign Affairs Committee, *Sierra Leone, Second Report, Vols 1&2*, House of Commons, London: The Stationery Office, 1999.

Fowler, William, *Operation Barras, The SAS Rescue Mission: Sierra Leone 2000*, Weidenfeld & Nicolson, 2004.

Gberie, Lansana, *A Dirty War in West Africa – The RUF and the Destruction of Sierra Leone*, C. Hurst & Co, 2005.

Gberie, Lansana (ed), *Rescuing a Fragile State – Sierra Leone 2002–2008*, LCMSDS Press of Wilfred Laurier University, Waterloo, Ontario, 2009.

Geraghty, Tony, *The Bullet Catchers – Bodyguards and the World of Close Protection*, Grafton Books, 1988.

Hirsch, John, *Sierra Leone – Diamonds and the Struggle for Democracy*, International Peace Academy Occasional Paper Series: Lynne Rienner Publishers Inc., 2001.

Human Rights Watch, *Getting Away with Murder, Mutilation and Rape – New Testimony From Sierra Leone*, Vol II, No. 3(A), June 1999.

Legg, Sir Thomas, *Report of the Sierra Leone Arms Investigation*, House of Commons, London: The Stationery Office, 1998.

Médecins Sans Frontières, *Mutilations of Civilians in Sierra Leone – One Month of Surgical Activities in Connaught Hospital, Freetown, Sierra Leone*, May 1999.

Parris, Matthew, *Parting Shots*, Viking, 2010.

Penfold, Peter, *The Tangled Web of Sierra Leone's Special Court*, Africa Analysis, No. 491, April 2006.

Ross, Hamish, *From SAS to Blood Diamond Wars*, Pen & Sword, 2011.

Scully, Will, *Once A Pilgrim*, Headline, 1998.

Sierra Leone Truth and Reconciliation Commission Report, *Witness to Truth*, 2004.

Spicer, Tim, *An Unorthodox Soldier – Peace and War and the Sandline Affair*, Mainstream Publishing, 1999.

Index